Sputum Hill

Bob Shen

Sputum Hill

By

Bob Shears

Published in 2005 by Stamford House Publishing

A CIP catalogue record for this title is available from the British Library

ISBN 1-904985-35-1

Stamford House Publishing

1st Floor, 13 The Metro Centre, Woodston, Peterborough PE2 7UH

CONTENTS

FOREWORD

After a lifetime (well, almost a lifetime) of seeking the answer to his question, "Why am I here?" Bob Shears is a little wiser than when he first made his appearance in a council house in Hele Village as the unplanned offspring of wartime parents, where hostilities were continuous and Hitler didn't come into it.

Bob went with the flow, surviving schooldays, an unhappy apprenticeship, and horrendous operations in a sanatorium. He became a local pop idol, a wheeling-dealing businessman, a pillar of society, and an enthusiastic drunk. He was also the associate of high society, the local likely lads, and the gambling fraternity.

He was bankrupted twice and spent some time as a guest in HM Prison Exeter. You may not like him, you may not approve, but he tells it as it is, and now he is content and has found the answer to his question.

Les Jones

ACKNOWLEDGEMENTS

I would like to acknowledge Les Jones for his help in my writing this book. Les was born in 1924 and sadly died in 2003 before I had completed the book. Les was an all round entertainer. He was an artist, a poet and a musician who sang to the public whilst playing his ukulele. He was known locally in Torquay as the Bard of Babbicombe.

Les was an avuncular person, popular with all who he met and helped in many ways. A park bench with a brass plaque commemorating his life was donated by the local community and is sited in a meadow near the Babbicombe model village with the inscription "Les Jones The Bard of Babbicombe".

I first met Les when I approached him for his advice on art, and during the conversation I told him that I had started to write this book. He offered to help me, and being a dyslexic I jumped at his offer. I soon learned that 'spellchecker' on a computer doesn't know the difference between 'new' and 'knew', and many other similar words, but fortunately for me Les did.

Fortunately Les wrote the foreword to this book before he died, and I thank him for all his help.

Bob Shears

INTRODUCTION

When I was a young man, a famous musician who I admired told me that he was the master of his soul and in control of his own destiny. I thought that I was the same until events taught me that I was a victim of destiny and a master of nothing . . .

CHAPTER 1

THE GRIFFITH SPLIT

Hawkmoor, a sanatorium built for the treatment of Tuberculosis was situated on the outskirts of Dartmoor in the County of Devon. Dartmoor is a place of divergence, austere and dismal or beautifully picturesque as the weather and seasons permit. Located in the heart of Dartmoor, the stark reality of Dartmoor Prison with its grey granite walls predominates as a bleak sight in a forbidding wilderness. The prison was built to contain French prisoners of war and is used to this day as one of Her Majesty's Prisons. During the episodic years of the Consumption, most people would have chosen incarceration behind those grey prison walls, in preference to the nightmare of Hawkmoor.

In the early 1960s, tuberculosis was being eradicated with the use of the newly discovered drug streptomycin. The sanatorium however, was still more than half-full of TB sufferers. Its reputation as an outpost for the Consumption sufferers, far away from towns and cities, rang out like a death knell! In some way or another, the death or the suffering of a friend or relative from the Consumption had affected most people. The surrounding population throughout Devon and further afield thought of Hawkmoor as a death camp.

Two connecting wards named West Block A were a part of this complexity of buildings that made Hawkmoor. As the Consumption waned, West Block A was used primarily for diagnosing and the treatment of other chronic lung disorders, mainly cancer. In 1963 this became my home for approximately six months.

After five months of enduring tests (some of them experimental) in the form of biopsies (or minor operations) I was well aware that every cancer-suffering patient whom I had met in West Block A when I had arrived was dead. All the tests carried out on me had proved negative. What was I doing here? I began to wonder. I was now the old lag, the longest serving patient. New patients now looked to me for advice. I had arrived in summer, autumn had passed, and now winter had settled in. Having outlasted all the others, my thoughts suggested that my number would soon be up. I was aware that my health was slowly deteriorating, and that I had lost a great deal of weight, but considered that I was still reasonably fit enough to attempt a return to work. I suggested to my consultant Doctor Litler, "If there is nothing wrong with me, doctor, I'll go home!" I felt like a fake!

Brought up to keep quiet and take everything that was dealt out to me by my elders, I was too ignorant to understand the gravity of my situation. My parents had been brought up in this way and they had passed it on to me. Born during a world war and brought up in its aftermath instilled respect in me for those who had suffered its torments at first hand (I knew my place?)

Doctor Litler took me into his office and pointed to the X-ray display unit mounted on a wall. Exhibited within the illuminated cabinet was a photo X-ray of a chest, "This is an X-ray of your lungs, Robert," said the doctor. I had never understood what intricacies doctors were looking for on these X-rays. With a vacant stare, I gazed at the X-ray until the doctor brought my attention to a large black shadow on the bottom lobe of my left lung and many smaller shadows all over both lungs. As he ran his index finger across the X-ray he explained.

"These shadows show there is definitely something wrong with your lungs, Robert!"

I was fascinated by his summation. For the first time I could see the anomalies in the form of faint shadows and felt privileged to be enlightened.

"Don't worry," said the doctor, as he turned to face me with a smile. He gave me a confident nod of his head and assured me, "We will find out what it is." His encouraging brief filled me with trust. I was like a lamb being led to the slaughter! (Imagine being a fake in a death camp, I mused!)

The following day, I attended an appointment in the laboratory of another consultant, Doctor Trowbridge. I had seen Doctor Trowbridge many times up until then, but this was the first time he had attended to me. He was a man of about forty years of age and leant towards the scientific side of medicine. His laboratory was brimming with apparatus built by him out of scrap materials. Austerity had not excluded the experimental sciences of medicine during the post war years of our country's economic recovery. After the formality of our introduction, he eagerly introduced me to one such appliance. It was obviously a newly-constructed apparatus and I was to be its primary test subject. Doctor Trowbridge seemed a likeable man to me, and I feel sure that many constructive advances in medical tests have derived from his intriguing contraptions.

"It's an apparatus I designed for measuring the capacity of one's lungs," he explained, gesturing towards the appliance.

The structure laid out before me was built primarily out of a discarded coffee tin, about the size of a small bucket. The tin was floating open end down partially submerged in water. Measurements were scrolled on one side of the tin starting with a limit of submersion (like the Plimsoll line on the side of a ship).

"When you blow the full capacity of your lungs into this tube, Robert," the doctor explained, holding a rubber tube in his hand that led under the water and into the tin, "the tin will rise like a gasometer and the measurements on the side will record the capacity of your lungs."

Quite intriguing, I thought. I nodded my head in approval to the doctor.

"I tested the apparatus on one hundred students from Exeter University," proclaimed the doctor. He had assessed that these preliminary tests would provide him with the average lung capacity of a healthy person.

My dad came to mind as I examined the apparatus. He had worked on the construction of the local gasometer. Dad was very adept at making things and could have constructed a model equal to this, I considered. However, I was intrigued by the fact that a doctor could be accomplished with his hands as well as intellectually competent. As an accomplished craftsman, I had found that the professions were generally ham-fisted.

As I made ready for my attempt at testing the appliance, I wondered how my lung capacity would compare to that of the average student. As a child I could hold my breath for three minutes and out-swim all of my friends under water by far.

Inhaling air to the full capacity of my lungs, I started to blow into the tube causing the tin to rise. The tin rose, nearing its full volume as my lungs were still deflating. Suddenly, it toppled and fell from its mounting, meeting the floor with a clatter!

"Good grief!" said the doctor, as his eyes followed the plummeting tin to the floor, "I've never seen it do that before!" He turned towards me, staring with a look of amazement and exclaimed, "My word, Robert, you've got the largest lung capacity I've ever seen!"

Standing back from the now defunct apparatus and gawking at my innocent effect on its destruction, I commented jokingly, "Back to the drawing board, doctor." He looked perplexed but made no comment. Perhaps he should have tested his apparatus on fully-grown workingmen instead of students, I pondered.

The doctor moved me on to the second part of his test. He inserted a needle into a vein in my arm and was attempting to insert a second needle deep into the centre of my arm into an artery. During this procedure, his forehead developed a pinkish shine through hints of sweat and his breathing became heavy and agitated. I sensed that he was struggling with this task and becoming frustrated. For fear of making his job even more difficult, I was trying to control my feelings by suppressing the pain and my own anxiety.

After ten minutes or so, he withdrew the second needle from my arm and slumped back into his chair. Breathing a heavy sigh he began to explain his difficulty to me.

"Robert, you're not helping me by suppressing the pain you know!" He said it appealingly, as though I should have conformed to his design through telekinesis or something extrasensory. He looked down for a moment, shaking his head to collect his thoughts. He was searching for a way to convey his requirements from me, "You must realise," he began, looking up at me with his hands emphasising his every word, "I cannot see inside your arm!" He then paused as if waiting for an answer from me.

I was dumbstruck; my suppressing the pain was generally helpful to the doctors, "What is it you want me to do, doctor?" I asked.

He then suggested, "Well, if you indicate pain when I strike a nerve, it helps me to assess my whereabouts."

"Oh, OK, doctor," I said, and he then commenced his second attempt with the needle.

Over the past five months, I had become accustomed to pain. I had endured many minor inconveniences of painful tests. The art of mind over matter I had mastered, providing I didn't enter into shock (in shock, you have control of nothing). He had given me a choice of either arm for the tests, indicating that the arm would be out of use for a few days, so I was anticipating pain. A few healthy screams from me at the appropriate time complied with the doctor's request, and together with his skill and my co-operation, the job was done.

Now that the needles in my arm were secure, tubes were attached to the needles and I was instructed to lie on a table on my back. Facing me at my feet was another contraption in the form of an old bike. It was rigged with its frame in a vertical stance (what next? I thought) I had easy access to the treadles. Apparently, as the doctor explained, a patient could pedal the bike at a controlled degree of restraint in order to record a measure of one's energy output.

A pointer mounted on a wooden dial above my feet indicated the rate of speed that I should pedal. I did this with ease, for quite as long as required. An old RAF pilot's oxygen mask was strapped to my face to collect my expelled air for later analysis. The doctor certainly knew how to utilise old junk.

As I understand it, Doctor Trowbridge was monitoring the amount of oxygen passing through my lungs and into my bloodstream in ratio to the energy used pedalling the bike. This was pioneering research (front line technology at the time). Having completed the test and receiving a handshake and a reassuring pat on the back from the good doctor, I returned to my ward to await the test analyses.

Up to this stage of their investigations into my ailment, the problem with my lungs was still a mystery. Tuberculosis had been dismissed at an early stage. The possibility of my problem being cancer was uppermost in the doctors' minds, hence all the biopsies from all over my body. They were searching to see if the suspected cancer was malignant. (Of course, I was not privy to their reasons for the tests at that time.) I was so unenlightened that I thought every negative test was a failure to diagnose my illness. In fact every negative test was a bonus in their eyes. They were more or less convinced that I had cancer. Their only quest was to determine if the cancer was malignant or benign.

Approximately two hours after the test, Doctor Trowbridge called to see me in my ward. Something was wrong; he was full of apology. Apparently, his equipment had malfunctioned. The results he had compiled were way too abnormal to be correct. He wanted to repeat the whole test the next day.

Having witnessed the failure of his miniature gasometer equipment, I was a little apprehensive as to where this test was leading. My arm by now was turning black from my shoulder to my hand, and he again gave me the choice of which arm to use for the repeat test. I elected the same arm. I reasoned better to have one really bad arm than two mediocre ones.

With the second test duly completed, the doctor summoned me to his office the next morning.

"Take a seat, Robert," he said, offering me a chair. He was accompanied by a Sister and began to sum up the results of his test, "I have some very bad news for you, Robert." He spoke with a solemn tone to be sure of my full attention. I was oblivious to any notion of danger. How could a simple little test like this be of danger to me? I thought that I had heard it all before. He continued with his declaration, "The results of the second test are the same as the first, Robert!" He hesitated for a reaction. (I thought, 'Blimey, surely I don't have to go through all that a third time?') "The results are quite shocking," he said, nodding as if to indicate a need for a response from me. I remained po-faced and

6

he resumed his grave message, "I would expect a patient in your condition to live for no longer than six months." He paused again for response but my brain was suddenly stunned into silence! My number was up? Although I had half expected this, the shock completely pole-axed me. He now had the full attention of my shocked brain.

From this point on, he began to sound like a judge with the black wig on his head, I felt sure he was going to end his sentence with the words, "You will be hanged by the neck until you are dead."

He continued his deliberation with an account of my forthcoming schedule, "You will now leave this ward and go to the surgical block (known as New Block) where you will receive major surgery to remove a part of your left lung, an operation known as a sect-ectomy. (This is the removal of a small cube of lung.) After this operation, you will be administered a treatment that is as yet untested. I'm afraid it will be your only hope of survival." (All he had to do in my mind now was to say to the Sister, "Take him down!")

I just sat in my chair mesmerised. Again came the silence and this time it seemed never-ending.

"Is that it," I said, breaking the quiet.

He nodded his head.

"Can I go?" I said, nodding towards the door.

"Yes," he replied. So I thanked him for his frankness and left. I couldn't get out of that office quick enough.

To the other patients I must have looked like a zombie as I walked through the adjoining ward and into my ward. My mind would not focus on what I had just heard. All I could think over and over was:

What did he say? Did he say die"

As I sat on my bed trying to slow down the collision of erratic thoughts bouncing around my head, some of the older patients came to my side and asked me if I was OK. They knew the look on my face; they had already received their final judgement from the good doctor. Over the last five months I had seen the expression I now wore many times on the faces of others. In that short time, I could count the survivors of West Block A on one hand. They only survived because their X-rays gave false readings. There was nothing wrong with them in the first instance. I rounded my response to my fellow patient's question with a synonym, "Same as you, my friends, I got the Griffith Split."

The Griffith Split referred to the cut of the surgeon when performing a lung operation. It left a scar, which extended from your side in a curved line, terminating halfway around your back. The surgeon's name was Griffith. Hence, the Griffith Split.

It seems that in West Block A, all the patients had one of three choices of treatment available to them. One treatment involved being irradiated, the second was an injection with an obnoxious substance, and the third was the chop. I was for the chop.

All the older patients did their best to console me by making all the usual comments, "You're young and strong. You can fight it," they all assured me in agreement. I had heard all this before. At the age of twenty-one I was the youngest patient there. Memories surfaced in my mind about the experiences of the past patients that I had known. I thought of a patient from Seaton, a small town on the south coast. He had been responding to one of their experimental treatments and had started haemorrhaging. He was now on his way home to die. I had not seen anyone respond favourably to any treatment.

Two weeks prior to this, a new patient asked me for a drink of Guinness (I kept a store of Guinness in my locker). He was facing the same operation as I was. In preparation, we had a swab sample taken from our nose, to check for some kind of infection. He had received treatment for his nose but mine was all right. We all cheered on the day he got through the operation. Three days later (two days before my operation) he died on the toilet. (There wasn't any good news!)

The news of my impending doom I kept from my parents. They were preoccupied in keeping their marriage intact at the time. It seemed to me that the other patients were more genuinely concerned about my well-being. The doctor had given me the news personally because I had reached twenty-one, the age of consent. This was the second time that a doctor had confided details of the outcome of my medical tests to me.

Prior to entering the sanatorium, I had completed a five-year plumbing apprenticeship and ventured into my own plumbing contracting business. I was unhappy serving my apprenticeship and hated the job of a plumber.

Although the new business venture was a success, it was a temporary arrangement, embarked upon with the sole purpose of raising money for a new future. I didn't intend to continue in this detestable trade into which I had been forced by circumstances.

For the past five years I had also played the guitar and sung in various bands as a semi-professional musician. I was undecided on two options regarding my future. One, to move from my home in Devon to London and pursue a full time career as a musician. Two, to travel the world seeking employment on building sites, engaging in whatever jobs were available. The whole world was to be my oyster.

The manager and members from my old rock band visited the sanatorium, to ask me if I could join them for a six-month tour of Germany. The boys remarked on my weight loss and I lifted my shirt to show them my new figure.

"Christ, you could play a tune on them," said our lead guitarist pointing at my ribs. They were all quite shocked.

I hadn't contemplated a trip to Germany as a professional guitarist with my old band. Although lots of rock bands did the Germany stint in the sixties, some of our band were married with children and this was a big step for them. Up until then the band were semi-professional. This trip meant giving up their day jobs, and their families stood to lose financially as much as they did if it all went wrong. I would have jumped at the offer but had to tell them that I was facing the final curtain. I'd be dead by the time they returned.

My manager broke the news of my fate to my father. My father stormed into the doctor's office condemning him for telling me. My father's normal reaction would be to punch the doctor on the nose forcing him to change his diagnosis. He picked on the wrong man when he saw Doctor Litler, who told him to calm down and that he would do everything possible to get me back to work.

It seems strange now when I think about what he said, 'Get him back to work?' To hell with work! I just want to live!

At my age, I thought my adult life was about to begin; death was not even a consideration.

Eventually everyone in the ward seemed to leave me in peace to ponder over my demise.

People all around me were dying, and I saw the stark reality of my mortality. I was really confused. Foolishly I had thought up until this moment in my life that the whole world revolved around me. If it did not, what was the point of everything? Why was I born?

I had some urgent thinking to do and very little time to do it. Should I read the Bible? Is there something I have missed in religion? Is there a God? These are some of the questions that ran through my troubled mind.

A drawer in my bedside locker contained a small Bible and for the first time since entering the sanatorium I attempted to read it. I have always struggled with reading from childhood and soon tired of it.

Later, I purchased a large book entitled World Mythology. A statistic quoted in the early part of the book stated that over four thousand religious cults were registered in the world. I considered that they couldn't all be right, so I dumped the book. I reasoned in my desperate thoughts, what is the truth? I had to know. How do I find out? I came to the conclusion; I must ask myself the question. Why?

My thoughts suggested that a man who lies to himself is a fool.

CHAPTER 2

NO BULLS HERE

Could the answer to my problem be buried in my past experiences? I mused. At the age of twenty-one, there wasn't much past to mull over. That's all I had to go on though. Some of my youthful days of yore could be enlightening.

It all began for me on the ninth of August 1942, the day of my birth. My mother tells me that she brought me into the world in the front bedroom of number twelve Salisbury Avenue, with the aid of a midwife. My mother had five children and nine miscarriages. I was supposed to be the tenth miscarriage but survived. Out of the nine miscarriages, two of the babies lived for a short time. One, a sister, lived for a few days, and a brother for three weeks. In my youth my mother had repeatedly advised me that she had tried to get rid of me also. Families were very large in those times; one family just up the street from our home had twenty children. There was no pill in those days, and if there had been a lot of families would have been smaller, and I would not have been born. This gave me the inclination that I must have been a real champion to survive this primary ordeal!

Due to the lack of space at home, I had slept in a cot for much longer than most children did. (I got used to life behind bars!)

From the very beginning I had continually suffered from chest complaints. These were always diagnosed and treated by our family doctor as colds or bronchitis. The doctors in the sanatorium however, discovered scars on my lung from contracting pneumonia during childhood. My parents were unaware of this. Nobody knew that I had suffered from pneumonia until then. So much for our family doctor's diagnoses!

The only fireplace in our house was situated in the lounge. In winter the condensation from our breath froze on the inside of our bedroom windows. The houses were Jerry-built with no thought for conserving heat. When the ice on the window of our bedroom thawed it left pools of water on the windowsill creating a damp atmosphere in the room. All these things were damaging to my susceptible lungs.

As soon as the doctor told me about the pneumonia, I could relate it to my childhood. I was so ill and so young; I had nightmares about it right up until entering the sanatorium (where they gave me worse things about which to have nightmares!) I assume this was my earliest memory of life. It was so catastrophic; it became etched in my mind. As I lay in my parents' double bed repeatedly struggling to raise my heavy eyelids to remain conscious, the bedroom window appeared to flicker up and down in front of me. As the daylight from the window shone intermittently into my palpitating vision it created a sickening stroboscope effect. I was struggling to hold on to consciousness and life itself.

Even at that young age my life was almost forfeit. Later, when black and white televisions first arrived, the picture on the screen often flickered up and down emitting a strobe lighting affect. This induced memories of my childhood illness. I'd feel nausea and turn away from the screen.

During one illness, my father picked me up and shook me like a rat.

He screamed into my face, "Are you really ill?"

"Yes," I whimpered. He was worried about the doctor's bill; it seriously affected his boozing kitty (there was no National Health scheme in those days).

During the process of my father urinating in the chamber pot one night, after returning home from the pub sozzled, my coughing angered him. Work for him started early in the morning, so he was understandably annoyed.

He screamed at my mother, "Can't you shut that fucking kid up?" I still couldn't stop coughing. In temper, instead of returning the chamber pot back under the bed, he threw it at the wall above my head where it smashed into a thousand pieces. I was covered in broken china and his piss, and that's how I stayed all night (still coughing).

Our home was a council house in a district of Torquay named Hele Village. The village was then situated on the outskirts of the fast expanding town. My parents had first lived in the slums of Torquay, in the back streets of the very heart of town. As the slums were being cleared up and redeveloped into shops and luxury homes, we were shipped to the outskirts of town to the new reservation of council homes. The largest graveyard in town was situated virtually on our doorstep. Locals humorously remarked, "We moved from the dead centre of Torquay to the centre of the dead!"

There were thousands of American servicemen stationed in Torquay during the Second World War. My earliest memories of the Americans came when a young American sailor named Bob was courting my eldest sister Sheila. It was just before D-Day 1944. He arrived with his mates bringing cigarettes for my father. It was wise to bring gifts to my dad. I saved the empty packets as toys. I was barely two years old and I still remember Bob burning the toast in our kitchen. No doubt his thoughts were concentrated on my sister. Flames still licked from the toast as he snapped his teeth into the charred embers. With a big smile aimed directly at me he announced, "That's how I like my toast!" I was quite shocked by his madness. From that moment on, to me, Bob was etched in my mind as someone special. Bob later died during the Normandy landings. Much later in life I learned from my sister that Bob was only eighteen years old when he died. This was the start of my sister's depression and drug addiction, brought on when the family doctor introduced her to drugs. It was a habit that was to continue throughout the rest of her life.

On VE Day, my mother had fashioned a suit of clothes for me from an old Union Jack flag. She entered me into the local carnival and fancy dress competition as John Bull. Union Jack flags hung from every window in our street. Where did they all come from, I wondered? Seven of the nine children next door dressed up as the Seven Dwarfs. They pulled their father along in a cart during the carnival procession and I followed them. Unlike my neighbours I was unable to win a prize. After the procession led by the carnival queen ended, I watched the maypole dancers and listened to the brass band. I have never seen people so happy as they were that day. The long, ghastly war was over. Will it always be like this, I thought? I was so happy. Of course, I didn't know why at that age, I was barely three years old.

Our terraced house had three bedrooms. My two brothers shared one bedroom, my two sisters another and I shared my parents' bedroom. When both of my brothers were called into the Army to serve their National Service I was four. This enabled me to move out of my cot into their bedroom. (I was pleased and so was my dad!)

My mother often took me to Torquay harbour after the war. I loved to visit the harbour. It was a hive of activity, bustling with pleasure boats coming and going and trawlers unloading their catch, yachts sailing, and liberty boats bringing sailors to and from visiting naval ships. I was allowed to go inside an American submarine moored alongside of Haldon Pier. It was very cramped inside. Dials, levers and metal handles packed every space on either side and above the narrow walkway. As small as I was, I banged my head and was prodded and poked by hard metal protrusions from all angles. There was an awful smell of rotting feet and I couldn't wait to get out into the fresh air again.

Two hundred warships were anchored in Torbay during one time, a peacetime sight never repeated to this day. The liberty boats were in and out of the harbour all day. The American sailors stood on the bow of the liberty boats with their boat hooks across their chest. I was amazed how they stood so upright in the choppy water that was created by their wake. Naturally, I wanted one to fall in.

British engineers constructed the two concrete slipways for the Americans in Torquay's outer harbour, specifically for the embarkation of approximately 23000 American 4th Infantry soldiers on D-Day. The slipways exist to this day. I fished there for Smelt as a child, dangling my hand line through surface water drainage slots built into the slipways. I could see the little silver fish take the bait from my hook as I peered down through the slots. A magical memory!

When the Americans landed for shore leave, the liberty boats docked on the American slipways. It might seem incredible nowadays, but when the sailors returned to the liberty boats the worse for drink, they were thrown as far as fifteen feet down into the boats off the harbour wall. The shore patrol couldn't be bothered to carry them down the slipway. It's a wonder that they didn't break their necks.

US Navy shore patrols always seemed to be in groups of three men. They swaggered up and down the main streets with their big truncheons swinging from their hips, surrounded by kids shouting, "Got any gum, chum?"

Aeroplanes from the aircraft carriers anchored in Torbay packed the skies at times and now and then jet planes with twin tails and sometimes bombers filled the skies. The kids knew all the names of the planes by sight. We had official identification documents showing black silhouettes of planes and warships, probably home guard surplus issue. To the amusement of passing adults, all the kids yelled, "It's one of ours," every time that aircraft flew overhead.

I later saw the Brabazon Air Liner fly over Torquay. She was flying a test flight from Bristol where she was built. I knew it was her because of her eight engines, four mounted on each wing. She never flew commercially because her eight engines were not powerful enough for such a big plane.

Kids had tyre inner tubes from army vehicles to play with in the sea. Lucky kids managed to get big tubes from a Lancaster bomber or an American Flying Fortress. We didn't have toys like kids do today but there was plenty to play with.

My mother had relations in Birmingham and in the summer of 1946, she took my sister Jean and me to visit them. Somewhere in the city centre, my sister and I held my mother's hand whilst waiting to cross a busy road. A military policeman suddenly stopped his motorcycle right in front of us. He dismounted the bike and ran into the centre of the crossroads stopping all the traffic. It went quiet for a moment. Then we heard a rumble in the distance getting louder. Armoured tanks suddenly appeared. There were loads of them. They thundered by at a fair pace. As they rounded the corner their tracks screeched on the surface of the road. The noise was deafening and the ground shook beneath our feet.

"Americans!" my mother yelled, "Wave to the Americans," and we all waved.

After the tanks had passed us by, I looked down at the black tarmac road and was perplexed at seeing white powder. Their tracks had scuffed the limestone in the road surface into white dust.

My mother said to my sister and I one morning, "Come on you two, we're off to the Bullring today."

"What's that?" I said, full of trepidation at the thought of being in the presence of bulls.

"You'll see," said my mother. After arriving at the Bullring, I was surprised! I remember thinking, why was it named the Bullring? There was no bulls in it.

"Mum, where are the bulls?" I asked.

"There's no bulls here," said my mum, stooping down to look me in the face, "It's a market place, it's a flea market," she said. Now that, I thought, I could understand.

To me the Bullring was a bomb-site; just flat ground where an open-air market with stalls was held. I was attracted to a big, unexploded German bomb. It was laid out horizontally against the Bullring wall on display and had a money slot in the top. I had never seen a bomb before, it was massive; the size of a big cast iron bath turned upside down. My mother allowed me to sit on top of the bomb as if I was astride a horse and she gave me a penny to put in the slot.

The River Cole, a shallow tributary of a main waterway, was my favourite playing area. Most of my holiday was spent there, playing with my cousin Gordon who was about the same age as me. My Uncle Arthur kept an eye on us from his riverside vegetable allotment. My cousin and I caught Stickleback fish under a bridge and put them in a jam jar to take home.

My relations were gentle and kind people. Through higher wages that were available in the industrial cities they appeared to be so wealthy compared to people in Torquay. They owned their own houses. Uncle Arthur had his own decorating business employing forty men. He once gave me half a crown; I had never held one in my hand before. I can't remember what happened to it but I bet my mum does.

Unlike my father, Uncle Arthur came home from work happy. My father often said to my mother, "I don't want to see them kids when I come home from work, make sure they're in bed!" My mother would pack us off to bed by six o'clock in the evening saying, "Quick, your father will be home in a minute." My father never came with us to Birmingham. You can't blame my poor dad for being so abrupt; he worked so many hours for so little.

George and Percy were two of my older cousins. They taught me to load and shoot their BSA air rifle. It was too heavy for me to hold but they held it for me while I pulled the trigger.

I became aware of a problem with George when he fainted in their lounge, "Go into the back room," said my mother and I waited there until he came too. Later, I learned that he'd been shot in the head on the first day of the Normandy landings and spent a lot of time in mental homes. If it wasn't for his brother Percy caring for him, I don't believe he'd have been allowed out.

Sweets were in short demand during the rationing. We seldom saw any except for chewing gum whilst the Americans were here. When they left it was more often than not a homemade toffee apple, or sherbet.

Anything that looked edible we ate. We even ate tar off the roads because it looked like liquorice and everyone pretended it tasted beautiful. Berries from the Hawthorn tree were sampled and they were repulsive. Gooseberries were so sour; you screwed your face up at every bite. We sampled everything.

When my friends and I went scrumping apples, they always seemed to be cooking apples. As sour as they were, they were eaten! We chewed the stem of a plant for the juice and referred to it as wild rhubarb. (Who knows what that really was?) The same stems became hollow and bone dry when the plant died; it burned slowly like a cigarette, so we smoked it and called it smoking cane. Smoking this cane often burnt our tongues when a flame shot down the hollow in the middle into our mouths. We looked for cigarette ends on the streets to pack into the hollow, thus providing a better smoke. We often followed people nearing the end of a fag and fought for the discarded dog-end.

Smoking was OK in those times; if you didn't smoke you were a 'sissy'. The slogans on adverts read, *"Smoke Wild Woodbine and be a man"* and other similar attributes suggested vigour and power. When sweets started to appear on the market, some of them were shaped to look like fags so that the children could emulate their elder's habit of smoking.

Kid's saved cardboard milk bottle tops, cigarette cards and comics, or anything that could be swapped or bartered.

In 1947, when I was five years old, my sister Sheila married Charles Taylor, a master butcher. Charles held the ship's charter authorising him to supply meat to warships from all over the world that anchored in Torbay.

Charles stood on the end of Haldon Pier in Torquay harbour sporting an old naval captain's hat and a Buccaneer cutlass that was tucked into his belt over his butcher's apron. This was his ceremonial welcome to a ship's purser. His eyesight was so bad; he looked like Barney Magoo with his thick horn-rimmed glasses, only taller. He appeared to be looking out to sea for his ship but usually he was actually searching for the end of the pier in case he walked over the edge.

Charles was much older than my sister was and as a child I thought he was much too ugly for her but Sheila had a background of which I knew nothing at that time.

To be fair about my sister Sheila (and another reason for her drug addiction) she did have a very bad run of luck after the loss of her American boyfriend Bob. She fell pregnant to a married man who was a taxi driver. That doesn't sound like much of a big deal by today's standards but it was scandalous then. I heard my father flattened the bloke and left my two elder brothers to give the man a good kicking. Sheila lost the baby through a miscarriage but the scandal remained. She had pains after that in her stomach and repeatedly went to the doctor but the doctor, who was as disgusted with my sister as everyone else was, ignored her complaints and told my mother that my sister wore her corset to tight. Sheila was rushed into the hospital in the end with a cyst on her ovaries. She suffered a major operation, a hysterectomy. She was only twenty years old and it must have been devastating for such a pretty young woman. As a child I loved Sheila more than anyone else, she had such a kind nature but her destiny was already written after her antisocial mistake.

Charles had a licence to slaughter livestock from the nearby farms in any of the many small abattoirs situated in the towns out in the near Torquay. He had secured contracts to slaughter a set number of animals, that he had purchased direct from the farmers, for his and other butchers' shops. Now and then I was invited to accompany him to the abattoir. I really enjoyed my day out, which started with a ride in his posh van.

At the slaughterhouse, the animals entered the slaughter room to be shot (they were shot with a pistol that fired a bolt into their brain). Charles let me play with the gun, which to my small hand was very heavy.

During the processing procedure, the pigs were hung up on hooks side by side along a metal rail. When their entrails were hanging down from their stomachs, I was permitted to walk along the row and pick the biggest bladder to use as a football. Once it was blown up and tied off, I spent the rest of the day kicking it all over the place. All the kids played with pigs' bladders for footballs; after all, a real football had a pig's bladder for an inner lining to its leather exterior. (Plastic balls had yet to be invented.)

Norman, a friend of Charles, was a bandleader on the first class deck of the Queen Mary liner. The ship sailed from England to America and back like a ferry. I would say to my friends, "I know the band leader on the Queen Mary, and he visits to our house!" He was the most famous man in the world to our family.

My youngest sister Jean and I thought that Norman and his wife Cherry were aloof from us. Cherry became a close friend of Sheila's and although my sister was naturally the more beautiful woman of the two, Cherry made up for it with fancy American clothes and make-up. Cherry was a very smart, sophisticated woman. Some of her refinement wore off on my sister Sheila, making her even more attractive to men.

The most memorable thing about them for me were the presents they brought home from America. There were boxes of sweets and tins with cake in them, biscuits and all manners of goodies.

Norman brought home a viewfinder. This was a handheld slide projector that was held up to your eyes like a pair of binoculars. The photographic slides were mounted on a circular disc. The disc rotated the slides as you flicked a lever on the side of the viewfinder. Some of the slides displayed pictures of film stars. The stars were mostly women but at that age I had no interest in them. The best disc for me was of Vancouver National Park. The scenery was like nothing we had ever seen and there were pictures of real totem poles. The whole family passed that viewfinder around in our lounge on many an evening.

The family sat around a large round table in our lounge some evenings playing cards. They mostly played solo or cribbage. Norman brought home a game of canasta; a game played with two decks of cards. We soon learned how to play and it became our favourite game.

We played other games like shove halfpenny on two different boards; one board was made of wood and the other of black marble.

All the games were put in the background when Norman brought home a Chinese game of mah-jong. The house was full of visiting family every night. It was a fascinating game with one hundred and forty-four ivory tiles like dominoes. As a child I found them to be beautiful to touch. The beautiful ivory seemed to slide off your fingers; they were pleasurable to handle.

One thing that really tickled me about Charles was his incredible appetite. He would call into my home at lunchtime and was always invited to sit with us for a meal and he never refused. He was always hungry. It became a regular thing. My mother said to my sister, "Don't you feed him at home?" As it turned out Charles sat down for a meal in every place he was invited, he never stopped eating. He never let on, "I haven't eaten all day," he'd say. I liked old Charley.

CHAPTER 3

STARTING SCHOOL

In 1947 just after my fifth birthday, I was enrolled at Barton Infants' school. My parents had purchased a new pair of boots for me that was two sizes too big to allow for growing room. They were meant to last for years. My father had the cobbler's tools for hammering in the usual seventeen studs per boot and renewing the new soles and heels with rubber when necessary. I hated having to wear hobnailed boots.

My sister Jean, who was seven, had moved from the infants to the adjoining junior school with its own entrance. She chaperoned me as far as the entrance to my school and instructed me to walk up the school driveway to a waiting teacher. The teacher told me to join a queue of children lined up outside a classroom.

My father and elder brothers had trained me in the rudiments of self-defence and gave me strict instructions to stand up for myself should I be bullied. One of the other children (an ill-mannered mutation) tested my resolution by trying to relegate my place in the queue. (A form of bullying, I thought.) As instructed by my family, I leaped into action and as he pushed me from the queue, I punched him on the nose. This resulted in my gaining respect from the boy, reclaiming my place in the queue and enduring the cane from the headmistress, Mrs Dimbleby. (This was my first experience of receiving the cane.)

There must have been a shortage of qualified teachers due to the demands of our country's armed forces during the war. Shortages of building tradesmen led the government to introduce crash courses in the allied trades. During my apprenticeship later on in my teenage years, I heard time-served tradesmen comment many times on the poor quality of fast-track tradesmen. I am sure there must have been fast-track teachers trained in the same way. I assume I met some of them.

Also on my very first day at school, having survived the caning, I became a victim to a masterpiece of misunderstanding at school dinner. A roast dinner was laid out before me and looked quite appetising, until I turned over the cabbage and discovered *onions!* Everything else was OK but onions to me were detestable. This fact I brought to the attention of the teacher Mr Sanders but my plea to remove them from my plate fell on deaf ears; he insisted that I should eat everything on my dinner plate. (Remember that these were the days of rationing, and to turn down food was looked upon as tantamount to a crime.) As Mr Sanders wandered off and checked on the other children's progress, I ate the lot and was sick on my plate. Having not witnessed my regurgitation, my plate seemed full to Mr Sanders when he returned. I suppose he thought that I had mashed the food up and messed about with it instead of attempting to eat it. He demanded aggressively, "Eat it, boy," and remained at my side to make sure I did. Eventually, after repeated regurgitations, I kept the vomit down. From this point on I hated carrots, greens and teachers as much as I hated onions.

This same teacher was also a master of miscalculation, and I believe he was responsible for developing my rebellious nature as a pupil. Small yellow cards illustrating mathematical sums were placed in four boxes beside the blackboard. One box contained adding equations, the next subtraction and then multiplication and the fourth contained division. After a preliminary explanation of the rudiments of arithmetic the children were told to take a card from the first box, being adding up, and after completing the sum take it to the teacher for inspection. This went on throughout the term from adding to division but after one month I had completed the lot. I was so far ahead of the rest of the class; he stopped providing me with lessons on maths. He chose instead to isolate me from the rest of the class, providing me with a book of basic spelling. He assumed that I was bright enough to learn the rudiments of reading and spelling on my own, thus allowing him more time with the other children to improve their arithmetic. (In all fairness to Mr Sanders, there were at least fifty children in our class, a daunting task for the very best of the teaching profession.) Alas I made no headway with reading at all; I simply had no idea how spelling was put together, it was nothing like the logic of arithmetic that I understood. It was at this point, that the first sign of what I now believe to be dyslexia occurred.

Mr Sanders instructed me to pronounce a word in the book to the rest of the class; the word was shirt. I did not comprehend the word as shirt. All I could see, was every letter excluding the R and this was known to me as a rude swear word, so I refused to speak the word.

The teacher kept bashing me around the head with the flat of his hand shouting, "Say the word," but I kept silent. He screamed in my ear as he whacked me for the last time. "SHIRT, you stupid boy." I thought, SHIT! As soon as he said, "SHIRT," and I saw the R and recognised my mistake. In hindsight, I have always believed myself to be a dyslexic since that day but I have never had a test to verify my theory. Just after the war, dyslexia was foreign as an extenuation for illiterate disposition.

From this point on, my education was relegated to the bottom division. As far as the teachers were concerned, I was the echo, reverberating amongst a background of discord. I was the dunce excluded from the elementary rewards of scholarly pursuits, a reject from the attributes of society. My answer to this was to always play the dumb fool. This seemed to lead to a more peaceful existence until the end of each term when I had to face my father with my school report. *Your son Robert is very backward* and *Robert does his best to be a nuisance*, were common teacher comments. One such comment was followed by; *I don't know why you bother to send him.* I remember my father tearing up that report and giving me a hiding. My whole family then started to treat me as the family idiot.

My mother seemed to be working from morning to night, washing, cleaning, ironing, and all manners of things. My sister Jean and I did jobs around the house but our help was minimal considering the enormity of her chores. During my first school summer holidays my mother was glad to get me out of her way by sending me over to the gasworks to see my dad. He worked in the depot doing yard and governor house duties and general work to do with the daily upkeep of the gasholder. When he started at the

Gas Company he had been a labourer digging trenches for new gas mains.

Behind the gasholder lay two meadows, sloping away from the holder down a slight incline. All the leftover rubble from roadworks was tipped into one of the meadows. Ashes from the work's large coke boiler was spread on the tip surface to soak up the rain and prevent the area from turning into a quagmire. This formed a hard, black plateau, rising above the meadow.

The plateau became an open-air workshop for men to work unhindered by mud. The plateau workshop was now almost obsolete since a large, unused blacksmith's forge building was converted into an undercover workshop. Old workbenches fitted with pipe benders and vices, etc, lay scattered around the plateau. A selection of obsolete haywains, carts, traps and buggies were also dumped haphazardly about. What happened to all the horses? I wondered.

My father used the plateau now and then to break up massive old iron pipes with a fourteen-pound sledgehammer. The noise of hammering was deafening and hurt my eardrums. One day he put me into the back of one of the traps and ran around the plateau, dragging me behind him as though I was on a chariot. I was hanging on to the front seat for dear life and cheering like a cowboy. He ran in and out of the benches and right along the edge of the tip that dropped steeply into the meadow (perhaps to frighten me but I loved it).

During the winter holidays, I watched my father light the big Robin Hood coke boiler that heated the water into steam to keep the gasholder free from ice. The steam was piped up to the gasometer and connected by flexible hoses to heat exchangers in the wells of water around each section of the holder. These wells acted as water seals that each frame floated on. As gas came into the holder the giant telescopic stages rose rotating around spiral guide rails. The guide rails were safety precautions in case the seal should break and the holder collapse. If it collapsed it would spiral sideways and down, decreasing its rate of descent instead of dropping directly downwards.

The steel plates groaned with a deafening rumble as the sizzling steam hit the heat exchangers next to the freezing-cold steel plates, causing them to rapidly expand. Standing right next to the holder, I was terrified by the noise. It was like a mighty drum-roll from the gods as all the steel plates shuddered. There's nothing more frightening than thousands of tons of steel grumbling, and I thought that the whole thing was going to explode.

Sometimes, at the end of the day, I was given the job of punching all the cards for the gangs of roadworks labourers clocking off work. They were the men my father had worked with until his promotion to depot duties. Punching cards for me entailed grabbing a brass handle (meant for a man's grip) which protruded horizontally out from the wall-mounted time machine just above my head. I could hardly reach the handle and had to jump every time and swing on it to get the pressure needed to punch the holes in the card. There must have been a hundred men waiting for me to pull the lever and I was becoming tired. They all seemed to insist that I had to punch their card. My father was on a different shift to these men and didn't have to clock off at that time. They probably insisted on my punching their card as their sign of personal homage to my dad. By the time the last man was done, I was completely exhausted.

Rainwater and condensation that collected in a sump beneath the gasholder had to be pumped out by hand. The solid iron pump handle was about a metre long and moved in a sideways motion. I have seen my father pumping for what seemed like hours. The water discharged into a one-foot deep by ten-foot wide moat that encircled the gasholder. The moat had a tiny outlet that slowly drained the water into a nearby stream. My father always filled the moat with water. He sometimes primed the pump so that I might have a go, whilst he emptied or set his Goldfinch or Bullfinch traps. (He captured Finches to crossbreed them with his canaries). My best effort at manning the pump resulted in one inch of water discharging into the moat.

That gasholder seemed to have a strange hold over my father. In the awful winter of 1947, all the other gasometers in the southwest were frozen solid; my father kept his gasholder free from ice. He came home one morning with his fingertips frozen black with frostbite. He had been up on the holder all night, hanging over the gantries freeing the steam hoses and repairing broken ones. Eighteen inches of snow lay on the top of the holder. No one would accompany him on the holder; he certainly appreciated his job.

At home I was generally instructed by my mother to play in close proximity to the house and whilst climbing over a wire fence at the back of our house I snagged my scrotum on a strand of sharp wire. It tore my scrotum open and it bled heavily. I returned indoors and my mother made me sit on a chamber pot, whilst waiting for the doctor. I was not a happy child.

In those days, the doctor carried everything to administer first aid in their bag and so she stitched my scrotum up. I protested in every way I knew how to no avail, until I struck a chord when the doctor said to my mother that I should have a bath after she had finished her job. I just wanted to be left alone so I said to the doctor, "I can't have a bath because our bath is full of coke!"

That really did strike a chord with my mother who had just cleaned the house from top to bottom for the doctor's visit. She insisted on taking the doctor into the bathroom to inspect. My reason for mentioning the coke in the bath was well-founded.

Coke purchased by the ton was cheaper and most people would save up enough money for a one-ton delivery. Being a commodity the price of coke fluctuated and ranged between seventeen shillings and sixpence, to one pound a ton. The pilfering of coke on the gas board was rampant, as coke was a by-product of coal when coal was used to make gas. Gas was made at Hollacombe gasworks, which was situated between the towns of Torquay and Paignton and large stockpiles of coke accumulated. This created a black market in coke.

Rumours abounded about people having exhausted all their storage space in their coalbunkers and storing coke anywhere, even the bath. This was a standing joke that became stigmatised. The health authorities for lack of hygiene prosecuted Mr Crispo, our local ice cream man. The locals blamed him for making his ice cream in the bath, which he also allegedly (according to the locals) kept his coke in. His homemade ice cream was better than anyone else's was but he had tiny bits of ice in the cream. When a child's tooth crunched a bit of ice, they would say, "I've got a bit of Mr Crispo's coke in mine!"

A few weeks before our doctor visited me, we had two bags of coke stored in our bathroom. We too had stocked up so much coke we had nowhere to put it. After this day I had a hold over my mother every time we had visitors. If I wanted something, then was the time to ask.

Like many people, my father had his good side and his bad side, but I cherish his memory. My eldest brother Ron tells me he positively hates our father. I can't say I blame him. My brother has a different nature from me and my mother told me of an incident that happened before I was born when my eldest brother frightened my father.

My father was administering a beating to my brother with his leather belt and no matter how heavily he laid on the punishment, my brother wouldn't cry. He just kept staring expressionlessly at my father. My brother even messed his pants because of the pain and fear! Apparently my father told my mother afterwards that he would never harm him again. It had frightened him. My brother has never forgiven my father for what he did, to this day.

I cannot justify another man's action; things have to balance in life for us to recognise our own imperfections. What my father did was wrong and his fear told him so, but he had received worse treatment from his own father and knew no better until that day.

My brother I can pardon for not forgiving my father but I cannot forgive my father on my brother's behalf, that's my brother's prerogative.

The leather belt was still used as a deterrent for me by my father. As soon as he reached to get the belt from the top shelf in our kitchen, the fear registered in my mind. Next came the deafening whack, as he struck the seat of a wooden chair with it!

27

Knowing what my elder brothers had been through, that threat was enough to get his message across!

My sister Jean was disturbed by my arrival into her life. She naturally felt I was stealing her thunder (having had all the attention of my parents up until then). Unfortunately, as you may well imagine, she being so clever and me so stupid, I always came second in any argument and won the punishment prize. She was a snitch for my parents.

A measure of her contrary lack of tolerance to her baby brother took place on my second summer holiday from school. Whilst sitting on the floor of our back porch, I was painting with a child's palette of water colours when my sister pushed passed me and the little paintbrush smudged her new summer dress. She hadn't noticed this until she turned to look at me and saw the look of concern on my face as I peered at the paintbrush and her dress. Instantly she presumed that something had happened and expected the worst. It was an accident and I told her I was sorry. The dress was patterned with so many multiple coloured flowers that I was unsure if I really had touched her dress after all. I had however, but the paint mark was so small that she really had to search her dress to find it. When she located the tiny smudge, she let out a scream like a wounded whale and I heard my father respond with a bellow that sounded like a raging bull, so I was off and running.

My father could overtake a cheetah in full flight but he toyed with me just like a cat playing with a mouse. He allowed me to get as far as the gasworks before he grabbed my ear and lifted me off the ground, belting me around the legs with the copper stick. (This was the first time he'd used the stick on me.)

Unlike my brother Ron, I cried all the way home. All this delighted the neighbours, who tried to impress my father by clapping and cheering him on. To think, I was being punished for a pure accident.

The copper stick was a round piece of wood about one and a half inches in diameter and two foot long. It was used to push the washing down in a copper boiler and was bleached white. The big copper tub had a gas ring under it and heated the water for laundering. (Sometimes, the water was transferred in metal buckets to the bath.) My father seemed to prefer the copper stick for punishing me.

A girl who lived next door playfully chased me into my kitchen, where I accidentally put my foot straight into a bucket of scalding hot water that had just been poured from the copper boiler. I sat on my bum on the floor watching my foot as all the skin split between ripples of the crinkled surface. It looked like my whole foot was becoming skinless. I was screaming my head off! It eventually did remove all the skin off my foot and I had to be taken to hospital. It seemed to take months to heal, maybe a whole year. A nurse placed little squares of gauze dressings all over my foot. Large yellow blisters appeared, about one inch in diameter, swelling up to a half inch high all over my wound; it looked like a messy pulp. Every time I visited the hospital, a nurse would pick off the one-inch squares of gauze dressings with a pair of tweezers and redress my injuries. It's a good job it hadn't been the girl next door hurting her foot instead of me, imagine the trouble that would have put me in!

There is one thing I noticed about my father's persona. He left the neighbours in no doubt that if his children did any wrongs, he would administer the punishment. He seemed to like terrifying other people; I think he had a strategy of marking his territory with his fist.

Gambling on horse racing off the track was illegal in those days. There were no betting shops and so naturally gambling went underground. My father often sent me to the house of an illegal bookmaker with his betting slip and stake money wrapped in a paper bag. On reaching the house, I had to say to the man, "This is from Jim Jam," and hand him the paper bag, for which the man thanked me and I returned home. I always viewed these transactions with suspicion; could they be stringing me along in some private joke? Why did my father refer to himself as Jim Jam? I was too young to understand that what I was doing was illegal. I thought they might be taking the Mickey as my brother Brian had done to me before.

Brian had asked me to go to the newsagents and purchase the Mid Week Mail, knowing it was a tongue twister. All the way to the shop, I was nudging my memory repeating in my mind "mid meek mail, mid week whale, wid week whale" and when I arrived at the shop, I spent half an hour trying to spit it out. Eventually, I managed to blurt it out, only to find there was no such newspaper!

The behaviour of children in my era revolved around the after affects of the war. I believe that parents during those times had too many other things on their minds than to worry about the petty antics of children. Despite the rationing and general shortages, children had more freedom than the mollycoddled kids of today do. Personally I'd rather play with something found on a bombsite than a plastic toy. There was very little in the way of organised recreation that's taken for granted today.

All the kids saved bullets and things to do with the armed forces and we, like most children, played with the gunpowder from shell cartridges. .303 cartridges were discharged in a bench vice on the tip behind the gas works using a hammer and nail to belt the percussion cap. We also had metal that burned, and all manners of similar volatile toys. Most of the kids went fishing in the lakes and around the coast and this became my main hobby, so much so that I have devoted Chapter 4 to fishing as the pastime lasting all my childhood years and beyond.

Chalk marks seemed to cover all the pavements with drawings of hopscotch games and arrows for chase the leader. Hopscotch was always played with a piece of bathroom tile that we named the clicky. Hopscotch was known as a game of clickies. The pieces of tile came from bombsites and the chalk was always found in big chunks, as big as your fist. I think there were a lot of broken chalk sculptures in those times, I am not really sure but there was plenty of it!

On reaching the age of seven, I moved from the infants' school to the juniors. On the first day, I had an altercation with a child who was two years my senior. He lived near the gasworks and my dad befriended this boy because his father and mine were mates. My father had always rammed this boy's achievement down my throat. He gave me the impression that he would rather have him as a son than me. He was a clever boy. The boy had sought me out to ridicule me for being so stupid. I knew my father had inspired the contempt in him, and I had to give him a good hiding to gain respect. This time I was singled out for the cane from Mr Ellis, the headmaster of my new school. I just couldn't win!

During the springtime my father took me to a tree in the meadow where a woodpecker had nested. Using a bent dessertspoon, he removed an egg from the nest for my egg collection. All the kids had loads of eggs that they kept in boxes packed with sawdust. The eggs were pricked with a pin at either end and the contents of the egg were blown out using your mouth. No one gave a thought about the preservation of species. Even the school biology teacher had his own collection of eggs neatly stored in boxes of sawdust with little labels for the bird's name under the eggs. It was a good law that was passed to stop people from collecting birds' eggs.

There was a baby boom during and just after the war. One of the cheapest presents a child could ask for was a mongrel dog. This resulted in packs of mongrel dogs numbering as many as twenty, roaming around the council estates without control. Jack Barnet (my first best mate as a child who lived just up the street from me) and I didn't own a dog of our own, so we played with the neighbours' dogs. We took them out into the countryside to a place known to locals as dip chic pond. This was a large open cesspool belonging to a large house, owned by a local squire (Squire Brown). Lots of birds nested in the trees and bushes that surrounded the cesspool. We collected Coot and Moorhen's eggs there. If the squire spotted us, he chased us on horseback, brandishing a horsewhip. (His house and land now belong to a Pontin's holiday camp.)

The sewage in the cesspool was covered with two or three inches of clear rainwater, giving it the appearance of a pretty pond. We threw wooden sticks onto the water, enticing the dogs to jump in to retrieve them. The dogs loved flopping about in what looked like black mud but it was really pure sewage. The smell was terrible. When the dogs were completely covered in effluent, we took them back to their homes. After knocking on the dog owner's door, we ran, leaving the dog locked in the garden. From a safe spot, we observed the owner's horror and heard their screams as the dog ran inside the house.

Jack and I were inseparable right up until the time he passed his eleven-plus exam. He was two years older than I was. My parents warned me against playing with Jack, because he was always fighting and in trouble. I suppose that's what drew me to him. The way I saw Jack was as a victimised person. He had a northern accent that drew ridicule from the other kids. He was tall and gangly whereas I was stocky by comparison. He was a good fighter and I saw him as fearless.

Jack had been a loner until I came along. We always seemed to be stone-fighting with gangs from other council estates on quarries and bombsites. A gang of kids who hung out on a bombsite near an allotment did battle with Jack and me one day. The bombsite was an old brick pottery with some of the kiln roofs intact. You could run inside the brick kiln and out of the other side. There were piles of broken bricks all around that had smoothed out over the years and grass had partially grown over them. It was great ground for playing on as we could hide behind the brick mounds. Two of the kilns had their roofs intact and were used as the gang's headquarters. It was like being inside of a small dome. We called the gang the Kiln Gang. In our battle we ran out of stones and retreated into the allotment where we found a pile of potatoes and started using them for ammunition. The owner of the potatoes suddenly appeared and gave chase. He caught me and gave me a good hiding. I was walking home afterwards with Jack and met my father. When my father saw the bruises on my face he asked me who had done this and I was too afraid to say. (I didn't want another hiding.) Jack told my father everything. It was strange but my father sent me home. I think he disliked the bruises on my face; he wouldn't do that to me.

Later that day, my father asked me to describe the person who had beaten me.

"He was a soldier," I said.

My father grunted, "Are you sure?" Apparently, my father had gone down to the allotment and beaten up a man in a blue overall. He had given the wrong man a hiding. I think he just wanted to vent his anger on someone. (Thank goodness, it wasn't me!)

Jack and I were playing in a swollen stream by the railway lines one day wearing Wellington boots. Whilst egging each other on to paddle into deeper water, we suddenly noticed a dead rabbit floating by and then another and another. We paddled upstream a little further and there were loads of them gathering where the stream was at its widest and the flow of water slower. They had contracted myxomatosis, a disease introduced by the government to control the spread of rabbits.

They looked hideous. Their heads were swollen and their eyes were bulging out! To think we had eaten more rabbit than any other meat! My mother would never eat rabbits again, nor would a lot of people.

Children in our neighbourhood swam at a coastal quarry beside Pettitor beach when the sea was running a heavy swell. We chose this location because the waves ran along the side of the cliff and not head on. This meant they didn't break against the rocks creating rough choppy water that was impossible to swim in. It was too dangerous to get in or out of the water anywhere else.

The water was brown where the bottom was churned up by the undertow of the waves. An old quarry chain hung from the rocks and was used to help us to get out of the water. The trick was to float up on the crest of a wave and grab the chain, whilst digging your feet into the rock face. When the wave passed by, you were left high and dry to scramble to safety. Without the chain, we would not have a chance of getting out of the water.

Generally there would be about twenty lads waiting around and looking at one and other, to see who was brave enough to go into the water first. It was a life and death situation that was normally decided by throwing the weakest boy into the water and waiting to see if he got out. If he got out (which he always did) we knew it was safe and we all dived in.

Children diving off of the harbour wall collected coins tossed into the water by visitors in Torquay harbour. The better the dive the more coins the visitors threw. That's something else you won't see today, for the harbour is so polluted, you would be poisoned. That's another beautiful play area not available to children today.

CHAPTER 4

THE PISCATORIAL ARTIST

My interest in fishing began in the summer of 1949 at the age of six; I was completely hooked on the hobby. My first experience in the art took place on Princess Pier at Torquay harbour. I used a simple hand line with a three-hooked paternoster. At low tide, mussels were collected for bait from around the Second World War anti tank concrete embattlements that remain in the harbour to this day. On the first day, I caught a Rock Blenny. The fish was green in colour, three inches in length and it looked untouchable! It was the most unsightly little monster that one could imagine. It had spikes on its gills and dorsal fin and a gathering of spectators insisted that it was poisonous, which was rubbish. The locals named these fish Boolies; all the kids were teased when all they caught was a Booly. I still took it home for the cat's dinner but Timmy was not impressed. From this small beginning I progressed to catching Pouting and Pollock. These were a little bigger and were easy to handle, and although they were not big enough for adults to eat, Timmy loved them.

My favourite spot for catching Pouting was under the Pavilion on Princess Pier (since destroyed by fire). The first half of the pier supported wooden decking suspended on steel girders four feet or so above the stone pier. The Pavilion was built on top of the decking at the end of the wooden pier. Where the wooden pier ended, a set of iron trellis stairs descended to the stone pier, which continued as far again as the wooden pier out to sea. My mates and I often crawled under the trellis stairs in the summer to see up the visiting ladies' skirts.

The wooden decking overhung the sides of the stone pier casting a shadow on the water enabling us to see right to the seabed. There was only about ten feet of water below us at a spring low tide rising to twenty-five feet at high tide. We fished near a sewage pipe under the ladies' toilet and could see all the fish feeding on the sewage as it came out of the pipe. Now and then a big fish would swim near to our lines and everyone dangled their bait in front of the fish's mouth hoping it would bite but the big ones never did. This filled my dreams on many a night when I'd hook the big one. This was the fascination of fishing. I can now imagine the ladies in the toilet listening to our idle chatter regarding the fish and their menu! I can imagine one of the kids saying, "Cor, look at the size of that one!" meaning the size of the fish. And the ladies above that were thinking, "What on earth are they discussing?" having just flushed the toilet.

Adjoining the pavilion, and just before the trellis stairs, was the headquarters of the Torbay Sea Angling Club. The club headquarters was about the size of a large garden shed. It held about six men before it became crowded. These men were real anglers with pipes and bushy beards. They were brewing tea when I arrived and offered me a cup. They encouraged children to join the club, which was hard for kids to resist when standing in a hut full of fishing tackle, waders, smocks, waterproofs and all manner of wonderful things. They encouraged me to enter a competition, but stated that competitions were for members only. Membership was one shilling per year.

Just before my eighth birthday, with shilling in hand, I joined the club and entered the fishing competition. The first prize was a fishing reel, which all the kids wanted awfully. At the start of the competition I activated a foxy plan to outsmart my opposition. I mashed up a rotting Mackerel to make a ground bait and coaxed one of the boys to stand guard whilst I entered the ladies' toilet. Half the mix I flushed down the pan and the second half I threw into the cistern above my head so that the next lady to use the toilet would flush the second half down the loo later on. I caught eighty-two Pouting from around that sewage pipe that day. I won a spool of fishing line, the second prize in the competition. The boy who won the fishing reel lived just up the street from me; he had a lucky catch of one big Pollock and ruined my crafty ploy.

In 1951, all the kids purchased aerials to make fishing rods. They were armoured tank aerials, surplus American Army equipment. These aerials came from a man we called Moses. Moses had a beard and reminded me of Fagin in Oliver Twist. He sat alone in the middle of his store surrounded by a mountain of junk that started at his feet and rose to the roof all around him. Only he knew where everything was. Everybody used Moses' store for bicycle parts, general second-hand accessories and American Army surplus stock. It was an Aladdin's cave.

The twelve-foot long aerials split into three four-foot sections, each joined together with a threaded joint. The full length of the aerial was used as a freshwater fishing rod. For sea fishing, we only used the first eight-foot of the aerial. We purchased corks for the handle and brass rings to hold the reel in place. Metal eyes with porcelain linings were soldered onto the aerial and bound with coloured cotton. The cotton was varnished to waterproof and preserve it.

In the village where I was born, a Baptist church flourished and one of my friends David Diamond (nicknamed Dinco Diamond) was a child preacher there. All the kids quizzed Dinco, asking questions about the scriptures in the Bible, trying to belittle his faith. As a last resort, when Dinco was lost for an answer, he would say in frustration, "It's true because it says so in the book!" The only pleasure Dinco had, was his religion and Mackerel fishing. The locals always held a competition for the first person (adult or child) to catch the first Mackerel of the season. It had to be caught from the shore using only a float and Mackerel strips for bait. Dinco always won the first prize. His favourite spot for catching Mackerel was Long Quarry just off Babbacombe Downs (a disused coastal quarry).

My childhood mate Jack Barnet and I were fishing at Long Quarry when it started to rain heavily, so we decided to go home. This entailed climbing two hundred feet up a narrow cliff path.

As we were climbing, a torrent of rainwater cascaded down the path like a river, making it slippery and too dangerous to continue. Jack decided to go out on the cliff face, which was almost vertical. Wheresoever Jack went, I followed.

Having climbed to within a few feet of the top of the cliff, we now faced a steep, ten-foot high bank of wet grass to reach safety. Jack climbed the last part and came down the path a few feet to my side. He watched me as I attempted the bank and crept

37

up the path just behind me. As I climbed the bank, the path to my right came closer to me and Jack kept watch over me. Just as I reached the top, I slipped back down the bank and had no chance of saving myself from certain death. I was skidding past Jack towards the very edge when he reached out and grabbed me and pulled me to safety. I couldn't bear to think he had done something that I could not achieve and said to him, "You nearly pushed me off then and killed me!" As I said it, I punched him on the nose. (I must have been a horrible little kid at times.)

As there were no deep freezers in those days, to be sure of having bait for the new season, Dinco always cured Mackerel strips with salt to preserve them through the winter. He alone did this and everyone called on Dinco for bait in the new Mackerel season. Dinco would always oblige by giving us free bait.

As kids, our circle of friends always tried to corrupt Dinco into misbehaving like us. For a very short period, Dinco succumbed to our ways, well, almost. To be one of us, he had to start swearing. We started him off with bloody and bugger and worked our way up to a full repertoire of bad swear words. We gave him several tests like jumping over hedges into gardens and pinching a flower, or climbing onto the church roof but after a week he went back to the church. That was Dinco. He died one morning of a brain haemorrhage; it was a real shock. He was in his early teens. At least Dinco had redeemed his faith before he died.

Everywhere that could be reached by walking, pushbike or bus became my fishing area. Grey Mullet were fluked at an outflow of hot water that discharged into the River Teign. The hot water came from the cooling tower of Newton Abbot Electricity Power Station. The Mullet shoaled in the warm water. No bait was required for fluking. A short rod was made out of the first four-foot section of the tank aerial and three large hooks were attached directly onto the main line, so they were rigidly fixed. A four-inch brass split pin we used for a weight because it slipped quietly into the water when cast over the fish lay. Repeated short jerks were made with the motion of the rod, forcing the hooks into the sides of the fish. The fish were foul-hooked. Hence, they were fluked.

One of my older friends Tony Crane, who was dating my sister Jean at the time, fluked one hundred and five Grey Mullet in one day, averaging two pounds in weight, and one big salmon. That was the record; I never managed to catch more than four in a day. Russians still use a similar method for catching Sturgeon but this type of fishing was banned in England on the grounds of cruelty. Fish were not always securely hooked and consequently swam away injured. It is a good law; it was a cruel way of fishing but like most things in those times, food was food, no matter how you acquired it.

A few years after the war, I used to fish off of Slapton Sands. The locals told me stories about lots of Americans being killed on exercises for the Normandy landings. There were hundreds of them killed on land and sea just practising. Bodies were floating onto the local beaches for weeks afterwards. One farmer told me that his barn was blown up and all the soldiers inside were killed. I have never seen that story made public. The whole exercise was kept secret for years.

My father generally worked seven days a week throughout my childhood, so he didn't take me out very much. In 1952, he took me sea fishing on the coast. I had a second-hand split-cane fishing rod that he acquired for my birthday present. The rod was so big and sturdy; it would have held a shark. I could hardly pick it up because of its weight. It was not such a good day out for me because he insisted on using the rod most of the time. The most exciting thing that happened that day was when a seagull ate the bait on his hook and got the hook pierced through its tongue. That caused a flap!

I borrowed a pushbike from a friend that was a conglomeration of spare parts obtained from Moses store and assembled into a girl's bike. No one had new bikes. For miles I rode that bike along with other kids; sometimes we pedalled fifteen miles up to Dartmoor and poached Salmon Parr in the River Dart. We'd fish and swim in the river all day and then pedal home before dark.

In the local lakes at Rakerhays, Newton Abbot, Tench was my favourite quarry, and in 1954 I became a member of the Newton Abbot Coarse Angling Association.

Before joining the club, I poached fish from the club's waters. I was too young to understand any other way. To me, at that age, everything was illegal. I seemed to be always running away from a bailiff, farmer, or gamekeeper. It seemed someone else owned every part of this world and did not want me on it.

My first sight of a Tench came when I was poaching. I knew what it was as soon as I landed it because I'd seen a picture of the fish in a book. It was a beautiful two and a half-pound fish, brown and bronze in colour with a gentle slime covering to its scales. It was nicknamed the doctor fish at one time because it was thought that other fish rubbed their bodies against the Tench to heal their wounds. I put the fish into my haversack and caught the bus home. It seemed that the fish didn't want to die. Every so often, it flapped its tail on the side of my haversack and it sounded like a drum. I felt sure I was about to be caught for poaching. Even on the bus, I thought the conductor would spot me and turn me in to the appropriate authorities. When I arrived home, the fish was still alive, so I put it in the bath in tepid water and the fish recovered.

The next day it looked in good shape in the bath, so my friends and I half filled a two-handled tin bath with water and transferred the fish into it. We carried it off to my new school (Audley Park Secondary Modern School) and put it in the school pond. One of the other children told the biology teacher Mr Jackman what we had done and I thought we were for the high jump, knowing that I had filched the fish.

To my surprise, Mr Rooks, the headmaster sung my praises at morning assembly for donating the fish to the school. The whole school applauded me. (If he only knew the fish's origin!) One week later, the fish was found dead by my mate; its bloated carcass was floating on the top of the water, along with all the dead gold fish in the pond. It must have been too big for the pond. This was a disaster! I collected all the fish and took them home before anyone else saw them. I buried the fish in my garden to make a maggot pit (to breed maggots for bait). Neither my mate nor anyone in the school ever mentioned the aquatic adventure again. It would seem this was the end of a fishy tale. Thank goodness!

Our biology teacher Les Jackman was well known locally for having a private aquarium beside Brixham harbour that he opened to the public. He also held an evening class at the school for youngsters that were interested in fishing. Guests appeared at the class from local tackle shops to explain the latest tackle and methods of using the gear. I was twelve at the time, it was 1955. The local kids had just discovered that there were fish in a clay pit situated just behind the school. They were very small and had recently appeared in the pit. There were Roach, Rudd and Golden Rudd. I asked the teacher if he was interested in buying some freshwater fish for his aquarium and did a deal with him. I caught a number of Roach from the pit and sold them to him for sixpence each. From the proceeds I purchased a Diana air pistol.

It was strange moving from fishing in a local pond for tiddlers to the contrast of fishing in the sea for much larger fish. Large Conger Eel were fished for using a thick clothesline and large, swivelled hooks purchased from Warren's, the local ironmongers. This was a very cheap way of fishing. The bait, Squid or Mackerel, was obtained free of charge from the local trawler men. The venue was a local coastal quarry named Hope's Nose.

Old iron drill bits were left inserted in the rock at the water's edge by the quarrymen of old. I assumed these were used to moor coastal barges alongside the quarry. These bits were rusted solid into the rock and came in handy for securing the end of our hand lines.

A pebble was tied to the clothesline to act as a weight. The whole Squid or Mackerel was put on the hook for bait and you simply threw the pebble weight as far out into the sea as possible. As a bite indicator, a second pebble about the size of your fist was loosely secured to your end of the line between the old iron drill bit and the water, balancing on the water's edge. The idea was that if you hooked a fish, the pebble would fall into the water, signalling that you had a fish on your line. As the line was secured to the drill bit, one could fish with a rod unhindered and just check the pebble now and then.

In 1956, I hooked the biggest Conger Eel I ever saw. The fish took all my strength to pull into the side of the quarry and I couldn't lift it out of the water. It's big eyes looked at me, and it rolled over and over at the base of the rocks below as I struggled to hold on to its thrashing body. I'll never forget those eyes. Eventually it bit through the clothesline and slowly swam away. I was left shaking like a leaf. I didn't realise it was possible to catch them that big.

A Conger Eel had been caught on a hand line at that spot previously, weighing one hundred and ten pounds. The British rod-caught record at that time, was eighty-eight pounds. I have no idea how big my fish was, it looked over six feet long and easily weighed as much as me. Everyone on the shore around me was shaken by its size. A holidaymaker who I had got to know that week sat me down on a rock and gave me a cigarette (I was a hardened smoker by now). He was a man of some forty years or more and he too was shocked.

I've heard stories about Conger Eels wrapping their tails around rocks to prevent you from pulling them in. Every time you snagged your line on the bottom, someone in the crowd always jokingly remarked, "Perhaps he's got his tail wrapped around a rock!" I disbelieved it, until one day I thought my hook was snagged on the bottom and when I eventually pulled the line free, there was a Conger Eel one metre long on my hook. Its skin along one side had been torn off, where it had jammed its body into the rocks. So the story is true.

Mackerel were so plentiful you could not give them away. They rotted quickly and people did not own refrigerators. Mackerel was the only fish that traders were allowed to sell on a Sunday! Seagulls have always been the scourge of the seaside and were culled in those days. Fishermen were paid a bounty for seagull eggs, which they gathered whilst raiding their nests on the cliffs.

Ex-soldiers played a game at the harbour side for the amusement of holidaymakers, involving the use of Mackerel and seagulls. They wrapped a chemical powder in newspaper (which exploded when wet) and put it inside a Mackerel. They fed the Mackerel to a seagull and watched it explode when their digestive juices got to the explosive. Imagine the uproar if that happened these days! This method of blowing up seagulls was something that the soldiers had picked up in the desert with a species of bird named the Shite-hawk!

In Torquay harbour, I can remember Porpoises in large numbers herding shoals of Mackerel so close to the boat slipway that you could scoop them out of the water in a bucket.

It's a pity that nothing was done to preserve the sea life in our harbours. As a child, it was an amazing sight to see all the varieties of fish and small crabs, now sadly denied to the children of today.

We had no television in our house until well after I had left school. I rode on a bus for seven miles to Tony Crane's house in Newton Abbot, just to watch the Quatermass films on the television. To occupy my time in the winter months, I spent hours making traces for hooks and trying out ideas for storing my fishing tackle, which always seemed to get into a mess. I collected feathers from all kinds of birds, to make feathered hooks for Mackerel fishing.

I was very keen on angling and all things to do with fish. I collected books about the subject, even books on keeping tropical fish from all over the world. My parents purchased two books from a collection of books from Lord Longdale's library. The books constantly referred to a book named The Complete Angler written by Isaac Walton. He was born on August the ninth in the sixteenth century, the same day as me in 1942. My father was interested in ornithology and kept racing pigeons, canaries and other birds. I could never afford such a luxury as tropical fish in our home. It was the beautiful colours of the fish that caught my eye.

My father brought partially used, unwanted stationery or various discarded books home from the gas board where he worked. Drawing books were hard to come by in rationing times. I drew all the hundreds of fish displayed in the books, using coloured pencils. All the adults that saw my drawings were amazed at their accuracy.

You could say that the talent shown in my drawings of fish would make me a "piscatorial artist," even at that age. (Some say I still am!)

CHAPTER 5

THE AG

In Audley Park Secondary Modern School, the teaching of religious matters was very lacking. One could see my teacher Mr Haywood, was not interested in religion. In Haywood's opinion, when Lot's wife looked back at Sodom and Gomorrah, she was turned into a pillar of salt by a fluke nuclear explosion set up by natural causes. With teachers like that and my being a dyslexic, what chance did I have?

There were a lot of nuclear tests going on in the fifties. The prospect of a nuclear holocaust hanging over our heads must have got to him. There was speculation in the Western newspapers, that a natural nuclear explosion had taken place in 1908 in Russia. It was later discovered to be a comet, or meteor collision with an impact force equal to a nuclear bomb of approximately thirty megatons.

In my view, Lot turned into a pillar of society, a society that was built upon the sale of salt. I'm no expert but I'll stick to my interpretation of the allegory.

In later life, I met a sailor who was at Christmas Island during an atom bomb test. He regularly drank in my local pub and he told me that he could see tons of ice cascading over the sides of the mushroom cloud as it pushed up into the high stratosphere. He must have been very close to the explosion; I've never heard anyone mention the ice before or since, and the sailor seemed to disappear not long after we met. Perhaps he was just too close to the bomb.

Being a plumber, I can't help but look at Jesus as a strong man, being a carpenter himself. The passage in the Bible about turning the other cheek suggests non-violence, and yet Jesus threw all those people out of the temple. He must have used some violence to do that. It confuses me!

As a young child, I learned the awful fact that Father Christmas did not exist and then moved on to Sunday School and heard the stories about Jesus Christ, who did exist. How can you deceive a child about Father Christmas, who to a child is so wonderful, and then expect the child to understand someone who can make the blind see and the dead live again?

The time for learning such matters should come much later in life I believe. The last of Father Christmas I would hate to see, or the last of Jesus for that matter. If only the teachers would leave a suitable gap between encouraging the fantasy and teaching the fact.

My class had agriculture as its main theme. The government wanted farmers and we were, by our own limited choice, being trained as farmers. From my point of view, I thought it would be a cushy number. The school had its own farm and I envisaged myself lying in the hay smoking cigarettes.

The standard of reading and writing was very poor in 'the Ag.' (Ag. is an abbreviation for Agriculture.) Inclement weather would mean that the outdoor farming activities were suspended, and on these occasions we were let loose in the school library. Half the class battled to get hold of the National Geographical magazine, to see the photographs of nude native women in the various jungles around the world. (Some of those pages went missing.) I suppose that the teachers thought that we would not have much time to read when being dragged around a field behind a plough?

Audley Park was a segregated school. Boys and girls never mixed for any classes or events. At the time of pubescence, our class was comparing the size of our individual sexual equipment. Dave Barter, a fellow pupil was blessed with the largest portion of equipment and could lift the desk lid without using his hands. All it took was one picture from the National Geographical to implement the feat. Our history teacher slammed the lid down on that era and brought tears to David's eyes. He never repeated the feat again.

The school was authorised by the government to pay a bounty of threepence for each butterfly chrysalis collected by its pupils. This was to cut down the population of green caterpillars who were eating the garden produce. Other children were bringing in three and four chrysalises but I brought in hundreds. My father was risking his life and limb, scooping them up in his flat cap from under the gantries all around the gasholder. They must have gathered there because the coal gas inside the holder was warm. It could have been because of the holders colour green. (Who knows?) My dad kept some of the money and I was able to purchase an air rifle with my share.

Most children feared Mr Haywood because of his violent method of administering physical punishment. During one whole lesson, he sat at his desk in front of the class, attempting to play a musical instrument without uttering a word to us. He had fashioned the stringed instrument out of wood to resemble a guitar. We all knew that if we uttered a noise, he would turn on us. Now and then he looked up from the guitar and did something I have never seen since. It was so funny we all wanted to laugh but we dare not, for fear of reprisal. The knot on his necktie he placed on his Adams Apple and wiggled the knot with his apple. It caused his tie to ripple all the way down his chest to his belly. It was murder trying to contain our laughter.

Our class was trained to march everywhere like miniature soldiers. We were marched onto a deserted playground during a lesson and brought to attention facing a sports field. The playground was higher than the sports field giving us a panoramic view of the field. Mr Haywood was armed with a longbow and carrying a quiver of arrows on his back. He proceeded to fire the arrows indiscriminately, in various directions, out over the adjacent sports field.

Each time he loosed an arrow, he looked at one of the children and commanded, "Fetch," whilst pointing in the direction of the flight. We were running in all directions, retrieving his spent missiles. That was another complete lesson gone. Can you imagine a waste of time like that today?

The pupils did not take sport very seriously in the Ag. It was the third and fourth year of that school class, known as 3 and 4 Ag. The class even made up songs about the Ag with words that rhymed with Ag (like shag and fag).

Our school was split into three categories of learning. After completing two years of basic education, we were given one of three choices regarding our future employment.

The choices were limited to a nautical future, in regard to the merchant navy, an engineering future, such as a garage mechanic, or farming, such as farm labourer. The whole school was geared up to provide work fodder, as the war was over and cannon-fodder was no longer required.

England needed a cheap workforce to build up its infrastructure to support all the businesses and industries of the fortunate side of its society.

After my first childhood mate Jack had passed his eleven plus exam and moved to a different school from me, I started knocking around with a new pal John Low. John, who lived in a cul-de-sac just up the road from me was in the nautical class. Charles my brother in-law, through his business activities in the meat market, obtained complimentary tickets every week for ringside seats to the wrestling tournaments at Torquay Town Hall. Charles gave the tickets to me so that my pal John and I could regularly attend.

John and I became ardent wrestling fans and always arrived early to obtain seats right in the front row. Mike Marino, an Italian heavyweight, was thrown out of the ring one day and landed right at my feet. He put his big hand on my knee to help himself back on his feet before jumping back into the ring. I was terrified!

One evening, John and I arrived at the Town Hall early and were the first in the queue. I was stood in the entrance alcove, leaning on a pillar next to the entrance door. The Black Quango, a big, black wrestler came through the door, opening it from the inside. As he came out of the building, the door bashed my nose. I was squashed between the door and a stone pillar. Big Bill Verna, Francis Sinclair Gregory and Masambula, all big wrestlers, swiftly followed him, each bashing my nose in turn. The Black Quango could turn one eye to the left while the other eye looked forward. He gave me the cockeyed stare and I stood silent and rigid with watery eyes from my throbbing nose. My pal John thought it was really funny. "Why didn't you tell them off?" he joked.

John and I practiced the wrestling holds and throws we'd seen in the show. They were very effective and painful. John was screaming his head off when I held him in a full Boston Crab and I thought he was joking until he held me in the same hold.

At a youth club named The Apollo Club, John and I took up judo lessons. After three lessons we were practising judo on a lawn in John's garden and I accidentally broke a boy's arm. The boy's name was David Rogers who was nicknamed Benji. Benji was a harmless person and a little retarded. He was also a little frail whereas I was not. It hurt me as much as it hurt anyone to see poor little Benji's arm completely broken in two and pointing the wrong way in an absurd fashion.

Benji was not endowed with good looks and although he was small he had a rugged appearance in his face that could fool a stranger into miscalculating his harmless nature. He lived in a fantasy world pretending that he was a hard person, a tough guy! He often bragged about always being in the company of "hard cases" and belonging to one gang or another. His father knew differently however, and understandably gave me a good hiding and made me cry. It was not that he hurt me; I was genuinely feeling sad for poor Benji. Mr Rogers heard my Dad's name mentioned by one of the other children and he gave me sixpence to dry my tears (and it did).

My judo training was getting me into trouble. After breaking Benji's arm a boy attacked me at school, and I threw him over my head onto a wall. The boy was two years my senior and suffered a broken leg. Luckily for me, the teachers regarded it as an accident (probably because of the difference in our age) but I thought it was self-defence on my part against a bully, and that I had reacted as I had been taught to respond. The next time I went to the judo club, the instructor told me to attack a brown belt (I was only a red belt, the lowest grade). I think the instructor wanted the boy to throw me to see if I had learned to fall properly. I attacked the boy and got him into one of the wrestling holds I had learned in the Town Hall wrestling bouts. The boy then screamed his head off to the instructor, insisting that I was hurting him. This incident caused me to be barred from the club. I was only doing as instructed and did not know that the sort of headlock I used was not allowed. (That was the end of my judo career, which was just as well, I thought!)

One of our sports teachers Jan Rid was a former captain of the Devon County rugby team. He watched me play rugby for my class, and although we were heavily defeated he must have spotted some ability in me to play.

After the game he suggested that I join the school team. I had to tell him that I had no shorts or money to join. He gave me a pair of shorts, which I wore, and he gave me a shilling to pay my membership fee. I spent the shilling on eight Domino cigarettes and that was the end of my rugby career. Domino's cigarettes were sold in packets of four cigarettes for a tanner (sixpence a pack).

The same teacher became aware of my ability to throw the discus, when the class was split up to make up two teams for playing a game we called rounders (a game similar to American baseball).

After the team was picked I was the odd one out and told to go to the other side of the sports field to throw rubber practice discuses. (These were smaller and lighter than the real discus.) I was instructed to throw the discuses towards the area where the rest of the class was playing their game.

"Are you sure you want me to do this?" I asked the sports teacher. I was a practised thrower of stone missiles of all shapes and sizes and knew they were in my range of throw.

"You do as you're told, boy," said the teacher. He seemed pretty sure I couldn't reach them.

The teacher and my classmates were calling out and franticly waving their arms to attract my attention as I threw the discus right in the middle of their pitch. My throwing ability impressed the teacher and he entered me in the sport championship there and then.

I became the brunt of the assistant headmaster Mr King's scorn. No matter which way I turned, trouble seemed to be my middle name. At the time I had no idea why this was happening. I'm sure now that he exceeded his authority.

Mr King had a cyst on one side of his forehead that had a diameter of about one inch and stood out about one inch. All the children said it was a horn growing!

His offensive against me commenced during my last term at school. He called out my name at morning assembly, together with that of Sam Tickle, one of my classmates. We were asked to appear on stage in front of the whole school, which numbered some seven hundred pupils. Also on the other side of the stage were two more boys.

"Hey, Sam," I whispered, "What have you done?"

Sam shrugged his shoulders and replied, "Nothing, what have you done?" I made the same gesture. Neither Sam nor I had any idea of why we were there.

We stood on the stage for a while awaiting our fate and Mr King, who was acting as headmaster in the head's absence, spoke to the whole school.

He asked the children assembled in the hall to gaze upon the two boys on his left (being Sam and me) and then referred to the boys on his right. After a half-minute pause he said, "Form your own opinion about their attire!"

That's all he said before dismissing the assembly. Sam and I were dressed in jeans. Sam wore plimsolls and I wore a pair of American trainers that Norman, the bandleader on the Queen Mary, had brought from America. He called the trainers American baseball boots that were unobtainable in England. Everyone was envious of my trainers. Our jeans had three-inch turn-ups that terminated just above our psychedelic socks. We wore zip up, brightly coloured cardigans that we tied into a knot in the front instead of using the zipper. Knotting the zipper was my homemade fashion of the day, that had caught on with some of the other kids.

The other two boys on the opposite side of the stage wore school uniforms, which our parents could not afford.

After the school assembly was dismissed, Sam and I received the cane, just because of the clothes we wore. Sam had his punishment first. We had six strokes on each hand and three across the backside. I never batted an eyelid at the punishment, even though the strokes on my buttocks stung. Sam's response was the same.

I held a smirk on my face throughout in defiance. Sam had already gone when I had mine. As I walked away from Mr King, I was dying to rub my buttocks but I didn't want him to see me show any sign of discomfort. I waited until I rounded a corner and then rubbed my bum, only to hear him shout, "By the way, boy, what's your name?" (As if he didn't know.) He just wanted me to know he saw me rubbing my buttocks.

Mr King was in charge of the engineering classes and he instructed us on engineering for a half-hour lesson once a week, as engineering was allied to farm tractors. He must have formed a real dislike for me because I was so cheeky and yet so backward.

I believe the only reason he called my classmate Sam onto the school stage that day was to hide the fact that he had embarked on a personal vendetta against me. He was not our form teacher and as we only saw him for one half-hour a week. What possible interest could he have in me?

To back up my theory of his personal hatred, he singled me out to be barred from the playground, the gymnasium, and the sports field for the rest of my school days. During these intervals, I was forced to spend my time sat in my classroom with a book on the English language to study. I was entered to throw the javelin and discus in the school sports but was not allowed to train. I have never heard of anyone at this school having these restrictions put on them before. Sport was a part of the school curriculum.

No teacher supervised me during these periods, so I became bored sitting in the classroom on my own with a book that I could hardly read. The whole thing seemed pointless. From my desk the sports field was in full view through my window, and after a while I found it too much to bear. I needed practice for the coming sports day event so I decided to ignore his prohibitive order and ventured onto the sports field.

I ran onto the field and started to practice with the javelin and, somehow, the assistant head got wind of my insubordination. He came onto the sports field shouting and waving his arms in the air. He was in the far distance and I was about to throw the javelin in his direction, so I did. I threw it as hard as I could, knowing that I couldn't quite reach him but it landed a few feet in front of him and gave him a fright.

He gave me the cane again but the restrictions were lifted. I believe the headmaster Mr Rooks became aware of his personal vendetta and warned him off.

Having received no practice due to Mr King's embargo on my sports activities, I didn't do so well on the day of the championship. It poured with rain just as I was about to throw the javelin. The grass was so slippery my baseball boots would not grip the ground. Some of the kids had spiked shoes and fared better, but I still managed to come second. I threw the real discus for the first time on that day and threw three no-throws that were just outside the target area.

My sports teacher took the trouble to check the distance of my throw, and later informed me that I had broken the Devon schoolboy's record by twenty feet, which was a considerable margin. He wanted me to take the sport seriously but I was now fourteen years old and more interested in earning a living than playing games.

CHAPTER 6

THE BALLAD OF BOBBY LANE

School wasn't teaching me anything of use any more; even if I had continued attending for another five years, I would have remained a moron. My future had to be gainful employment. I had no ambition other than earning an honest living. I now consider that chimpanzees might have acquired an equal degree of education to that of mine during one year of intensive cramming.

My schoolmate, John Low and I shared the same years progressively throughout our schooldays and yet he was almost a year older than I was. We must have been on the border of division in the selection of our annual school term.

In 1956, during our last year at school, John acquired an old acoustic right-handed guitar and was forever picking simple tunes from it that never amounted to much. He allowed me to play about with the instrument, but as he had reversed all the strings to suit his left hand, I found myself contorting my fingers in all directions to make the simplest of chords. I'd tire after a few minutes and lose interest in it. He later purchased a left-handed guitar and gave me his right-handed original. After rearranging the strings back to an orthodox hand I purchased a guitar tuition book, written by Bert Wheedon. I studied the book and really tried to get the hang of music and finally, I cracked it; I learned how to play.

It was at the start of the school summer holidays in 1957 that John and I finally left school and went in search of jobs. I applied for a job on The Great Western Railway. I wanted to clean steam railway engines. Cleaning steam engines was a sort of apprenticeship possibly leading to the job of a fireman. After several years as a fireman, if you were good enough or lucky, you became a driver. My reasons for wanting the job were as stupid as I was.

The Railway already employed my first childhood mate Jack Barnet and a few other pals. John Low had applied but failed the eyesight test. He had discovered for the first time in his life that he was colour-blind. Imagine going all the way through school and nobody noticing a thing like that. The money seemed good on the railway and my mates looked like workmen; they were absolutely filthy, covered in soot and oil. I thought my parents would be proud of me if I looked like a real worker.

I took a bus to Newton Abbot Railway Station for an interview and on meeting the railway official concerned with my application, I was seated at a desk and asked to fill in the application form.

The form required my name to be written in full but unfortunately I couldn't spell my second Christian name (which is Clive.) I thought K was a capital C and the interviewer stated, "You don't spell Clive with a K?"

"We do in our family!" I quickly replied, trying to bluff my way through.

He wasn't falling for that futile excuse and dictated a couple of paragraphs of the poem Mary Had A Little Lamb as a spelling test. On completion of the test, he took my test paper and retired to an adjoining room to examine my work.

For what seemed like ages I sat alone in the room waiting for the results and thinking about my options if I should fail. My fifteenth birthday fell during the summer holidays on August ninth. I was fourteen at the time of this test and school-leaving age was fifteen. If I failed to find employment by the end of the summer holidays, I was faced with the ultimatum of returning to school for another year. The room was relatively quiet, with the distant sounds of trains shunting carriages around the rail yard. Intermittently I could hear the muffled sound of my interviewer and some of his colleagues talking in the next room. Their chatter was interrupted now and then with outbreaks of laughter as they scrutinised my dismal scrawl. When the examiner returned to the room, he advised me to go back to school. That's the last thing that I wanted!

Whilst looking for a job and still aged fourteen, I was christened. My christening came late in life due to the Second World War. My mother wanted to get it done before I started work. It was performed jointly with my baby nephew Keith, the son of my brother Ron. He was less than one year old. I didn't have to wear swaddling clothes but I felt like a right prat all the same. My mother had purchased for me a pair of grey baggy trousers and a blazer so that I might look smart for my job interviews. Being a budding Teddy Boy I hated such square clothes and had to wear them to the christening. I remember saying to my mother, "Do I really have to be christened?"

"Yes," she said and continued to explain in a devout manner, "You won't be buried on consecrated ground if you're not!" My mother truly believed in such religious doctrine. I can honestly say now what a load of rubbish!

During the hot summer days of our last school holiday before starting to work, John and I played our guitars in John's garden and in the cul-de-sac just outside of his house. Little Benji who lived opposite John (his broken arm now recovered) tried to sing with us but it sounded terrible. The three of us had our photograph taken and we all looked the part with our trouser legs sewn up to make drain pipes, which was the Teddy Boy style. Over the next few months, I couldn't put the guitar down. At times I practiced for ten hours a day until I couldn't press my sore fingertips onto the frets.

Mr Rooks, my headmaster had written a letter of recommendation that I carried with me for my job applications. It stated that I was punctual, reliable and very good with my hands.

I was chuffed with the letter; not realising it said nothing of my mental ability (I didn't have any). It probably implied that I was a dextrous pugilist.

From interview to interview I travelled, each time receiving the same negative response, "Go back to school!" They were unanimous, until my luck changed when I attended an appointment with a local building firm. Two brothers were co-owners of the firm, and the one who was to be my assessor was busy and had no time to interview me or look at my school appraisal. He just stated briefly, as he passed me outside of his office, "Start Monday, at eight in the morning." He gave me the address of a building site and he was gone.

The job was for a trial period only, as a test for an apprenticeship. Had it not been for that builder's emergency, I would have had to return to school. I later landed the apprenticeship for the plumbing trade, and the deeds were signed on the twentieth of February in 1958. The deed registered my date of commencing my five-year apprenticeship as the seventh of October 1957. Although I started work aged fourteen in July, apprenticeships were only legal for fifteen-year-olds.

My success in landing the job was due to my size and strength. The firm wanted a donkey for the heavy work more than they wanted an apprentice and I filled that requirement.

On the morning of my arrival on site, a foreman directed me to a plumber whom later became my master. (The master was the term used on my indentures). He was sat on the first lift of scaffolding around a house, dressing lead flashing under a bay window.

What's he doing bashing lead sheeting around with wooden sticks I pondered? I thought a plumber messed about with the U-bend under the sink like I had seen them do in American comedy films. Later, I learned of course, that a plumber was the Latin word for a worker of lead. I was instructed on my first day to learn the names of all the wooden lead tools he owned. He had about forty different bossing sticks and mallets of varying sizes and shapes, all made out of Lignum vitae, Hornbeam and English boxwood. It was my job to learn the names of all the tools and hand them to him when asked. At the end of the day I would tend to their upkeep by cleaning them with a cloth well soaked in linseed oil.

The plumber was a cockney who, as a child, was sent to Torquay to get away from the Blitz in London. All these kids were a little sharper and cheekier than the locals were. They considered we locals as slow farmers with straw in our hats and this man, it seemed to me, still held that view, even in his late twenties.

He had attained the rank of a corporal in the REME during his National Service after the war and I could imagine him enjoying that little bit of power over other men. He was always shouting his big mouth off about everything and I could see that not many of the other tradesmen liked him. I thought that he was a typical know-all, and a creep when the boss was around. I thought of him as a pompous prick.

I was quite shocked and dismayed at the sudden realisation of the length of our working week and lack of holidays. The building industry workforce worked for five eight-hour days a week and four hours on Saturday morning, forty-four hours a week in all. During the school term apprentices had one day a week at the technical college and two nights after work. I enlisted to do two extra lessons at night during the first year, learning welding in three different metals bringing my total to four nights. We had one week's holiday a year and bank holidays: two days at Easter, one day on May Day, one day in August and Christmas and Boxing Day, being six days in all. This was equal to two weeks' holiday a year. After all the holidays we had at school, this was a shock. 'Have I got to do this for the rest of my life?' I thought. 'What have I signed up for? It's no wonder that older people relish their childhood days.'

Wages for the job had not entered my mind, as my father had always urged me to get a trade. I can understand this, as he was a labourer. My starting wage was two pounds five shillings a week and I had to purchase all my own tools out of that. The extensive tool requirements were set out in a small booklet as laid down by the trade union to make sure that your boss did not force you to buy other tools that would be to his advantage. I couldn't help thinking that my mates on the railway were getting a pound a week more than I was and they did not have to buy any tools. 'I hope my dad's right about this trade,' I thought.

I began to teach John and his brother Allen the things that I had learned from my music book, and being the budding entrepreneur taught three other boys also to play, for ten shillings an hour each. (My wages as an apprentice was forty-five shillings a week).

My sister Sheila left her husband Charles at about this time and lived with a drummer in a jazz band. What Sheila didn't know about drugs he did. John, Allen, and I practiced with him one day in their flat to try and get some experience at playing with a real professional. They had just bought the Elvis record Hound Dog and Heartbreak Hotel as a present for me and we played it for the first time in their flat on their hand-wound gramophone. He eventually took a fatal overdose, after which, Sheila went from one man to another, as most junkies do. This hit her husband Charles badly, but eventually he met a nice lady who really helped him back on his feet. I did not lose contact with Charles because I liked him. He was a good man.

John, Allen, and I decided to form a band and named it 'The Strangers'. We managed to get another boy Jeff Perkins (nicknamed Fego) interested in playing the drums for us. Two more lads were vocalists.

John had found a job working in a small workshop rewinding electrical motors (so much for him being in the nautical class at school). In his work's lunch break he once made a new steel spring for his air rifle using the firm's machinery. It was a lot more powerful than the original spring.

He turned this skill into practise when he built his own solid electric guitar, incorporating a tremolo arm. The arm raises and lowers the tension on the strings when pressure or relief is applied to it, thus changing the musical tone of the note. It's operated by a single spring. He incorporated a feature that was an improvement on the very best guitars available at the time. Most guitars fitted with the tremolo arm went completely out of tune if you broke a single string. All the strings were affected by the one master spring, which held the bridge of the guitar in place. This meant that it was impossible to continue playing with the remaining five strings, whereas you can on a conventional guitar. John overcame this problem by connecting each string to his own self-made spring, using six springs in all. I don't think he ever realised what a breakthrough in design he had made. I don't know if his design has ever been equalled to this day.

The guitar looked good and sounded good. His firm painted their reconditioned dynamos with mottled blue cellulose paint. John used the paint on his guitar and the effect of the mottled paint twinkled in the stage spotlights. The left-handed feature looked good on stage too.

In 1957, we began playing at small gigs, like the YMCA, and Church halls, which helped us to purchase better equipment. We chopped and changed vocalists until we ended up a four-piece band with me as the only vocalist. I played rhythm guitar, John played lead guitar and his brother Allen played bass guitar. The drummer Fego, was the youngest at fifteen years of age, I was fifteen, John sixteen and Allen eighteen.

When I meet with old rock and roll guitarists nowadays, we refer to our musical prowess in the early years as the "three-chord trick". The most popular chords were the major ones of E, A and B7. We learned to play for hours juggling the three chords, which were ample for most early skiffle and rock and roll tunes. Some of the best rock guitarists in the world started in this way.

We wore black trousers and shoes, black suede waistcoats and black, string bow ties on white shirts on stage. This was the cheapest gear we could get together. We already owned most of the gear; we only needed the waistcoats and ties. John and I always wore black cavalry twill trousers as our best trousers.

Apart from the one pair of cavalry trousers, we wore jeans. At that time, we decided to learn ballroom dancing at the Castle School of Dancing. Our trousers were showing signs of wear and the odd stain, so before going to the dancing school, we thought we would smarten up our cavalry twill trousers and brushed black boot polish into the stains to hide them. There were no girls from our neighbourhood at the school and I think we stood out like a sore thumb. The girls soon became polished off with us. Black polish didn't look too good on their dresses and we were finding it hard to buff up a partner!

During my apprenticeship, I saw many of the other apprentices leave the firm to serve their two-year compulsory National Service. It was abolished, fortunately, just before I came of age. There was another plumbing apprentice who was older than me and he later joined the Devon and Dorset regiment.

The stories I had heard about National Service from the returning soldiers gave me the impression that everyone was treated like dirt. It was the old cannon-fodder thing, you were nothing and expendable (just like being an apprentice, I thought). Most of the tradesmen returned from their National Service with the same opinion, it was two wasted years.

National Servicemen, on returning to their jobs, had a guarantee of six months' work with the firm they served their apprenticeship with, and usually that's all they received before being sacked.

Not one interesting story did I hear from these ex-servicemen, it was all 'spit and polish' whilst stationed at home and all 'flies in your dinner' when serving abroad.

The only good stories were from the older veterans, who had served in World War Two. I listened intensely to their fascinating tales. One such veteran was Johnny O'Hagen, a man with pure white hair. He had loads of great stories. He was once a top class boxer who had fought Freddie Mills, a world champion. He was a sergeant during the war and had served in Burma. When he joined the army, his hair was black. His fear was so intense whilst fighting in the jungle that it turned white overnight.

Later, when my hair was falling out in clumps in the sanatorium, I was reminded of Johnny. It's something you have no control over. No matter how you try to hide your fear from others, inside, that other you shows its fear in its own way.

My master, according to my indentures, had power of attorney over my life (I believe it exceeded that of my parents and my employer) and he used the power to boost his ego, instead of looking after my well-being. He called me a dogsbody and that's how he treated me. How I ever managed to complete that apprenticeship, I'll never know. I believe it was partly due to those times being harsher than today, and the army training that made bullies out of little men with stripes on their arms.

He often played tricks on me to amuse his fellow workmates. He'd heat a metal tool with a blowlamp without my knowledge and then, ask me to pick up the tool and hand it to him, resulting in me burning my hand. The last thing that I needed was burnt fingertips when playing the guitar at night and weekends. Time and time again this would happen. He kept me so busy, I was always too occupied to notice his pranks until I got hurt.

I often worked under Brian the other, older apprentice plumber. I learned something from Brian that has bugged me all my life. After the first year of my apprenticeship, I received a rise in pay of just over one pound a week bringing my total pay to three pounds ten shillings. For the first time in my life, I had one shilling income tax deducted from my wages.

"What's this?" I asked Brian.

He explained what income tax was and how the more you earn the more you pay.

"How much tax do you pay?" I asked, knowing he earned twice as much as I earned.

"Nothing," he replied.

"What!" I exclaimed. "Why?"

"Because I am married and have a child," he replied. Brian had married at the age of sixteen.

"So what?" I suggested. "What's that got to do with me? You chose to have a baby and you chose to get married. I chose to be single. This is not right. If I have a child, I'll pay for it myself!" I could not understand why I, who was earning less, should pay for his choice of lifestyle. I was most upset, to his amusement.

I still find society inflexible for the single man. He's the last man off the ship. He's the example when punishment is doled out and the last in line for benefits. I considered that he is the champion and the punch-bag of society both at the same time.

Our little band played a half-hour stint on Saturday night at the Co-op Hall, behind Union Street in Torquay, which was to Torquay what The Cavern Club supposedly was to Liverpool. These half-hour stints were trials where other people with interest in booking groups could study our progress.

The Co-op Hall was opened in February 1957, and was the first rock and roll dance hall in the southwest of England. It belonged to a promoter, Lionel Murrell Digby, who managed most of the local rock bands and performers. All the local bands played at the Co-op. I remember Screaming Lord Sutch and

Johnny Kidd and The Pirates appearing there. Lord Sutch was carried on stage concealed in a coffin. It was stood upright and he appeared through the coffin door as his introductory music played.

Peter and Gordon with Lionel Digby
my Manager centre.

The Co-op Hall had a reputation for fights between the locals and visiting gangs from Exeter and Plymouth. Some of the locals nicknamed it the "Bucket of Blood". It was all a part of teenage culture with Teddy Boys and rock and roll.

We played at Haccombe House, which was a large, private estate out in the countryside. It had its own private church and a very large outdoors swimming pool with a marble statue at one end and marble steps leading down to the bottom of the pool. I had never seen such extravagance. Apparently an Arab sheikh once owned the place and had installed the pool.

This event epitomised the swinging fifties and sixties to me. Bikers with their black leather jackets came from all around carrying girl pillion riders to the gig. A barbecue was laid on and it felt as though everyone knew each other in the friendly atmosphere.

A large proportion of the bikers came from the Kawilodi Café. We referred to them as the Kawilodi gang. The Kawilodi was a coffee bar that sold snacks, Espresso coffee and Coca-cola. It was the "in place" for teenagers, situated in the main street in Torquay. At times there were as many as fifty motorbikes parked outside. Some of the Kawilodi gang still have reunions to this day. Even gang members that settled in Spain turn up for reunions.

Most bands had a talent spot in the evening, and Benji always came on the stage and sang Muleskinner Blues. Benji had a terrible voice but everyone cheered Benji more than anyone else. He really believed he was Elvis Presley.

We were becoming known locally as a reasonable band and were given a live audition at the old Regal Cinema in Exmouth. The cinema had been converted into a dance hall. A well-established band topped the bill that evening and we were given a half-hour slot during their interval to show our merit.

We were auditioning for the established promoter Lionel Digby, who owned LMD Entertainments, a theatrical company. He had taken us to an outfitter and kitted us out with new outfits to wear at the venue. He also lent us his brand new Zephyr Six car to get to the venue, which was twenty miles from our hometown. We had played for Lionel before at smaller gigs, but he wanted to upgrade our band and take us under his wing.

This was the first time we had been in charge of a new car. Lionel could not attend the show himself. The main band was to be our judges on the night. John was the only one of our band holding a driving licence and it was only a provisional licence. We bluffed Lionel into thinking he had a full licence and took a chance on being caught by the traffic police. Like film stars, we cruised around the town of our debut posing to the local girls. We felt like millionaires.

On reaching the cinema and setting up our equipment on the stage, we nervously awaited our cue. We pondered over the clothes that Lionel had given us to wear. John, Allen and Fego liked the coats and kept them, everything else was thrown into rubbish bins at the back of the dance hall. I wore the clothes I stood up in. Jeans, white zip up coat and green, high-heeled winkle picker shoes with a large silver buckle on the side. Under my coat I wore the top half of a black tracksuit (we later told Lionel we had lost his outfits en route).

I was very nervous as the time of our slot arrived, we all were. At almost the last moment, I was took short and had to run to the toilet. My mates were calling out for me to hurry up. I sat there for what seemed like ages. Finally, the time for our debut arrived and we stood on the stage and started to play as the curtains opened. I was singing a number entitled 'Twenty Flight

Rock' which was sung by Eddy Cochran on record. We had never played under these conditions before and the screams from the audience, coupled with the sudden glare of the stage lighting, almost took my breath away.

The crowd thought we were great and our tenseness ebbed away. Our half-hour stint seemed to flash by and to our surprise the main band would not return to the stage. We were going down so well with the audience, they insisted we continue playing.

We played the whole evening and were a hit. The band now had a good manager to look after our interests and find us more lucrative work. From now on, the venues and the money improved. The main band that had judged our performance even followed us around, turning up at our venues, just to watch us play!

Ex-army sergeant Johnny O'Hagen kept me amused on the building site. He was employed as a bricklayer's labourer and tended a big gang of bricklayers. They were on piecework, which meant they were paid according to the amount of work they completed.

On one occasion, the gang was working on a site of town houses. The bricklayers, who were on the top lift of scaffolding around a house, were demanding more bricks and mortar. Johnny couldn't meet their demands for materials fast enough and became mentally frustrated at the impossible task before him.

He turned on the bricklayers screaming at them, "If you want me to work like a horse, I might as well look like one." With that said, he stripped naked excluding his Wellington boots; picked up his hod full of bricks and climbed the ladder; it was some sight. I wouldn't say he looked like a horse but he came pretty close to a donkey!

Windows were swinging open on all the occupied houses on site. Housewives were drawn to the windows by the sound of all the men cheering. They were looking on in amazement. It was a sight to remember!

After a couple of years of training, I became useful enough for my master to employ me on his private moonlighting jobs.

One of my tasks was to make ready and light the petrol-fuelled blowlamp. I performed this function early one evening and was extremely fortunate to escape from a blazing inferno. To light the blowlamp, petrol was poured into a small well at the top of the lamp and ignited. After a short time, the heat from the flame vaporised the petrol inside a sealed chamber at the centre of the well. On releasing the vaporised petrol out through the nozzle, a spark of ignition produced a fierce blue flame. It had been a hot, sunny day and some of the petrol in the well of the lamp had vaporised into the air in the room. There was a large flash on ignition that erupted around the room and made me jump. I accidentally kicked over my spare can of petrol causing the uncapped can to spill petrol onto the floor and that too ignited. I watched the flames spread across the room as the petrol flowed across the floor. Being young and inexperienced, I tried to beat out the flames with my bare hands, causing my hands to catch on fire.

Fortunately, my master and the electrician working with us were auxiliary firemen. They saw me prancing around like a red-hot disco dancer and came to my rescue. They threw a large old carpet over the flames and me and extinguished the fire. I escaped relatively unscathed.

I called on John one evening and heard some bad news regarding our band. He had fallen in love and could not give his attention to anything other than this girlfriend, and the band was to split up.

It was a great pity, as we had built up a good following and I think the band had good potential. We had played for about two years together.

John's romance did not last for long and he regretted breaking up the band and thought it would all start up again at his command, but things move on.

Our drummer joined The Vampires, a band whose members were great friends of ours. I did a twelve-month spell of singing in cabaret, backed by various bands including The Vampires, under the name of Bobby Lane. I had adopted the name in the Strangers band because I was said to look like Ty

Hardin. He was a film star starring in Bronco Lane, a cowboy series shown on television.

Bobby Lane performing
at the Town Hall Torquay

During the time our four-piece band was together, I had been learning to drive a motorbike. My father owned a motorbike and he allowed me to practice riding the bike behind the gasworks on private land. I was not old enough to learn on the public thoroughfare.

To transport me to work each day, I had managed to purchase a drop-handlebar, six-geared racing pushbike. I loved the thrill of speed and always pedalled flat out, just for the thrill of it.

In the mornings, I usually rushed to work after oversleeping, owing to my late nights with the band. One morning I was halfway to the building site and overtook two cars whilst pedalling downhill. In doing so, I approached a right hand corner too fast and crashed. The next thing I knew, I was in hospital!

My injuries were superficial, just a few stitches in the face and skin grazes on my cheek and chin. I was sent home the same day but had to have a few days off work because I had been concussed.

The news of my accident got around and John, who was so vain he wouldn't venture out of his house if he had a pimple on his face, thought I was scarred for life.

One side of my face was black and blue and swollen to twice its normal size but I knew it was superficial and wasn't bothered. It was John who noticed a difference in my face when the swelling was gone. When I smiled, there was an indent in my cheek muscle. I thought my cheek muscle was split and might need stitching together so I mentioned this to the nurse on my final check at the hospital. She just laughed and said, "What are you moaning about? You've got a dimple in your cheek!" She turned me to a mirror and said, "Look!"

As we both gazed into the mirror, I cocked my dimple with a smile. "You're right you know," I said, and she was; all the girls seemed to like my new dimple.

A stream of girls bringing me flowers and fruit were lined up on my garden path, at times forming a queue outside my front door (which was rather nice). Unable to invite them into the home (because my parents were too embarrassed to let them see how we lived) I thanked them for their gifts and said I'll be back on stage soon. I had never regarded my life as poverty-stricken; we were an average family. Poverty to me meant being hungry and having no home. I regarded my life as rather fortuitous. My father was a very good breadwinner and the whole family, as they grew older, contributed what they could. My parents and their three young children had moved from a one-roomed flat in town into a three-bedroomed council house with no furniture. Our furniture was all second-hand or scavenged from the local refuse dump. Other young families did the same. That's how things were just before the war when they moved in. We had no carpets on our floorboards and only linoleum in the front room. These girls, on the other hand, were a little more fortunate. We regarded them as posh birds. They lived in private homes away from the council estates. I didn't care about class distinction and I don't think the girls did, but my parents did.

After suffering two more accidents where I ended up in hospital that year, I realised that a motorbike was not for me. My lusts for speed were too great and I don't think I would have lived very long on a motorbike.

Injuries received on my second accident were similar to the first, but on the third occasion I broke my kneecap and ended up in plaster of Paris from my crutch to the tip of my toe. This meant I had to get around on crutches for what seemed like ages.

I decided to buy a car and purchased an old Rover for ten pounds; I again practised behind the gasworks and my brother Ron gave me driving lessons on the highway.

Because of my driving lessons before the qualifying age, I applied for a test immediately on reaching driving age, thinking I would pass easily.

On the day of my test my brother instructed me, "Above all, don't let the examiner think you're scared." Bearing this in mind, I drove around the course like a maniac, the examiner turned as white as a ghost. He gave me a form to indicate the points on which I had failed. Which was everything, except a lack of confidence!

My brother had learned to drive whilst in the paratroopers and the civilian requirements for driving were less focused on quick escapes from nuclear bursts.

I resorted to taking professional lessons and the first thing I was taught was to open the door for the examiner (I had nearly left the last examiner behind). Needless to say, I passed my test on this attempt.

In 1959, John, Allen, and I spent our summer holiday camping in the Doone Valley, a remote part of Exmoor. We still knocked around together even though the band had split up. My brother Ron had lent us his tent. It was a large, brown bell tent that slept eight people. He had purchased it in a second-hand shop for his family outings. John had hired a car off of one of his workmates.

My father had given me his old electric shaver to take with me. I had not used any other form of shaving and of course, an electric shaver is no good when camping in the wilds of Exmoor.

We had camped just off a small lane by a stream near the start of the Doone Valley. On the other side of the lane was an ancient forest. The tree trunks and main branches were hideously bent and tangled. They were covered in green moss and grey lichen. I had never seen such a sinister looking forest and was dying to explore it.

The first chance we had we entered the forest but couldn't make any headway. It was too overgrown and wild, we were

69

trapped by the mass of tangled branches. It must have been centuries old and had never received husbandry.

We called into the towns of Lynton and Lynmouth after the first day of camping for supplies and spent the day sightseeing and shopping. Local people were eager to tell us about a great flood that had happened in 1952. It swept away a part of Lynmouth town killing many locals. It was a national disaster. The town was back in shape and functioning normally when we arrived. The two roads descending down to Lynmouth were very steep. The locals also told us a tale about their old lifeboat many years before when it was dragged up one of the hills during a storm by loads of people. They had to launch the boat out to sea from a safe harbour to save mariners in peril. The road was so narrow that walls had to be demolished en route to navigate the bends in the road.

Come evening I was still pondering over how to use my electric shaver when an idea struck me. We had one round three-pin wall socket in our house and nothing to plug in it. Everything electrical including the shaver was plugged into the light socket. Why not use the light socket on a lamppost I thought? After dark, I shinned up an old-fashioned lamppost and sat on the crossbar. I removed the light bulb and plugged in my razor and it worked. The silhouette of me shaving against the starlit sky must have been quite an unusual spectacle for the locals of Lynton.

The next day we called into a small cafeteria in Lynton named The Woolly Lamb. It had a jukebox with all the latest rock and roll music. It played three records for a sixpenny bit. I had a farthing in my pocket, which was more or less the size of sixpence. I just had to try it!

To my surprise it worked, it played three records for a farthing; you could exchange one sixpenny piece, for twenty-four farthings. I thought, there's money to be made here!

Farthings were being recalled as non-legal tender and they were hard to come by. Taking the cliff railway down to Lynmouth Post Office, I purchased all the farthings they had in stock and having acquired a good pocketful returned to The Woolly Lamb Café.

My luck was in, a gang of bikers all wanting to play the jukebox, had settled in the café. I sold the lot at two farthings for a sixpenny bit. My friends and I were rocking all the way to the bank.

The next day, we called in at The Woolly Lamb and the jukebox had a sign hanging from it, which read, 'OUT OF ORDER'!

"Where are the bikers?" I asked the proprietor.

"They're all barred," said the proprietor.

"Why, what happened?" I said.

"The bastards were putting farthings into the jukebox!" He replied. If only he knew where they got them I thought, as I sat down at a table with my coffee! Things were quiet in The Woolly Lamb!

A farmer called in to our tent on the third morning and charged us a fee of one shilling for each day's camping. He sold us fresh eggs and a bottle of milk.

"Where are you off to today, boys?" he said, just making light conversation.

"We tried to explore that forest but it's too overgrown," I explained. "We're going to walk up the Doone Valley today to look for the waterfall. You know, the waterfall that John Ridd and Lorna Doone hid under when being chased by Carver Doone."

He probably never knew what I was talking about. We had seen the waterfall in the film, Lorna Doone. The people thereabouts capitalised on the film and book. There was a small church with a window missing a pane of glass, allegedly the same glass broken in the shooting at Lorna Doone's wedding. The Lorna Doone Farm with its sale of cream teas was situated in the valley.

"Good luck," said the farmer, as he climbed back into his Land Rover. As he drove off he called out, "Mind out for my bull, he's grazing some way up the valley."

We all looked at each other thinking, BULL?

After parking our car in the Lorna Doone Farm, we set off on foot up the valley. From here on the footpath was the only access.

Five miles up the valley, having edged our way along the side of the stream playing about along the way and taking in the beautiful scenery, we came to a fork in the valley and decided to go right. By now we were thinking that there was no waterfall. That scene in the film must have been shot at another location.

As we rounded the bend we came across the only bit of grazing pasture we had seen that day. We all froze as we saw the bull fifty yards in front of us. It was looking right at us. There was nowhere for us to hide. No fences to jump over and no trees to climb. The bull was tethered with a very long rope attached to a flimsy stake driven into the grass. He started lumbering towards us. Not knowing how long the rope was and thinking, surely that stake won't hold him, I'm not talking bull when I say we all ran like hell back down the valley, shouting to each other in turn.

"Is he coming?" said I.

"Fuck knows!" said John.

"Will that stake hold?" said Allen.

"Fuck knows!" said John.

"What about the waterfall?" said I.

"Fuck the waterfall!" said Allen and John.

Eventually we stopped to catch our breath and realising we were now safe contemplated our next move. I suggested, "Let's all go and look for the Golden Fleece back at The Woolly Lamb," and we all vacated the valley.

During the middle years of my apprenticeship, I had a narrow escape from what could have been a fatal accident. I had just acquired a Calor gas blowlamp. The gas bottle contained thirteen pounds of high explosive liquid gas when full. It was a round metal bottle, with a thick metal rim attached to the bottom to act as a level base for standing the bottle upright.

My employer was inundated with distress calls from customers with burst pipes, due to frost. Although I was not fully trained to take on this sort of work I was coerced to aspire above my station to appease the unprofessional aspiration of my employer. I had been summoned to a local bakery to repair leaking lead pipes in the attic space.

The building was very old and sited near a railway track. The soot and smoke from the steam trains had penetrated the roof space, leaving every nook and cranny covered in a thick layer of black coal dust. I could see water leaking from pipes everywhere but despite this, the bakers were still working below.

I crawled along the narrow loft with a candle in one hand dimly lighting my way, whilst dragging my gas bottle behind me with my other hand. I managed to struggle to my feet, although I was still crouched into a stoop because of the shallow roof space. Suddenly, there was a blinding flash; the whole roof was lit up with a bright blue light!

A bare electric cable had penetrated the supporting rim at the base of my gas bottle, leaving a quarter-inch hole in it. I didn't feel a thing! I believe my Wellington boots and a tremendous amount of luck saved me from electrocution.

The old lead-covered electric cables were falling to pieces in disrepair. An experienced plumber would have been more insistent, and made the baker (who was hell bent on maintaining his production) shut the electricity supply off before venturing into the loft.

If the cable had touched my gas bottle one inch higher, it would have penetrated the gas chamber and the whole bakery would have blown up and me with it! (Like a plum flambé!)

John, Allen and I were on a camping holiday a few days before my cabaret debut. I was to appear in Looe, a small town in Cornwall, with a well-known band called The Wild Cats from Plymouth. Performing in cabaret was a mixture of experiences, some of which we appreciated more than others. Our holiday had begun on Exmoor and then we moved to Brighton, where we camped on the outskirts of the town. We had our first experience of Whisky A Go Go Clubs in Brighton and noticed the locals had a weird way of dancing. Modern trends were always on our minds, being from the remote county of Devon. As it happened, we later realised they were all smoking pot! Finally we drove down to Looe and camped on the verge of the main road leading into town. I wanted a sneak preview of the town and the people there before making my appearance.

I was pleasantly surprised when confronted all over town with posters, advertising the event and proclaiming me as the star attraction. The posters had two-foot high pictures of me on them.

At the age of seventeen, I thought this was marvellous. Imagine me, walking around the town in mid-summer, with people pointing at me and saying to their friends, "It's him, Bobby Lane!" And then they were asking for my autograph.

What a contrast to the building site where I was a dogsbody, and always covered in mud in the winter and dust in the summer.

John regretted breaking up the band now as he witnessed me in awe of myself. He could only watch while I received all the young ladies' attention. He had ditched his girlfriend by now and started to court Liz who was a nice girl. I latched on to a beautiful blonde girl back in Torquay, and like most teenagers I fell in love.

The girl's name was Corrine and I was besotted with her. She was the one for me, the one I would marry. She felt the same way and after a couple of weeks of dating she invited me to her middle class home to meet her mum. I treated her with respect, and Corrine and I were celibate. 'No more one-night stands for me,' I thought, 'I'm going steady. This is how things happen,' I believed. 'This was the road to marriage.' Then I ended it! She casually made a comment about a singer in another band. "If he asked me for a date I would have to go out with him," she said. I replied, "He's all yours," and walked away from her for good.

It turned out she was just teasing me but it hurt me so much that in my mind I would never let anyone hurt me like that again. I was crazy about her, and her friends told me that she felt the same way about me. She broke my heart and although her friends all approached me on her behalf I stubbornly refused to even talk to her. I'd see her opposite me in a dance hall crying her eyes out and sending her friends to talk to me but I stuck to my ground. From now on I made a vow to distance myself from love, it was too painful. Up until then I had never realised I could be so stubborn and unforgiving. (I'm sure I've mellowed just a little with age.) Fortunately, at that time I had my new life as a cabaret singer to take my mind off of Corrine.

My master at work was still playing his stupid little tricks on me, burning my fingers with tools, and I was getting pissed off with him. I thought, what's good for the goose is good for the gander and planned my revenge. I was inside a bathroom helping my master to install waste pipes to the suite, and he was outside the house sat on scaffolding. He was shouting instructions to me through a hole in the wall to pass one tool or another through the hole to him. Most of the time, I was sat on the side of the bath awaiting instruction, so I heated the end of a two-foot steel engineering rule with my blowlamp. When he called for the ruler, I made him wait for a while to annoy him and sap his concentration. I passed the hot end to him as his screams for attention grew to a crescendo. I was delighted when I heard his screams change in definition from anxiety to agony!

I thought he would take it in the same way that I was forced to but instead, he demanded that the builder terminate my apprenticeship. The builder had to arrange for my master's car to be driven home whilst the builder took him home in his own car. He said his injuries were too painful for him to drive. His hand was bandaged like that of an Egyptian Mummy and the incident was logged in the site accident book. The builder, who had been a prisoner of war to the Japanese, was fortunately sympathetic to me. He was smiling when he asked me, "What have you done to your master?" Apparently the whole building site was laughing at him.

After years of his abusive acts of inhumanity towards me, my master could not tolerate my one act of defiance. I now saw him for exactly what I had thought he was, an arrogant shit-head. The boss's father who had started the building firm was a director of Torquay United Football Club. He took me to the football ground and handed me over to a maintenance man and told me to follow his instructions and carry out small plumbing maintenance jobs whilst he found a new master for me on site.

The highlight of my cabaret era came as a result of Richie Valance (a well-known singer) contracting a throat infection whilst on tour in England. Richie came to fame with the song 'Tell Laura I Love Her'. He had to cancel his contract in the southwest of England and I was selected to take his place. I appeared at the top of the bill in three locations, starting at Bristol.

The backing group was a band from Exeter named Gary Kane and The Tornadoes. I had known them for many years and we got on well together. That was not the first time I had appeared on stage with the Tornadoes.

The show in Bristol went down really well with the audience and after the show I wandered off around the city centre looking for a restaurant. Starving as usual, I ended up in a Chinese restaurant eating a steak and chips.

Afterwards, I casually strolled back to the venue and noticed a large crowd outside the building; it looked like a riot was in progress.

Lionel my manager, was stood at the stage door and I asked him, "What's happening, Lionel?"

He was all hyped up and demanded, "Where have you been? I've been looking everywhere for you. These are fans of yours demanding your autograph, you twerp!" As he spoke, he shoved me into the screaming fans.

The fans pulled and pushed me in all directions as I signed my autograph on autograph books, pieces of paper and every part of young ladies' anatomy. When I eventually boarded the bandwagon for the journey to our next venue in Exeter, I still had one of the young ladies in tow.

The vehicle we were travelling in was a converted van with windows added to the sides. One of the engine pistons had broken and we drove all the way to Exeter averaging a speed of twenty miles an hour. It took half the night to complete our journey. To add to the dilemma, I was being actively amorous with my newfound fan on the back seat of the van. To emphasise my ardour, I inadvertently pushed one of my feet through a side window, breaking the glass, and there it stayed throughout almost the entire journey.

Motorways did not exist in those days and we negotiated every little town and village. The van must have been a spectacle, trundling through some of the small towns. Our engine was making a deafening noise in the still of night, drawing the attention of anyone who was about at that hour. My foot protruding through the broken window must have added to the spectacle drawing all sorts of conclusions to mind from any onlookers.

I never knew what happened to that young lady after we reached Exeter. Lionel saw her safely home to Bristol I expect!

Lionel found lucrative venues for me in cabaret but given the choice, I wouldn't dream of undertaking some of them. I preferred being a member of a band, as opposed to performing solo. He sometimes put me in situations performing with ballroom dance bands, entertaining people who were dancing in bath chairs!

Rock stars sang ballads but these were few and not the songs for ballroom dances, and of course, these venues were nearly always with bands that did not even like rock and roll! Although I knew a couple of the dance bands, I missed the crack. (By that I mean the ad-libbing and the banter between pals.) I carried on doing cabaret for a year but I missed my regular mates.

Lionel often drove me home at night when he was very tired. Loads of singers and guitarists were being maimed or even killed in road accidents in the fifties and sixties. Often I had to nudge him when he drifted over to the wrong side of the road when falling asleep at the wheel.

One time, he drove up a bank on one side of the road, then swerved back across the road and drove up the opposite bank. This resulted in my staying alert; I dare not take my eyes off the road and being an apprentice plumber by day, I needed sleep.

My Birmingham cousin Percy (who looked after his war-wounded brother George) sang in dance bands as a crooner in those days. He had to have elocution lessons to get rid of his broad Birmingham accent. Percy was in a fatal road accident. He was returning home late after a dance, in the back seat of a friend's car. The car collided with another and Percy was decapitated. I don't know what happened to George after his death. The family had drifted apart by now and we seldom heard anything about relations nowadays. I remember them as soft-spoken gentlemen.

It's no wonder, years later, when I entered the sanatorium with a high temperature and in need of sleep, doctors were interrogating me, making allegations about my possible involvement with drugs. The interrogation took place in a small room with my parents as witnesses. They couldn't understand how I maintained the pace of my lifestyle without drugs. No member of the band had taken drugs. Some mornings when my father saw me come home when he was sat at the breakfast table, he warned me that I was burning the candle at both ends and that it would lead to trouble. I never took a scrap of notice.

Eventually, I also joined The Vampires as a rhythm guitarist and singer, the same band as our drummer Fego had joined. I was happier with my mates, it was more enjoyable travelling around with people you knew and with whom you had common interests.

The picture above is of the Vampires Rock Band from left to right, Adrian Hall, Bobby Lane, Johnny Hondo, Jeff Perkins, Mel Fear, and Johnny Carnell

78

The Vampires band had been established for years. They had a great following of regular fans that always turned up wherever they played no matter what the weather or location. John, Allen and I had played with The Vampires lead guitarist in jamming sessions in his home in Teignmouth before we had played in our first gig. This meant that I was well familiar with their style and traits.

The Vampires were promoted as a packet show. The lead guitarist Adrian Hall (nicknamed Gunga) had a brother Trevor who managed the group, and my old manager Lionel acted as one of his agents. Johnny Carnell played bass guitar and Mel Fear, Shadrack and Johnny Hondo were resident singers. We performed on stage all night and backed various acts. On occasions we backed people who had current hit records in the top ten.

This band was never going to be famous; it performed an all-round musical variety show, unlike my first band The Strangers, who I believe did have potential of stardom.

The police had labelled The Vampires with a reputation for inciting trouble wherever it went, but this was now the early sixties, and rock and roll was enough for the police to get the hump about anyway. On occasions, various band members became involved in scuffles with the locals, mainly over the local girls. We more than once jumped off of the stage to defend each other but mainly to protect our equipment.

We were still struggling financially to maintain our equipment at times. The total cost of all our equipment including costumes amounted to approximately three thousand pounds. You could purchase a new house for less than two thousand pounds at that time. We nicked the odd microphone or lighting equipment from some of the halls and theatres to compliment our gear. Consequently, when we were invited back to venues to perform, the local constabulary turned up to interrogate us about a missing item that had strangely disappeared on our last visit.

We had taken a nice rope from one location that looked very suitable for tying the tarpaulin down on our trailer. We were invited back to play and sure enough, there was the policeman waiting for us.

"Excuse me, boys," the policeman said. "When you were last here a rope went missing, I don't suppose you accidentally took it?"

Our little drummer Fego replied, "Oh no sir, if we'd taken it, we'd have pinched it!"

The boss of the firm that I worked for eventually took me to another building site and put me with a new master Lou Stanton, who was a gentleman.

For three years I had put up with the first master. The new master was older and wiser. He struck me as a clever considerate man and a much better tradesman.

People referred to Lou as Teapot Louis. He carried a tin kettle around with him and before he commenced work on any job, he would roll a fag and boil the kettle using his blowlamp. He always stood back from the job while the tea was brewing and said to me, "We'll give it a coat of looking at before we start, Bob." He remained my friend for years.

When I talk about the crack in relation to being with your mates in the band, all-night cafés come to mind. We were always racing around day and night with hardly a moment to spare. Snacks were grabbed here and there whenever possible but hunger always dogged our day. The one place you could rely on for a pause in this hectic scramble for a hot meal and a moment to reflect was an all-night transport café. Our favourite café if we were travelling to Cornwall was the Indian Queen's all-night café, if we travelled through Somerset we stopped at The Black Horse all-night café.

Often we would meet with other bands at these cafés, returning from their gigs. Opportunities arose for us to twaddle about the thing we all had in common, rock and roll and the venues we played at. There were always new songs and stars emerging to chat about.

On one occasion in the Indian Queens Café, we were sat at the table eating our meals, when four men sat at another table started to sing. It was an old cowboy song, the sort of song that cowboys sang whilst sat around the campfire at night.

It was about two o'clock in the morning and they turned out to be a professional Barbers Quartet. They sounded absolutely beautiful. The whole café was filled with atmosphere. One of the guitarists brought in an acoustic guitar and accompanied the Barbers. It was not long before many of the musicians were joining in, with drums, mouth organs, saxophones and other instruments. In the end the whole place was swinging with county and western, rock and roll and jazz. That's what I call 'the crack'!

Can you imagine the comedown when I was in a situation like this during the middle of the week? On reaching home the following morning, I'd barely have time to change into my working clothes and get to work. Back to the mud and dust of the building site to start a hard day's work, instead of getting some much-needed sleep!

My family had labelled me a sissy because of my interest in playing the guitar. All my efforts and progress were reviewed with slight. This was just a follow-on from the days of my bad school reports. The label that was given to me then had stuck permanently. The only time they ever saw me perform live on stage was as a result of my mother being taken to hospital with acute appendicitis. I was appearing with The Vampires at the Bradley Hall at Newton Abbot. My family came to tell me she was in hospital and to have a sneak look at me in my band. All of them came including my father, my two brothers, two sisters and their husbands and wives. Naturally I wanted to be informed about my mother's urgent dispatch but one of them would have sufficed to deliver the message. I suppose they were hoping to ridicule me about what they saw, but they were silenced.

I saw them enter at the back of the dance hall, just as our singer Shadrack was walking on the stage to sing 'Jezebel'. We had started to play the heavy rock beat of 'Lucille' to the song and Shadrack had a very powerful voice. He had a tremendous following wherever he went. Attired in his gold lamé suit he looked every part a top class rock star. We were dressed in silver, green and red glitter suits. I could not get off the stage at that point, and my family had to wait. Everyone in the dance hall crowded the stage when Shadrack was on.

Shadrack first sang with us in a talent competition at Ford Hall, Newton Abbot. His mates goaded him into singing after he had consumed a substantial amount of Dutch courage in the bar. He was a tree-feller and was still dressed in his working clothes. His baggy trousers were tied at the knee with string and his hobnailed boots were falling to bits. He wore a chequered shirt and had a spotted handkerchief tied around his neck.

His voice was fantastic and his rugged appearance was popular with the locals. We noticed he was slightly tone deaf. The band asked him to call in to our practice session one afternoon for an audition. He did not have a clue about singing in key but he soon learned.

Trevor, the manager of The Vampires, owned a black Wolsley 680 car. We used the car to travel to gigs. At that time, the police were using the same make and colour car (black) for their highway patrols. It was a powerful car in its day and we once reached a speed of one hundred miles an hour on a flat, straight road.

In the middle of the night, during our return home from gigs, we used to imitate the police! In those days there was very little traffic at night. Our driver and front passenger donned two imitation police caps as soon as a bandwagon was spotted and the boys on the back seat ducked their heads. We'd give chase and pull the bandwagon over to the side of the road and have the crack with the group!

Gunga our lead guitarist had a double-barrelled shotgun, and used to fire it out of the car window into the sky as we passed through quiet villages at night. That was just being a teenager. Imagine what would happen today in this world of gunmen.

Gunga carried a six-volt motorcycle battery in a satchel to power a lamp to hunt hares and rabbits at night. One night, we visited Hope's Nose (a coastal quarry) in Torquay to lamp rabbits. A rabbit or hare freezes when caught in the beam of light. All you can see is its eyes and you blast away.

Gunga gave me the gun and I spotted two shining eyes and shot. I killed my first hedgehog! The problem was, the quarry was common ground and surrounded by luxury houses with coastal views.

A crescendo of screeching seagulls alarmed by my gunshot breached the calm silence of the night as they took to flight. All the lights in the houses were being switched on. Shocked by the sudden change from serenity to chaos, we now felt that we were the hunters who were about to be hunted. We took our usual stance and ran like hell.

Night school as an apprentice was now over and this gave me more opportunities to play. Courtney Park, Newton Abbot became the venue of our first open-air gig. We played to what our manager said was thirty thousand people on a stage sited in an open-ended marquee. It was a fair, a big public celebration for something. Our drummer Fego was over the moon because if ever there was a complaint about the volume of noise, it was always blamed on him!

The volume of our amplifiers could be easily turned down in small buildings but Fego liked to put his heart into his drums. On the day we played in the marquee he put the drum pedal right through his bass drum skin. He always seemed to break a skin in big events. Our manager said we were the first rock band to play in the open-air events. We once played in the Royal Arcadia Ballroom at Bournemouth, with an orchestra behind us.

Another band told us to stop off at a venue in Somerset on our way to another gig. It looked like a large, prefabricated building and was packed with people. At the far end on the stage, we could see the unmistakable bowler hat of Acker Bilk. There he was with his jazzmen entertaining the crowd. It was fantastic (and this was in the daytime!)

Lympstone Marine Barracks held an officers' ball, to which we were invited to entertain. We shared the bill with a jazz band. I drove home that night in my own car accompanied by Keith Setters (a keyboard player and friend of mine). It was a stormy night with torrential rain and trees were being blown down. The road home from Exeter was a treacherous bendy road and I hit a deep patch of water that stopped the car dead in its tracks. Keith and I had to push the car out of the puddle to the next downhill gradient to get the car started again. What a sight we were in that storm pushing my car with a double bass on the roof rack! It was at times like these that I could understand why some people gave up the game!

Paul Raven was a rising star with a record in the charts entitled 'Tower of Strength'. Frankie Vaughan (who was higher in the charts than Paul) also sang it. I hated the song! I remember doing several shows with Paul, who later became Gary Glitter.

Paul kept pestering the secretary of my fan club after a gig in Redruth in Cornwall. I had a fan club as Bobby Lane and the secretary was a Redruth girl. Paul was younger than me by over a year at the age of seventeen and the girl was not interested in him. Pissed off with his over-exuberance, I left him alone with her, but she stayed faithful to me.

Mattresses were laid out on the floor of the dancehall for our accommodation that night. Starving and rummaging for food as usual, we found a serving hatch leading from the hall to a kitchen. We searched the kitchen and found tea and sugar but no milk. This was two o'clock in the morning and the whole town had closed down for the night.

A service road ran through a tunnel under our dance hall giving access through an arch leading to the main road. A café under the dance hall had a side door that opened onto the service road in the tunnel. Shadrack was nearby and tinkering with the car engine that had been missing a stroke and he mentioned to us that the café might have some milk inside. After casing the joint, a decision was made between us to break into the café and pinch a bottle of milk! We could be seen from cars if they stopped at a set of traffic lights on the main road and so we had to control them. Two members of the band went around the corner and jumped up and down on the rubber pads, to keep the lights by the arch on green. Paul and I, meanwhile, tried to push Shadrack through a skylight over the café door.

Eventually, we managed to push Shadrack through the window to an awful clatter of pots and pans that sounded deafening in the still of the night. He pinched the milk from the fridge, leaving his oily handprints on everything. I don't know why we chose Shadrack to climb through the skylight; he was about the biggest member of the band! (Perhaps he had the bottle?)

Over the years when asked by friends about my rock and roll exploits, I have often mentioned Gary Glitter and said his name with pride. How sad it is, when someone who had everything, let himself, and everyone he has ever been associated with, down.

In the band's heydays, we also shared the billing with some of the stars from America whom I had idolised in my school days. Gene Vincent of 'Be Bop A-Loo La' fame was one such star that we appeared with in Torquay Town Hall. At the same venue, on another night, we were with B Bumble and The Stingers, of 'Nutcracker' fame, who we found to be great people. B Bumble allowed us to use all his equipment, which was made in America and far superior to ours. After the gig, he wanted to give us all his equipment but his manager pointed out that the reason we could not obtain the gear here was because of an export ban and he could not allow us to have it.

CHAPTER 7

A BRIEF BUSINESS ENTERPRISE

My years of business began when I was barely twenty years old. The master, who was so noxious towards me at the start of my apprenticeship, having got over his burnt hand, knew my potential as a hardworking tradesman.

Out of forty-four apprentices in my class at the technical college, I was one of two who passed the City and Guilds examination. Both of us received a second-class pass. The practical teacher was an old plumber and was replaced the following year with a young teacher with modern training. All forty-four students in that class passed the same exam that following year and received first class passes. In the eyes of a potential employer, I was relegated to a second-class plumber in one year. It didn't matter to me later when I became a self-employed man but the time of paper qualifications had arrived. If I had applied for a job, I would have come second to all those pupils with first class exam papers.

In other subjects such as technical drawing and mathematics, we had competent teachers that were very concerned about the students understanding their lessons. One teacher told me to write what was in my head. He said he would unravel my spelling. He just wanted to know if I understood what he had tried to teach me. I learned more in the technical college than I had in all my years at school. I still could not spell, and dyslexia was still an unrecognised handicap. I went from the bottom of the class at school, to the top in the technical college. Some achievement for the college teachers, I think? The only thing the teachers had taught me in the infants, the juniors, and secondary modern schools, was the fact that I was stupid. The teachers in the technical college however, contradicted this diagnosis and taught me that I was not!

My master had established a plumbing contracting business and in the last few months of my apprenticeship, he enticed me financially to work for him on the odd weekend and evening. I had seen the builder that employed me purchase a brand new

Vauxhall Cresta car for one thousand pounds. I knew that if I worked for the rest of my life on a plumber's wages I could never own a car like that.

Apprentice money was very poor and the master was paying me more than double my earnings at the end of my apprenticeship with the promise of much more.

He had entered into a partnership with Brian Kneil, the older apprentice with whom I had worked before. Brian had completed his National Service and also completed his six-month guaranteed rehabilitation work with our employer.

Brian was already acquainted with the business venture set up by my master and recommended that I should accept an equal part in a three-way partnership. I felt I could trust Brian, so accepted the offer. The fact was that Brian and I were chasing the same carrot.

It was not very long before things started to go wrong with the partnership. I was working on my own building site and getting my payments regularly. These were pooled for the three of us to share equally. Brian did the same but the master rarely made his contribution. He made excuses, saying he could not get his money. Consequently, the money we were earning was way below what Brian and I had been expecting.

I recommended we all three called on the builder who was not settling his account on the following weekend, to clear up any misunderstanding that might exist between us.

The three of us met at the builder's home and were stood at his front door. After ringing the doorbell, the builder opened the door to face us and, to my surprise, I was stood there on my own. My partners had walked off down the road. I had no idea of the details of the work completed on our account, only the amount of money the builder owed to us. I had assumed that my partners, through their Army training, had recognised the builder as a toff and therefore their superior. He was not a toff he was a gentleman.

When I asked him for the money, he explained that he had a counter bill for damage to his property, caused by the bad workmanship of our firm. I now realised the real reason why my master had disappeared and coaxed Brian to go with him. He had obviously cocked the job up! I had no way of refuting the builder's assertion. I apologised for my ignorance of the account and offered to accept whatever, if anything, that he was willing to pay (what else could I do?) The builder had a good reputation for settling his debts, and I thanked him for his patience, shaking his hand, and left with a small cheque.

There and then, I decided to leave the partnership and establish my own business. Fortunately, I landed a very nice contract with a lady hotelier who owned three hotels. She took to me kindly and found work to last me for months. It was not long before Brian asked me if he could join my enterprise, to which I agreed.

My new partner and friend was an ex-schoolboy champion of England amateur boxer. We took over the work on the building site that my ex-master had messed up. It seems the builder recognised my honesty in dealing with the misunderstanding.

In the early part of 1963, I was beginning to find it hard work to continue playing in the band. My mother commented on my stage shirts, saying she could not understand why they were soaking wet in the summer. It was sweat, caused by the heat from the stage lights among other things.

We were playing at more and more venues and I noticed the audiences appeared to get younger and younger. Having started building up my plumbing business I felt too old for rock and roll; it was time to move on. Our bass player Johnny Carnell had left the band at one time. It was just through a tantrum, a thing that happens with many musicians. John Low my schoolmate and lead guitarist from my first band, stood in on bass guitar and he had never played bass before in his life. We had to travel for miles out of our way en route to a gig, just to pick up a left-handed bass guitar. We rang all the local suppliers but being left-handed always created obstacles for John. He hardly played a note on stage all night. I walked in front of the footlights on stage that night, to the very edge, where the fans could reach my toes. I played my heart out to try and draw attention away from John. I was shattered come the final curtain. It was harder to provide the standard, which we were being paid good money to provide.

The last night I appeared on stage, our lead guitarist Gunga and regular drummer Fego could not make the venue. Malcolm Dodd the new lead guitarist was very good, but it's not the same as playing with your usual guitarist. I decided this would be my final night with this band and that there would be no looking back.

My business partner Brian and I started working seven days a week from then on, from seven in the morning until nine in the evening. My plan was to save enough money to get away from plumbing, to see the world, or become a professional guitarist in London.

I had been having problems with my chest for about a year and constantly visiting my doctor. The first signs of trouble came during the lunchtime football kick around with the lads on the building site. We were working next to a full size football pitch and being so few in numbers to make up two teams, there was a lot of running around to do. Whilst struggling for air, I noticed pains in my chest.

Eventually, when working all those hours with my partner, I felt utterly exhausted as I walked off the building site at night. I could easily have lay down in a trench, or in the gutter at the side of the road and comfortably gone to sleep.

The disease in my lungs had taken a real hold on me. For a year my doctor had insisted that it was just a smoker's cough. She had passed this information on to my parents, who totally worshiped the omnipotent doctor, and I became the object of ridicule for everyone.

This all climaxed on the day that my doctor asked me nonchalantly, "Which medicine do you prefer, the one in the red or the green bottle?" I blew my top and demanded an X-ray of my chest stating, "If the X-ray is clear, I will never bother you again."

To work abroad, as I was contemplating, I would have to be fit. The results of the X-ray and a notification that I was to be admitted into the sanatorium with all haste came in the post the next day.

I have always remained very sceptical of doctors since those days (who could blame me?)

If only I could have secured an X-ray through my doctor a year earlier, all the butchery that I had to come might have been avoided. You would think that having experienced all those years when the whole world was battling against the Consumption, my doctor would have paid attention to my persistent pleas for help! Only a few years before, mobile X-ray units had regularly visited every town in the country in an attempt to combat the Consumption.

A lot of class distinction existed in those days; the doctors were a class above us working class, and my mother was used to cleaning the house from top to bottom just for the doctor's visit. Fast-track training after the war came to mind, just as it was with tradesmen and teachers.

Before the National Health scheme, my parents were always apprehensive about the cost of the doctor's treatment and that's why they had learned to grovel to the likes of this pompous parvenu. They could not distinguish the difference between a decent doctor and a quack. We had a quack, and my mother waddled after her until the day she died.

After I received the news of the shadow on my lung and it's potential consequences, people began to rally around me. Some were referring to the 'wonderful things they can do nowadays in these sanatoriums'. Others were less well disposed. "You'll never come out of there alive," they stated cynically. The place did have a notorious reputation because of the Consumption. Nearly every family had been affected by the epidemic.

It was at this time I was urged to move into the sanatorium and soon realised I was going to stay for a long time. I informed my customers of my misfortune, and handed my business temporarily over to my partner.

CHAPTER 8

THE DEATH CAMP

Having packed everything needed for a short stay into my old A40 van, I had arrived at the sanatorium with instructions from my doctor to report to West Block A ward. It was the beginning of the month of June. My doctor had led me to believe that I would be staying there for a fortnight, just for a few medical tests.

The residents' car park was situated on the outskirts of the complex, and after parking my van, I walked past a row of chalets towards a large building. It was a sunny day and I asked a man strolling in the grounds for directions. It turned out he was a fellow patient. He pointed to a large building and suggested I walk along a narrow path at the side of the building and round a corner to a set of French windows.

"That's your ward," he stated. I thanked him and trundled on my way to the ward with all my gear.

The French windows were a back entrance to the ward serving as a fire escape. As I entered, I was confronted with a vision of two lines of beds, stretching away from me on either side of the ward. The reception office I sought was at the opposite end.

Hanging all about my person, I was loaded down with an air rifle, fishing rods, nets and tackle. My friends and neighbours had informed me that there were facilities for all these activities readily available. They probably thought I needed some encouragement to enter into this notorious establishment. I looked like Jungle Jim; I had everything barring his pith helmet and a native bearer.

On entering the ward, the patients looked at me in amazement.

"What are you doing here?" they asked.

Confused at so many inquisitive faces and short of an answer, I asked, "Where's the lake?" I certainly looked a chump, as if I had arrived in a holiday camp! There was no lake on the complex, or any other sporting facilities.

A nurse appeared on the scene and when she stopped laughing at this misguided piscatorial big game hunter, she escorted me to the reception room, where I was put wise to the joke.

The nurse registered me into the sanatorium and the doctors (after having their twopence worth of laughter) gave me the most thorough examination that I have ever received. They established that I had a very high temperature and ordered me to bed for the next two weeks, to allow my temperature to drop. I needed no persuasion to go to bed and relished the chance to sleep. It annoys me to think that something as simple as taking my temperature was deemed unnecessary by my own General Practitioner. General Prat, more like it!

I surveyed the patients in the ward around me, there wasn't much else to do whilst confined to my bed. At this stage of my ordeal, I did not realise that all the people in my ward were destined to die very soon and some of them already knew that.

One of the patients came to my bedside and said, "You're Mrs Shear's boy Bob. Don't you remember me? I'm Les Thorn, your local butcher from the Co-op."

"Well I'm damned," I said. "I haven't seen you since I was a kid, Les." We had a chat and Les tried to reassure me about all the wonderful things they were doing for patients in this place. I had heard it all before from my neighbours but it was better to hear that than the opposite, which I had also heard.

My mother often took me as a child into the Co-op shop where Les worked. He always had time to lift me up to the metal cups that held the cash and receipts inside and let me pull the handle that made the cups zoom along on wires to the cashier and back to the counter. They zoomed all over the shop; they spellbound me!

All the other patients were at least twice my age. One of them told me that the man who had occupied my bed before me was twenty-seven years old and that he had died the day before I had arrived.

Some of the regular cleaning staff seemed cheerful enough. The main man was known as Yorkie; he was always laughing and joking. Yorkie washed and polished the floor mainly. This was done with a bucket and mop and old rags wrapped around the mop when polishing. Yorkie didn't get a lot of free time but did talk to the patients whilst working and found moments to become a bookie's runner for the racing enthusiast. He had a finger missing on one of his hands that he had lost during the war. His wife Audrey was also a cleaner and generally did the furniture and windows. Audrey was deaf and reminded me of Lester Piggott the famous jockey when she spoke. Her deaf aid seemed to echo as she spoke, like a feedback on a microphone. They lived in a nearby village.

Three patients, who were nearing retirement age, told me they were farmers from nearby farms. They looked pretty ill and I gathered from our conversation that they had already received a diagnosis of their problems. They were familiar with the running of the ward and I assumed that they had been here for quite some time before my arrival. Farmers are a close-knit community and they all seemed to either know, or knew, of each other. They seemed to rule the roost in our ward. If they formed an opinion about anyone, it stuck. Each one in turn seemed to be a 'yes man' to the other's suggestion. My life was in danger as much as theirs was at this stage but I was a nothing in their eyes, they seemed bland towards me and had no respect for me (or so I thought). They were probably preoccupied with their own destiny and that of their families; I learned to respect this as time passed. I respected their age and fell in line with everything they decided. I look back on them now and realise their ignorance. They meant no real harm and they simply knew no better.

One of the farmers who lay in the bed opposite me had a glass eye. His real eye was lost when an ear of corn lodged in it during the winnowing of the chaff from the grain at harvest time. Two days into my stay, I was watching him during the morning as he coughed up some phlegm and spat it into his metal spittoon (we all had one at the side of our beds). His phlegm was tinted with blood and I witnessed a look of surprise on his face. He spat again and this time the spit was bright red. This truly made him frown in a chilled disbelief as he examined the contents of the spittoon. In the next moment, blood gushed from his mouth like an open tap; it filled the spittoon and splattered all over his bed. The ward was unattended at the time and I pressed the emergency bell by my bed to summon the nurse.

The nurse soon appeared and witnessed the bloody mess. She quickly swept into action and seemed to be doing ten things at once. She was only eighteen years old and was a true professional. Things were soon under control.

Apparently the haemorrhage was caused by the treatment he was receiving. An experiment that had failed!

The patients who were fit enough sat around a table eating lunch and talked about a man called Jim Spry who had been a patient in our ward. Apparently he was moved to a surgical ward on the other side of the complex named New Block, and I had yet to meet him.

"Have you seen Spry?" one patient asked the rest.

"Yes," said one of the listeners, "doesn't he look rough?" They all agreed. The patients were reflecting on how sturdy and proud a man he was on entering the sanatorium and how his operation had bowed him. Jim believed he was about to have one of his lungs removed but the cancer was in an advanced state. The surgeon had closed his chest with his lung intact. Everyone had agreed with Jim's family to keep up a charade about his state of health. Jim thought he had one and a half lungs removed.

When Jim left New Block and returned to our ward for treatment, it was one week after my arrival and I found out that Jim had a habit of greeting new patients with an explanation of what treatment to expect. Realising their anxiety, he tried to put their minds at ease in their new surroundings. Unfortunately, he invariably created the opposite effect.

In my own case for example, he greeted me by saying, "What are you in for?"

"I have a shadow on my lung," I replied.

"Don't worry, they look after you here, boy," he said assuredly, "They'll take you from this ward to the operating theatre and put you to sleep; they'll then operate on you but don't worry, boy, you won't feel a thing." Jim was reflecting on his own experience and by this time, he had your full attention as he continued earnestly, "When you wake up in the morning boy, it's all over, the operation's done, they've cut out the bad lung and you're in BLOODY AGONY!" He emphasised the bloody agony, whilst contorting his face in an agonising pose with his hands clutching his chest.

After this introduction it became a habit for the patients to watch Jim carry out this procedure on new patients. Someone would say, "Look, there goes Operation-Spry," and we'd all watch the expression of fear on the new patients' faces as he came out with the punch line. It seemed that everyone had to go through the Operation-Spry experience.

The patients adopted the anecdote derived from Jim Spry? Whenever pain was involved with minor operations or tests, other patients would ask, "What was it like?" "Nothing to it, it's just bloody agony," was the reply!

Jim Spry was in his mid-sixties, he had been employed in Appledore Shipyard in North Devon all his life and was a shop steward. He was a big, powerful man who had worked hard all his life. It must have been a physically demanding and rugged job, from which he inherited the apparel of endurance in his stature. He beckoned respect and emitted dignity.

My first diagnostic probe was a simple test for tuberculosis. This was a series of pinpricks on my arm set out in a small circle. It took two weeks to determine if I was infected with TB, the same period of time it took for my temperature to return to normal. The test proved negative and I now learned that I was to stay in Hawkmoor for a long period for many more tests. I rang Brian my partner, to tell him that I would not be coming home for some time and that he was now on his own in the business.

With my temperature back to normal, I could get out of bed and move around the sanatorium to explore. I walked down my two adjoining wards nodding to the patients on either side that were confined to their beds and finally came to an area used by the staff. On my left was the office where I had received my medical and on my right was the slop-out room. In front of me, I viewed the opposite wing of the building named East Block A. It consisted of two wards identical to mine. These were full of male TB patients. They were all confined to bed for a minimum term of six months and some of them for much longer. Two of the patients were around my age and I waved to them but I was not freely allowed access to the ward. It was generally accepted that those in my ward should not venture into the TB wards. I was now standing at the main entrance to the building for the first time.

The complex was quite extensive, like a self-contained village with its own shop, café, pub, dance hall-come cinema, snooker room, church and outdoor bowling green. It took me most of the day to get my bearings. The pub only opened at night and was reserved for staff and visitors only. The bar was situated at the opposite end of the cafeteria counter and had shutters that were pulled down over the bar during the day.

One of the chalets I came across was full of bottles containing human lungs in all shapes colours and sizes. They were immersed in a preservative solution! There was even a baby in one bottle! The resident patients usually asked the new patients, "Have you seen the baby in the bottle yet?" I assumed this was for students and doctors to study. The museum was always locked to patients but you could peek through the drawn curtains that were too small for the window.

There was one recreational area of the sanatorium that became notorious to the patients.

"Did you walk up Sputum Hill?" asked the patients on my return to the ward.

"What's that," I asked. They told me it was a country lane, leading from the back of the complex up a very long steep hill. The patients had christened the hill 'Sputum Hill', owing to the nature of the products of their chest complaints, being deposited on the hill.

I never heard of a patient that managed the scale the entire hill during my stay and I never even attempted it. The thought of walking up a hill splattered with bloodstained gob didn't appeal to me. I was told that at the summit of the hill there was a lake and that's where the idea of me angling in the complex was conceived. The patients used the hill as a fitness test. Every so often they would make an assault on the hill to see if they were improving in health by beating their previous records attempt, or beginning to fail in strength. I became accustomed to this in time. The general consensus among the patients was that if you made it to the top of the hill, you lived! No one made it whilst I was there.

Doctor Litler was my principal doctor throughout my stay in the sanatorium. He was about forty years old and looked quite fit. He reminds me now of Edward Fox, the actor that starred as the Jackal in the film 'The Day Of The Jackal'. He had acquired the nickname of 'Spiv' before I had entered the sanatorium. I gathered from our general conversations that he did a bit of sailing from his yacht that he birthed at Shaldon (a small town at the mouth of the River Teign). After my two weeks in bed, he performed my first operation, which entailed the removal of a small piece of muscle from my shin. After a pre-med sedative that made me feel drunk, and a local anaesthetic, the doctor commenced the op. I began singing on the operating table and persistently sitting upright during the operation. I was as high as a kite and tried to watch Doctor Litler at work, but he kept putting his left hand onto my chest and pushing me back down on my back. I think he was taking my jocular nature in the right context; there was a good atmosphere in the theatre. When it was over, I had gained my first scar; it was three inches long. Doctor Litler seemed quite chuffed with the operation and asked me to acknowledge his accomplishment, which I did.

During the operation, I felt no more pain than a few sharp pinpricks as he touched a nerve now and then. After the op however, it was painful enough for me to enlist the aid of a walking stick for a week, What was the point in having an operation on my leg? I wondered. It's my lungs that are at fault. The doctors would not explain anything to me at that time because I was twenty years old.

The age of adulthood was then twenty-one, which meant my parents had to sign for my operations, and they alone were privy to information regarding my condition.

Instead of handing the walking stick back when my leg had healed, I kept it as a toy. In fun, I whacked the young nurses across the buttocks with it now and then, which annoyed some of them. Mr Beaumont, the Sister in charge of my ward, had received many complaints about my tomfoolery with the young nurses.

Mr Beaumont was the one person that seemed to take a particular interest in my case along with Doctor Litler. They were a great team together. I often heard them making arrangements to meet on the weekends to go sailing together. Mr Beaumont looked like the film star Clint Walker, who was currently staring in a TV cowboy series and I nicknamed him after the cowboy star of that series Cheyenne Bodie. Doctor Litler and Sister Beaumont had a great rapport and lit up the daily moil of our existence.

The sanatorium had one Matron and two assistant Matrons. The two assistant Matrons towered over the Matron who was a petite tiny little woman. She was prim and proper and in my eyes everything a Matron should be. She was unblemished, the picture of truth, and the grand matriarch!

It was the procedure in those days, for the Matron and her two assistant Matrons to do the rounds, inspecting the wards. Everything had to be spick and span. If the Matron found fault with anything, the ward sister had a severe reprimand. Persistently I had hung my flat cap on the overhead wall light at the head of the bed and my walking stick hung from the curtain rail that surrounded my bed, which made my bed space look untidy. My air rifle was kept beside my bed and I practised firing it out through the window at targets now and then.

After a critical inspection by the Matron, Mr Beaumont took my stick and hat and carried them out through the French windows at the end of my ward, throwing them out across the field in frenzy. He also confiscated my rifle. Everyone seemed to see the comical side of the kafuffle.

The next day Mr Beaumont called me into the slop-out room where a number of young nurses had assembled. A whole batch of nurses were transferred from hospitals all over the country to do a three months stint of specialist training. They came en bloc four times yearly and lived in a block of flats within the sanatorium grounds. These nurses with Mr Beaumont had just arrived. In all, I was to meet three separate groups of these budding angels, so there was some sport to be had in the grounds of the sanatorium after all.

"Robert," said Mr Beaumont, "I need your body for a few moments for a demonstration."

"OK," I said, not wanting to appear shy to the nurses. Mr Beaumont was about to teach the nurses the procedure for removing blood from patients' arms. He then began using me as a guinea pig, drawing my blood into a syringe and then squirting it down a sink. The nurses lined up and copied the performance, each one puncturing my arm and squirting my blood down the sink. I think that this was supposed to be punishment in Mr Beaumont's eyes for my untidy bed space but I didn't mind playing the tough guy in front of the young nurses.

The next day I was sat opposite Jim Spry at our lunch table and he was grumbling away as usual about his operation. Jim noticed I was struggling to cut the meat on my plate. I was encumbered, due to the nurses' bloodletting on my left arm. It was so stiff I couldn't even use my knife. It was then that Jim showed how kind and considerate he was.

Despite his illness, he got out of his chair and said, "Forgive me, Bob, there I am moaning about my troubles and forgetting that you have yours." He came around the table and cut the meat on my plate. How can you forget people like this?

The problem that I found in being surrounded by gorgeous young nurses was finding somewhere private to be with them. I would see them around the grounds or at the cinema on Mondays and sometimes in the cafeteria but there was nowhere to be alone with them and I wanted to flirt. At the base and to one side of Sputum Hill, there was a field with long grass that I sometimes visited to lie in the sun and be on my own, and I thought that this would be a good spot for a romp. One nurse in particular I had coaxed for two weeks for a date, with no luck. I told her all about my secluded spot but she would not accompany me to my love nest and I fancied her even more. She was a flirt and teased me as much as I teased her. She suddenly received news that her family fortune had changed and she was cutting short her three-month term of training to go home. Things were looking bad for a chance for us to get together but on the last day of her stay she consented to go to my field for a romp. I had arranged an assignation by the dance hall come cinema and from there to walk her to my field.

I was really excited when I set off to the dance hall for our date. As we spotted each other, I was right next to a public toilet near to the hall and bursting to go. I had not been to the loo for three days and was suffering with constipation. 'Oh God, what do I do now?' I thought. I don't know if it was my excitement that had brought it on, but I literally ran to the toilet. I noticed a look of shock on the nurse's face, as it appeared that I was running away from her around a corner. Lots of patients had suffered with constipation. One old guy went for fourteen days without going. He was in a serious state and had a minor operation to relieve him. I think it was because there were no locks on the toilet doors and therefore no privacy. People would walk in on you whilst you were trying and put you off. I spent ten minutes of bliss in the toilet and returned to the dance hall where the nurse had vanished never to be seen again. I often wonder what I missed that day. I'll never live it down, but I felt as light as a feather with relief.

It was July and my next few days were spent eyeing up the rest of the new batch of nurses but there were other things that also occupied my mind. I had got to know a patient named Henry who had more than his share of ridicule from the three farmers before they were all sent home to die. Like most of the other patients, I had given my weight to their constant jibes. Henry was a grumpy old bugger, who wouldn't wash and stayed in bed all day. He wouldn't co-operate with the nurses who wanted him to take part in therapeutic exercises. The farmers looked upon him as a dirty, lazy old man and often told him so.

I did not pay so much attention to Henry after the farmers had left. He seemed to spend most of the time sleeping. Things changed however when I had a dream about Henry one night. In my dream, Henry was shaking his fist and cursing me on his deathbed. The dream disturbed me so much it played on my mind when I awoke. The following morning, having felt guilty about falling in line with the farmers' biased condemnation of Henry, I walked to his bedside for a chat. To my surprise, he started to curse me there and then, just like in my dream. I showed interest in his ranting and he calmed down. He then began to unravel an enthralling tale of an adventure that he had experienced in his youth. It was a tale of endurance, involving a very famous explorer.

The adventure had taken place during the early part of the twentieth century in the Antarctic. He and his colleagues had lived through a tremendously long, arduous ordeal. For many months they were unsure of their very survival. He kept shouting the name Shackleton and saying, "I met him in Australia." I didn't know to whom he was referring at the time, I had never heard of the explorer. Henry was seventy-three years of age and after three years of suffering as a patient in the sanatorium, died later that day. Patients received a bottle of stout each day as a part of their treatment. Henry however, was allocated brandy instead of stout, perhaps because of his past history. Later in life, I learned of Shackleton.

Jim Operation-Spry had moved into the bed opposite mine and I loved to play games with old Jim. I'd be staring directly at his face all day some days. His eyes seemed to be fixated in my direction like he was daydreaming. I used to get fed up with his stare. I'd get out of bed and place a flowerpot on our dining table that was situated between us, just so I couldn't see his face. I'd walk to the table and back to my bed a couple of times to adjust the position of the pot.

"What's the matter with you, boy?" he'd say, as I aligned the pot.

"I don't want to look at your ugly face all day," I'd say. This used to make him mad.

He would hold up his big clenched fist and say, "I'll give you one of these, boy!"

When facing a new test or minor operation, for consolation I would ask the other patients who had already endured the test,

"What was it like?" After the Spry anecdote, they invariably did their best to terrify me. One such test was to be my next experience, the bronchoscope!

The bronchoscope was not like the modern TV scopes that are used today. It was a rigid metal pipe about eighteen inches long and a half an inch in diameter, with a light on the end. You had to swallow the tube rather like a sword swallower. The doctor would peek down the centre of the tube into your lungs.

Before the tube was inserted into your lung, a nurse wrapped a cotton cloth around your tongue and yanked it around the side of your head. The other patients emphasised this, as if your tongue painfully reached the back of your neck.

Sat on my bed with my hanky wrapped around my tongue, I tried to pull it out as far as it would go, thinking 'Blimey, how can they pull it all the way around there?' This made me anxious before the actual experience. It turned out however to be nothing like the patient's description and I was pleasantly relieved afterwards.

It was now mid-July and I received news from other patients that all the farmers had died. It turned out that they had all died before old Henry. I seemed to be always playing host to newcomers.

Having had more tests than the new patients, I was often asked by them, "What was your test like?" Being young, I wanted to show off my courage to the young nurses and implied nonchalantly, "Nothing to it, I didn't feel a thing!" I was due to have a small operation on my throat to remove samples of flesh for laboratory examination. It was something to do with my lymph glands. Bearing this in mind, the other patients asked the young eighteen-year-old nurse who was in the operating theatre that day, to check what I was really like when under pressure.

The standard procedure, for this type of minor operation I knew well. I was instructed to sit on my own down-turned hands on the operating table and two assistants, then pressed down on my shoulders, to make sure my hands were trapped under my buttocks. They wrapped a surgical cloth the size of a bath towel around my head to act as a blindfold, pulling the cloth down at the back of my head, so my face was pointing at the ceiling and my throat fully exposed to the surgeon. At this point you're secure and not going anywhere. (It was the same procedure as for the bronchoscope test!)

The nurse in question was stood to one side pressing on my shoulder with one hand and squeezing my wrist with the other, in a reassuring way. Someone on the other side was gripping my tongue with the cloth and gently pulling it to one side. I suppose this was done to prevent me from swallowing it.

The surgeon (Doctor Litler) began to cut into my throat whilst talking to me, explaining what he was doing. I remember him describing at one point, how he was removing a small muscle and how he intended to sew it back later on. I felt the odd twinge of pain and bled a lot. I could feel the blood running down my body but that was to be expected with a throat op. The nurse meanwhile, disappeared.

When I arrived back at the ward and started bragging about how easy it had been the other patients turned to the nurse for confirmation about my alleged bravado.

"What was he like, nurse?" they asked.

She blushed and replied, "I don't know what happened; the operation was so messy, I fainted." I think she had a soft spot for me. She probably felt more pain than I did.

George a fellow patient, who was a roof thatcher from Honiton in Devon, was obsessed about a ladder he had left on a roof. I had experience in fixing the lead flashing around chimneys and renewing zinc guttering under the eaves for thatchers in Cockington Village in Torquay. You can't rest your tools on the thatch because it's so slippery. George and I had plenty to talk about.

We both experienced a similar test on the same morning and were in our beds, lying on our right side. They called this the recovery position. We had to spit the bloody phlegm into our spittoons. Tiny samples had been cut from our lungs. The doctor used a bronchoscope to look down our throats into our lungs. You could hear the long scissors rattling against the side of the rigid metal bronchoscope as they slid them down our throats to cut the samples. George had his back to me and heard me coughing. He turned and said, "Oh no, not you!" He had just been told he had three months to live and thought I was in the same boat. He never did get the ladder off that roof!

Something happened one morning that made me realise that bravery was only skin-deep. I was sat in bed after breakfast and felt an irritation on my face. I brushed my face with my hand and hair from my head fell on my chest. I swept my hand over my head and handfuls of hair fell on my chest and stomach. Drugs or treatment couldn't cause this, I wasn't on any. It could only have been the shocks to my system from the tests and my anxiety and fear that were causing this effect. My method of control over pain was to concentrate in my mind allowing all the pain, whether it was coming from my leg, arm or any part of my body, to focus in my brain. This left my body limp, helping the doctor or surgeon to work in relative peace from my anxiety. I suppose my hair was the nearest thing to the centre of pain and that's my only explanation of what happened. No matter what image you wish to portray to those around you, nerves have other ways of showing the strain, which you have no control over. This reminded me of my old friend Johnny O'Hagen the bricky's labourer, when his hair turned white overnight in the jungles of Burma.

A man about my own age from Teignmouth town came into my ward whilst I was recovering from one of my tests. He was bedded down on the other side of the ablution rooms and recreation room in the centre of West Block A, so I was unable to see him from my bed. He was undergoing the simple test for tuberculosis. He had received the all-clear on the day that I met him and was due to go home the next day. We visited the snooker room together and spent a pleasant afternoon playing snooker and chatting. It turned out that he knew some of my old band members in The Vampires who grew up in Teignmouth.

After our pleasant day, we were walking across the bowling green on our way back to our ward, when he suddenly attacked me! I was quite shocked! He had momentarily dropped back a pace and launched himself onto my back. He held my head in a headlock, choking me by pulling his forearm tightly into my throat. (The worst thing anyone can do to a person with breathing problems is to restrict their air supply.)

My adrenaline was up instantly, and I managed to throw him over my head, and in turn I restrained him in the same headlock. I was holding him on the ground from behind as I knelt on one knee. I did not restrict his breathing as he had done to me, I simply held him there and asked him, "What the fuck are you doing? Have you gone fucking mad?" He never spoke a word. Maybe he was embarrassed by his failed assault. I released him and left him on the bowling green, whilst I returned to my ward.

Why anyone would want to inflict harm on a sick person I couldn't imagine? I thought about an incident that had happened to The Vampires before I had joined the band. Apparently a local tough guy and our singer Mel Fear had had an altercation. Mel was a man who could stand up to anyone and often did. Friction had built up between him and this tough guy, probably over a woman. After a local dance, Mel had arranged to fight this man on Teignmouth beach. Mel followed the man onto the beach. It was a dark night. They were alone and the man had the advantage of walking into the dark. Mel being behind the man was silhouetted against the town streetlights. Mel didn't see the guy stoop and pick up a handful of sand from the beach. The guy turned suddenly, throwing the sand into Mel's eyes blinding him totally.

After a while, the remainder of the group saw the tough guy returning without Mel and rushed to the beach to see what had happened. They found Mel lying unconscious on the sand. He had been beaten pretty badly. I assumed that my assailant in the sanatorium was probably a friend of the guy who beat up Mel. He must have seen me on stage, he would have been unnoticed by me in the audience. He probably wanted to brag to his mate that he had beaten me up, just to gain favourable recognition in his friend's company. It must have been intimidating for him to fail in his attempt so miserably. I didn't see him again before he left the following day. Perhaps it's just as well.

The next day, I was strapped down on a table in a radiography room in preparation for a test. I soon forgot about my little scuffle. Two stone pebbles the size of your fist (like beach pebbles) were placed between a belt and my stomach. They were pressing into my stomach when the belt strap was pulled tight. I had no idea what purpose this served and it made things uncomfortable; I could not breathe properly.

Two doctors were standing next to the table discussing how much isotopic fluid they should chance pumping into my veins. This illuminated my blood vessels on the X-ray to determine my blood circulation through my kidneys. This was obviously the first time they had used this procedure.

After much deliberation, they decided on the amount to use and began pumping a very large syringe full (about half the size of a bicycle pump) into my arm. After emptying this syringe they unscrewed the fluid container from the needle (which was still in my arm) replaced it with a full container and continued pumping. Before they had completely emptied the second syringe, I went quite red all over; I was on fire, from head to toe. My lungs were full of a ferocious irritation and I coughed so much I thought my eyes were going to pop out as the two pebbles dug into my stomach.

My arms and feet were strapped down to stop me from falling off the table as it twisted and turned in all directions and at one point I was upside down. My feet were high above my head making things worse as I coughed and struggled to breathe. The two doctors had left the room whilst this was happening and were viewing me through a glass screen.

When it was over, they entered the room and were talking to each other in front of me, as if I weren't there. I heard one of them say, "We had better halve that dose in the future," and the other nodded in agreement. As they released my straps one of them said, "You can get up now and dress."

I was pole-axed! I couldn't move! All my energy had gone and they had to call two assistants to help me into a wheelchair. One of the assistants had to wheel me back to my bed. That's when I realised I was just a guinea pig, a disposable product for the use of research. If they had attempted this experiment on any of the older patients, I believe they would have killed them.

Doctor Midgley headed the sanatorium and I was informed that he had suffered the loss of a lung to tuberculosis. Also, I heard that my doctor, Doctor Litler, had had a lung removed. Apparently Doctor Litler was a teacher before he became a doctor and studied to become a doctor whilst he was a TB patient in Hawkmoor. The story goes that he had been confined to his bed for two years and this gave him the opportunity to study the profession.

Doctor Litler conducted most of the minor operations on me and being young, I suppose that I was an ideal specimen for him to practice his hand at surgery, an ideal guinea pig!

Another narrative commonly used by the patients originated from Les Thorn, my local butcher in Hele Village whom I had met on my arrival. He had a lot of weekend home leave. This was quite common among the married men. He was in his early forties and married to a Frenchwoman whom he had met in France during the war.

All the patients recognised Les as the one who put up the strongest resistance against the cancer. He was a real fighter, and every time when returning from his home leave to the sanatorium he'd remark, "It's doing me good, the treatment, I'm feeling much better!" He firmly believed he was on the mend.

It's strange but I remember him stating how bad the pollution from traffic exhaust was as he walked down through Torquay Town. I didn't understand what he had noticed; pollution was not an issue in those days.

His treatment consisted of large injections of a brown murky fluid that made him feel very ill and constantly vomit. He always forced down his food saying repeatedly, "If you eat, you live!"

This was the narrative we all adopted and yet there was I, still the fussy eater that I had been all my life, due to that stupid schoolteacher Mr Sanders, who had made me eat my own vomit. I was not eating enough hospital food and owing to my rapid weight loss, permission was granted for tins of food to be brought into the sanatorium by my parents to complement my diet. I was also permitted to boil my own eggs in the slop-out room.

In those couple of months, I could see Les gradually losing the battle for his life. He was very thin and weak. I sat by his bedside one morning, feeding him his porridge with a spoon; he was too weak to feed himself. I was struggling, trying to tempt the food down inside him saying, "Come on my old pal, if you eat you live."

He looked up at me and shook his head saying, "It's all over, boy, I'm finished." With that said, I called the nurse, who drew the curtains around him. He must have died within five minutes of his last words to me. Then came that awful sound of the electric razor. Why couldn't they use a blade to shave him? Noises like that we all hated!

A moment later all the curtains were drawn around our beds. I was sat with two other patients and we had started a game of cards on the bed. One of the patients was trying to peek through the curtains to see what was happening but I had seen the coffin on wheels many times through the cracks in the curtains, I had learned the ritual.

I called into the slop-out room the next morning to boil an egg and noticed my pal's pyjamas tied in a knot on the floor in the corner of the room. That picture is as clear in my mind today as it was then. May God bless you my old friend!

Some of the other patients were surprised at times, when they alerted me to my parents' arrival and witnessed my dismay at receiving the news. My parents were always arguing, even when I was in the sanatorium, and I hated their visits.

The patients thought I showed a lack of respect and commented, "That's your mother and father, they love you." Little did they know, my father had been unfaithful to my mother and contracted a venereal disease!

My mother, at any private moment, pronounced her disdain of my father for his infidelity and the consequences of his selfish act. My father on the other hand was his normal self. He wanted to occupy his time with me as a chance for him to elude my mother's nagging and invariably would challenge me to a game of snooker, when I was well enough to play. Failing that he would sneak off to some of the other patients for a chat and this gave my mother a moment to burden me with her problems. This enabled my father to both tolerate me and avoid confrontation with my mother. I was glad when my parents left, and felt far more comfort from the other patients in the sanatorium who genuinely cared about me. To tell you the truth, this was the first time in my life I had ever felt at home in this way. I suppose it's because they all showed me respect. That's something I had never had at home, where I was still the family dunce. It's no wonder I miss them all so much now.

The doctors allowed me to go home for a weekend leave at my request. My sister Jean had asked me to complete a plumbing job on her newly acquired house. She was soon to be married and needed to move into her home. Naturally, I didn't tell the doctors the real reason for my home visit.

It was now early August, a few days before my twenty-first birthday. The temperature in the loft of my sister's new home was one hundred degrees Fahrenheit, and I nearly passed out whilst installing her cold water storage tank. During my apprenticeship, if the temperature was that high in the loft you were only permitted to work for ten minutes at a time because of the danger of passing out. The temperature would rise dramatically too, as much as one hundred and fifty degrees, when using a blowlamp. I was not fit but I managed it.

Whilst at home, my mother's nagging about my father drove me to the point where I offered to fight him when he came home from work. She sounded as if no less than patricide would suffice. I observed my father through our kitchen window nearing my home as I built myself up for the conflict. He walked through a grove dotted with dwellings and I could see him intermittently through the gaps between the houses in the foreground.

At the last moment, my mother fell to her knees and begged me not to proceed. What a relief; I was in no fit state to fight my father. After this terrible experience I hoped to hear less of their problems. I had enough of my own.

I was relieved to see that they really loved each other after all the years I had witnessed them battling like Spartans. I was shocked however, at suddenly becoming aware of my position in the family hierarchy, being second to my father who she always defamed at every opportunity. What a time to grow up when I was so confused about my own life. That's how things were between my parents.

When I returned to the sanatorium, a new patient near me emitted an awful pungent smell that filled the whole ward when he coughed. It was almost unbearable and all the patients were complaining in front of him. He knew of everyone's discomfort and must have been embarrassed but he was helpless to do anything about it. He had an undiagnosed contagious disease and was transferred to the operating theatre. We later heard on the bedpan express, that he was operated on all one night to save his life. He ended up in the isolation chalets with a two-inch diameter pipe in his back, draining out the awful stuff that created that smell. Fortunately, he later returned to my ward and seemed to be much improved, before being transferred to another hospital.

I struck up a close friendship with a new patient named Clifford Everly, who was suffering from lung cancer. Cliff was five years my senior at the age of twenty-six (I was now just twenty-one) and he was very tolerant of me. I was pretty dumb and inexperienced; anything outside of plumbing, fishing and rock and roll was a closed book to me. Cliff had been an English teacher in a grammar school. He had recently married a lady who was employed as a teller in a bank and joined her as an employee of the bank. They were very much in love.

Cliff and I often played darts in the restroom and he was better than I was, which surprised me! Regularly I had played darts in my kitchen at home with my father who was a top player in the local league. This led me to believe that I was an above-average player. Cliff and I were about even in the snooker room; you could say Cliff was my best mate while I was there.

I had been a patient for just over two months and endured a half dozen tests by now, all of which were reported as negative. My parents gave me the news after each test.

"Is that good?" I asked.

"Yes," they told me with their faces lit up. I just wanted the doctors to find something wrong so that I could have my treatment and go home. I really didn't have a clue as to what was going on.

CHAPTER 9

THE PASSING OF MY TWENTY-FIRST

Five men restrained me on my bed one day, acting on instruction from Doctor Litler. It was a rehearsal for a liver biopsy. Doctor Litler had sketched a drawing on my body with a biro pen, indicating the position of vital organs in my stomach and chest. He was reading the instruction details of the operation from a small manual and he explained to me, "I've never performed this operation before, so I want to rehearse the procedure before committing myself to the operation." Because he had performed many small operations on me prior to this, I was not unduly worried about his rehearsal.

He had to push this bayonet-like implement, with a grappling hook on the end, into the wall of my lower chest, through my rib cage and on into my liver, enabling him to pull out a piece of my liver.

He explained, "You have to inhale and hold your breath for ten seconds whilst I perform the biopsy. Your liver moves up and down when you breathe and if you breathe whilst I am in your liver, it will tear and cause a haemorrhage." He paused for a reaction from me at this point but I wasn't all that interested. He leaned closer to me and continued his review with an emphatic warning, perhaps to wake my concern, "We are a long way from the operating theatre, Robert, and if you haemorrhage, you would die before I could transport you there to repair the damage."

I was still uninterested, I thought it was just another op, another chance for me to practice my mind-over-matter skills. He then injected a local anaesthetic and inserted a metal sleeve between two ribs to gain easy access to my liver. I had become used to these mundane, though painful little experiences and, as usual; I wasn't taking a lot of notice. (I should have.)

When the rehearsal was over, all the people involved in the operation walked away for a while and then returned to do the real thing.

I was completely oblivious to any notion that this involved pain, as this was never mentioned. I was more concerned when, at the last moment, the doctor decided that I should exhale and hold my breath instead of inhale, which made things a little more difficult. I had never practised exhaling and holding my next breath.

So now we are set, all the assistants grabbed hold of one part or another of my body and the doctor instructed me to breathe in and out quickly, then exhale and stop breathing, he then said loudly, "I'M COMING IN!"

Bloody hell! You can't imagine the shock I felt! I heaved air into my lungs. Obviously the doctor was in my liver, so I assumed it tore as soon as I inhaled. I now realised why every one was holding me down!

I could vaguely hear Doctor Litler as he repeated to himself, "In twist, in twist, breathe away." I could see a red piece of meat on the end of his implement as he withdrew it from my ribs. It was just a fragment of my liver about half an inch in length. It looked like a little red maggot dangling about. My pulse rate accelerated to a critical level and I couldn't catch my breath. I was in shock with my head shaking from side to side and every muscle in my body strained. My mind had vacated my head and my body was out of control.

My friend Clifford Everly in the next bed, called to me through the curtains, "Bob, what are they doing to you?" to which I blurted out the Spry motto in gasps, "Nothing--to--it--Cliff, --its- -just--bloody--agony."

I even asked a nurse to put a lit cigarette into my mouth and she complied but I couldn't suck on the damn thing because I was blustering for breath, so I spat it out.

Other patients concerned about me pushed their way through the curtains to complain to the doctor and were quickly told by the doctor to go away.

For over an hour I continued in a state of shock. Exhausted and covered in sweat, I searched Doctor Litler's face for some sign of help but all I saw was despair and anguish in him. Up until now I had considered my life was completely in his hands but doubt began to touch my thoughts. He busily removed the metal sleeve from my ribs and put a stitch in my wound. He turned to look me in the face and began holding my wrist and timing my pulse rate, I could see there was nothing more he could do for me. I now realised that I was on my own!

It was now down to me to try and control my shock, or die through exhaustion. Concentrating all my thoughts on my feet, I gradually controlled my nervous system on up through my body finally reaching a reasonably stable state, to the relief of everyone.

Doctor Litler and nursing staff gradually drifted away, with the exception of one nurse. She was instructed to keep me under surveillance, which was to be maintained for a period of forty-eight hours, in case I suffered an internal haemorrhage.

Doctor Litler later returned for a chat, "Well, Robert, that was an unexpected reaction," he said.

"I thought I was close to death for a while," I declared.

"You had me going for a moment," he replied. He apologised for what had happened and said he did not understand the reaction it had caused in me.

"Why didn't you give me a general anaesthetic and open me up for the operation?" I asked. He said they had to perform so many tests on me in a short time that I would not recover quickly enough between operations. I thought that if they kept doing things like this to me I wouldn't last long anyway.

When I look back at this situation, I realise this was the first time anyone had discussed the tests I had received. I now realise this was the first operation I had signed for, it was well after my birthday and I was at the age of consent. What a twenty-first birthday present! If it weren't for the dramatic way this operation had turned out, I wouldn't have asked any questions and didn't intend to ask in the future. I was quite happy to put my life in their hands and for them to inform my parents about the outcome. Nowadays I think of that particular operation as akin to modern keyhole surgery without the keyhole to peep through.

I had many painful, frightening and shocking experiences for my body to endure, none of which caused me to feel in the least bit depressed. I seemed to be able to keep my pecker up all right. Later, my depression came from enduring the pain and grief of others, whom I came to respect and cherish in my memories.

One of three men I knew to have survived the sanatorium was a Merchant Navy Captain, serving on oil tankers.

He had coughed up a congealed lump of blood on board ship and was sent to the sanatorium by his employers for a medical examination. He was only there for two weeks and then received the all-clear.

He had witnessed the fiasco of my liver biopsy and was one of the men who burst through the curtains, demanding to know what was happening to me? On the day he left the sanatorium, he shook my hand and told me that he had been all over the world and seen many things but I was the bravest man he had ever met. I was a very impressionable young man at that time and his remarks boosted my ego, which was just as well, in view of all the things that were yet to come. I suppose I was just like a child at the dentist, being told he was a brave little boy but believe me, it was a fillip to me!

The captain looked one hundred percent fit, which indeed he was; he looked a youngish forty years of age and was a single man (that turned the nurses' heads!)

One sister in particular gave her attention to the captain but he liked the life he had chosen. People that knew him told me he was well known in his North Devon town for enjoying a tipple in the local pubs.

You may think that everyone pulls in the same direction when under the pressure that we were, but that's not always so. After the fiasco with my liver biopsy, the first nurse who was instructed to stay with me for the forty-eight hour period was drawn away from me on an emergency. Foolishly, I got out of bed to go to the toilet for a pee.

It was quite painful getting out of bed and staggering to the corridor leading to the toilet. Leaning my shoulder on the corridor wall for support, I slid along the wall slowly step by step and bowed in stature. Just before I came to the toilet Mr Nasty confronted me.

Mr Nasty was a patient about sixty years of age with a jaundiced attitude. "You don't look so cocky now, do you, boy?" he remarked in a derogatory manner. Luckily for me, some of the other patients, including the captain, were able to lead him away from me.

It was very rare to meet men like him but who knows what pressure he was under? Perhaps he had family and loved ones relying on him at home. One has to stay calm in a situation like that.

On reaching the toilet, passing water was arduous. My insides were still tender and suffering from shock. After the struggle, instead of returning to my bed, I went to a restroom and sat down with some of the other patients for a break, just to take my mind away from the ordeal.

Unbeknown to me at that time, the nurse detailed for my care had returned to my bed and was panicking because she had lost her patient. When she found me, she insisted I return to my bed in a wheelchair. This was the first time I had been wheeled back to my bed under these circumstances but it was not to be the last!

By early September, I was to attend my sister Jean's wedding. I was really poorly after my ordeal with the liver biopsy and felt every bump in the road whilst travelling home in my parents' old Austin car.

Saturday morning, I awoke in my own bed to the sound of my mother calling me to breakfast. I got dressed, walked to the bedroom door and as I reached for the door handle, I instinctively looked back, and saw myself in bed still asleep. It was the most frightening moment that I have ever experienced. I was terrified. The instant that I realised what I'd witnessed, I returned immediately back into my body! I had just gone through an out-of-body experience! Three times in succession this happened, after which I remained there in bed trying to move but could not. It was as if my body was paralysed. When I tried to call out in reply to my mother's breakfast call, I realised I was not breathing, so I had no voice. Eventually, I managed to break free from the paralysis and sat up in bed suffering palpitations of the heart and gasping for breath.

One eerie part about the event is that, on reflection, I remember looking at my big toe that was sticking out at the end of the blanket. I was trying to move it, willing it to move in my mind to no effect. I now realise I was on my back facing the ceiling, How could I even see my toe? I must have been slightly out of my body to even see my toe!

Discussing this with my parents was out of the question; they would regard my experience as a fantasy. My father had the same regard for me as a snooker player regards an unforced error. That's a mistake when everything else is going well!

Despite my out-of-body fright, I managed to visit the freshwater lakes at Newton Abbot on the Sunday and did a spot of fishing. Unfortunately, I was stung or bitten by an insect (probably a horse fly). It caused my hand to swell to twice its normal size and my leg was swollen from my crutch down to my ankle. I was glad to get back to the sanatorium after the weekend. I was given penicillin and my test was delayed until I recovered.

I had waited for my return to the sanatorium to inform Doctor Litler of my out-of-body experience. He attentively listened as I painstakingly revealed the facts. Anxiously I appealed to him, "Is it anything to do with the treatment here?"

Unperturbed he shrugged his shoulders as he turned away from my inquisitive stare. "Nothing to do with me!" he said routinely, as if I needed a psychiatrist.

The dilemma was left with me. My treatment was none other than biopsies and tests? No drugs were involved to induce the out-of-body effects. The experience repeated from time to time and it was no less terrifying. What with my hair falling out and now these out-of-body experiences, I was wondering what could happen next?

On the morning of the day after I got back from my weekend out, Clifford was in bed having fluid drained from his lung and although the curtains were drawn around his bed, I could just see him through a gap in the curtains near the head of the bed. The doctor had a needle inserted into his back and seemed to be draining an awful lot of fluid from his lung. Cliff began to moan in anguish. I could see he looked distressed, as if he was about to faint.

I honestly felt the pain and I called out to him, "Are you OK, Cliff?"

He painfully replied, "Bloody agony." This was all the narrative he could complete; my friend was too poorly to complete the Operation-Spry saying!

At least once a week, it was customary for all the doctors in the sanatorium to come around the wards and visit each patient. They gathered around each bed discussing individual cases. Some of them performed examinations on the patients and made suggestions for an alternative treatment or test. Doctors also came from other hospitals for the purpose of possibly transferring you to their hospital for specialised treatment.

A female doctor from another hospital created an ambience of fear in her presence. If she so much as looked in your direction, the hair stood up on the back of your neck. She was in charge of the cobalt ray treatment. She was quite pretty and wore loads of make up, which was unusual in those days, but that didn't mask the gruesome reason for her presence. We regarded her as the Angel of Death.

She selected me for treatment one day, just like choosing a piece of fruit from a market stall.

When she left the ward, I anxiously asked the other patients, "What do you think she wanted me for?"

The patients agreed amongst themselves to console me by saying, "Ah, she probably just wanted to dry some phlegm up off your chest!" I didn't fall for that. I was quite worried until several hours later I was relieved to hear that the other doctors had managed to change her mind.

The cobalt treatment was far from perfected in those days and they were killing patients with massive dosages of radiation. We regularly witnessed the patients on this treatment commute to the other hospital on daily excursions for their treatment.

They generally returned in the afternoon in a terrible state. They had blue marks similar to tattoos on their chests that were target indicators for the cobalt rays. In the vicinity of these marks they were inflamed and sore, as if they were still burning.

Some of them were vomiting and others just wanted to lie down. The rest of us patients looked on in anguish and nicknamed them as 'the walking dead'. We were all guinea pigs but sometimes it seemed obvious to us that they were not going to make it. Old Jim Spry was put on this treatment and had since gone home to spend his last days, God bless you Jim. Who knows what would have happened to me if the Angel had irradiated my lungs?

We all thought that some of those men should have been left to die in peace but most men would volunteer for treatment if it gave them the slightest chance of survival. This was in 1963 and this cobalt treatment was a relatively new way of treating cancer; it must be vastly improved today.

I had pretty well got to understand how the whole complex of the sanatorium was run by now. Because of its remote location engaging staff was a problem. Patients were often recruited from a local mental institution, as a part of their rehabilitation back into society. They were given the title of auxiliary nurses and used to help out the overstretched staff on the wards. They helped out by serving the tea, lifting heavy patients and other mundane tasks.

Convicts from local prisons recuperating from chest illnesses were also conscripted into completing their prison sentences as porters and general helpers to work outside the wards, tending the gardens and grounds.

One particular auxiliary nurse presented a problem; he was a big, strong man, who liked to perform feats of strength in front of the patients. Often he would hold a large heavy metal teapot full of scalding-hot tea at arm's length over the head of the patient. The patients were terrified and he expected gratitude and applause from them for his entertainment. As if the patients needed all that!

I witnessed him punch an old patient in the face on one occasion and complained to him, whereupon he threatened me. This happened when I was confined to bed after a small op. I thought it unwise to respond to his threat. By now, I had learned to keep my own council and decided to wait until I was fit enough to deal with him.

I could have mentioned the incident to my father, who would have leaped at the chance to batter him but he had just left hospital himself after a hernia operation. Although this would not have deterred my father, I thought it wise to keep the incident to myself.

The next day however, this man was at my bedside crying his eyes out like a baby. Another patient had complained to the Matron about his violent nature and he was sentenced to return to the asylum for more treatment. As I was known by now as the ward's longest standing patient, he pleaded to me to speak up for him to the Matron. The poor man was not ready to accept the responsibility of a job and he was acting just like a child. That was the last I saw of him.

My mate Clifford gradually became too weak to complete a game of snooker. Repeatedly he cut the game short to retire to his bed. After several weeks, Cliff was transferred to another hospital for specialist treatment. I can't imagine how he managed to decipher my spelling when I wrote to him, but my letters were answered until he became to ill to write.

For a while his wife replied to my letters on his behalf, but eventually she stopped writing. The strain of watching her husband approaching the end of his life was probably too much to endure. She thought no doubt that I was approaching the same end, and she had enough to contend with without enduring the addition of my demise. Although I felt sad about this, I understood her dilemma.

Two gentlemen of the road became the objects of interest during October when they were admitted to the sanatorium to undergo treatment. Presumably they were suffering from terminal illness. One of them was forcibly brought in against his will screaming and shouting blue murder as the staff locked him in a garden shed just outside of my ward.

At meal times, he had a habit of throwing his dinner back at the staff, plate and all. I suppose he just wanted to be left alone to die in his shed; after all he was a loner. It wasn't long before he had his final wish granted.

The other gentleman looked like Co-Co the Clown! His name was Ruby. He adorned himself with long dresses and put on women's make-up! His cheeks were heavily made up with thick red powder and he wore bangles all up his arms.

An incident occurred not long after Ruby appeared on the scene when all the other patients in my ward had gone home for a weekend's special leave. The Sister on my ward requested my co-operation in allowing Ruby to sleep in my ward whilst I was alone in the ward. All the patients in the other wards were so frightened of Ruby that they would not accommodate him.

"OK," I said but I was soon to find out why everyone was afraid.

In the middle of the night, Ruby had a slight haemorrhage and began screaming and blowing his blood all over the bed. Cautiously, up until then, I had been lying in my bed with one eye open expecting trouble. So being wide awake, I got out of bed and walked over to his bed to try and calm him down.

As I approached him, he was uncontrollably flailing his arms about like an overacting Hollywood film star. "Ruby, calm down," I said quietly whilst clenching his left arm firmly. I leaned close and whispered in his ear, "Your anxiety could worsen, Ruby, if you choose to ignore my advice." I was offering him a personal sedative if he didn't shut up! I didn't want the young night nurse to have to contend with his offensive attitude. He calmed down.

I turned on his bed light and proceeded to search under his pillow having earlier spotted something suspicious protruding from underneath. My notion turned out to be well founded. A wooden club with a big ball shaped at one end lay there. This type of club I had seen before when I was at school. He had concealed it under his long flowing frock in the daytime. The club was of African origin. Our teacher had informed us that this club belonged to a certain tribe. The significance of the ball (according to our teacher) was that it was said to crack a white man's skull but not a black man's.

Ruby had an old doctor's bag under his bed, which I checked out and found it was full of long, rusty knives. That's when I rang for the night nurse, who then confiscated the lot. You'd think the staff would have searched a man like this before admitting him onto the wards. I have often wondered what the consequences could have been if I had not searched him.

This crazy man portrayed a select education in his manner. He spoke with a privileged tongue and played classical music on the grand piano alone in the dance hall, which was normally locked when unattended. Perhaps he had an old school tie concealed under his frock to help him gain entry into the hall.

Ruby had a displeasing habit to the other patients of rummaging the ashtrays for cigarette ends. It's hard to imagine someone doing that in a place so ridden with lung disease.

Patients were always emptying the ashtrays to try and stop him. I rolled my own cigarettes and decided to play a trick on Ruby. Scraping all the ends off of a number of red matches, I placed them in the centre of one of my cigarettes. After smoking a quarter-inch of the cigarette and then extinguishing it, I left it in an ashtray. The trap was set. All the patients were in on my ploy and waited on Ruby taking the bait.

He didn't harm himself when he lit the dog-end but he nearly jumped out of his skin when the match ends flared up, nearly burning his nose. We all roared with laughter, causing Ruby to scurry off out of the ward. It was great to have some entertainment amongst all the gloom and if Ruby had asked me for a cigarette, even though times were hard, I would have obliged.

I had got to know Jim the sanatorium stoker, who was always black with coal dust from stoking the one large boiler that supplied all the hot water and central heating throughout the complex. He always had time for a chat. Jim was once the Royal Navy sausage-eating champion and told me he had eaten twenty-seven pounds of fried sausages in one sitting.

Harry was another prominent staff member who became listed among my friends. He ran the cafeteria-come-bar and delivered the newspapers in the morning. Harry would do anything for anybody. He would bring in shopping from outside the sanatorium and became a good all-round friend to everyone. He would regularly drive people to their homes on weekend leave in his pink Rolls Royce car. Harry had lots of flats that he let out privately.

Yorkie the cleaner enticed me to go into the bar for a drink one evening, on the pretext that I was leaving the sanatorium that night and was just waiting for my parents to pick me up. Jim the stoker backed up Yorkie, as Harry was a bit reluctant to serve me. Patients were strictly forbidden to use the bar facilities in the complex. Harry agreed to serve me in the end and both Yorkie and Jim (who were both inveterate drunks when off duty) proceeded to get me (who was tee-total) plastered. The first two pints I remember, the rest I do not! Apparently Yorkie and Jim had to carry me back to the ward and sneak in through the French windows to put me to bed afterwards. The worst thing of all was the fact that I wet the bed that night. I felt like a right fool the next day when the young nurses changed my bed in front of the whole ward. My head was splitting and I felt sick all day. The whole thing was kept a secret from the principal Doctor Midgley and the Matron, but I somehow believe they all knew what had happened. I suppose they can't kick you out of a death camp for what I had done.

The fact that we were permitted to smoke cigarettes in bed seems unbelievable today, considering the sanatorium dealt almost entirely with lung complaints! Smoking was still a socially acceptable pastime, many of the patients sat up in bed at night smoking cigarettes, and drinking tea when possible.

The patients regarded a male nurse named Jock Moran (who only worked the night shift) as a gentleman. He made arrangements with us, welcoming us to ring the emergency bell at any time of the night, and providing he was not too busy he would provide us with a cup of tea. Everyone appreciated his considerate nature.

I personally indulged in a cup of tea and biscuits at night, along with a cigarette; it was very relaxing and gave one time to reflect on what seemed at times, to be a non-stop barrage of grief.

There was the alternative to our kind night nurse. We had a male nurse who did nothing for us. He was always having sex in his office with the female assistant nurse who always worked on his shift. He ignored the bell even in dire emergencies; he only came when his assistant wanted him to (and that's not an innuendo!)

Eventually he left the sanatorium to start a new job in the Midlands. We, the patients, were very happy at hearing this news and had a meeting to discuss his going away present. It was decided that I, being the youngest and fittest, should pour valuable sugar (it was rationed at the time) into the petrol tank of his bubble car, such was the dislike of this man. We never heard from him again after our 'sweet goodbye'.

On my first home visit, I had driven my van because my tools were inside and I needed them to complete the plumbing job on my sister's home. I left the van parked in the gas company's car park for security and my father drove me back to the sanatorium in his car. It had become clear by this time that I was not going home for at least a while. At the end of October, I had my last weekend break and the Matron drove me home in her car. It was cold at home and noticeably colder when I returned to the sanatorium on the Sunday evening, especially in the Dartmoor wind.

On the following Monday, I was playing snooker for hours with a patient who was a champion of England billiard player. He taught me many things about the game. This was the only time that any one of the staff complained about patients smoking. Matron called into the snooker room on one of her routine inspection tours and saw the air in the room was thick with cigarette smoke.

She complained saying, "Good God, look at the smoke in here!"

My new friend and I had never given it a second thought! Snooker halls outside the sanatorium were always thick with smoke. It must have appeared like a thick mist to the Matron who was a non-smoker. She flung all the French windows wide open, letting the cold air in and left us to carry on playing. We were more in danger of catching pneumonia than dying of any other illnesses!

The Matron insisted on opening all the windows in the wards at night, no matter how cold it was. I threw my second-hand Army greatcoat on top of my blankets in the coldest nights to keep myself warm.

A detached radio shack stood in the grounds of the sanatorium, of which I was entrusted with the keys. The staffs generally ran the radio room but were glad to hand over the facilities to me because they were so shorthanded. This was my warm haven where I had control of my own electric fire. The conditions of this allocation of trust went as follows: Providing I was fit enough, I was in charge of the entire sanatorium broadcast. Twice a week I would perform a music request hour, run bingo on two other days, connect the local football team, Torquay United, through to the bedside headphones on Saturdays and connect our own church service on Sundays. Monday, being my only day off was matinee day and all the fit patients attended the cinema.

For every event I was paid an extra bottle of Guinness and this, together with my daily allocated bottle of stout, enabled me to build up a stockpile of booze, as I didn't drink.

Meeting the needs of men who were at times dying for a drink was a pleasure for me. I was able to run a free bar supplying virtually as much stout as they wanted. I managed to acquire by stealth a store of sugar because sugar was like gold dust at the time. I was a sugar and booze baron.

The patients from all the wards in the sanatorium relayed messages to me through the sanatorium communication system. We had our own internal postal system and a microphone in each ward enabling a connection through the radio shack to be transmitted to other patients. The sanatorium had an extensive collection of records.

During the show I opened the mail and received requests and messages live over the air, relaying them to the patients and playing the records of their choice, acting as a disc jockey. I think they had a laugh at my expense whilst listening to me stammering through their letters.

The shack was not only a detached building, it had a nice, spacious, furnished lounge and it was private. Often I invited a selection of young nurses to the shack, to play records and have little private parties. At that time I was not long out of my teens and the nurses, who were eighteen and nineteen were living a long way from their homes. In this respect, we were in the same boat and it was nice for me, as the only young patient there, to mix with people more of my own age. My love nest in the field at the base of Sputum Hill was never utilised for assignations in the summer and I was becoming too weak for anything other than flirting in my new love nest. The nurses liked to flirt just as much as I did.

Long-term TB patients lived in the chalets, and by arrangement I was permitted to visit some of them. There was a woman, who was known to my family, who had lived in Hele Village where I was born that I called on, and I was told to visit an old lady that was named Mary Tickle. Mary, a star patient, had resided in the sanatorium for twenty-five years before I had arrived. Prior to this she had been a hospital Sister. Her chalet commanded a beautiful panorama of Dartmoor, as seen from her bed. Mary had contracted tuberculosis in the first instance, whilst performing her duty as a Sister, but was more recently afflicted with the incapacitating disease of arthritis and confined to her bed. She was settled in a chalet with an end wall consisting of a glass folding door, which was a standard fitting to the chalets, to allow as much fresh air into the chalet as possible. It was always opened to its fullest extent throughout the year, except during the harshest weather conditions, fresh air being the order of the day.

The tests of varying types continued on different parts of my body and after the most recent one I was in pain and confined to my bed. Although I was by far the youngest patient there, being the longest stay patient in my ward meant that other patients came to me for information and advice about their predicaments. I therefore had no chance to avoid the confession of the ward bore whilst I was stuck in bed. He was a new patient named Mr Pitman, who sat on a chair beside my bed and commanded my undivided attention. He unravelled a tedious tale that took place during the Second World War when he was a soldier terrified of the prospect of dying and about to go into battle. He therefore decided to fake mental illness to avoid the battle and was consequently incarcerated in a mental infirmary. On being sectioned for medical care, he then realised that living with the authentic inmates was a living hell, and he couldn't wait to get released.

He was now awaiting a major operation to remove one of his lungs and was again terrified at his prospects. I was amazed to learn that within two days of hearing his confession he pulled the same stunt and was back in the mental home.

Still trying to make the best of my distressing situation, I enjoyed seeing the nurses laugh in this remote outpost. A lot of the nurses who lived in the flats became very homesick at times. Most of the patients were terminal and it was hard for the nurses to keep cheerful, but at times the funniest things happened!

A stream of toilet paper followed an old gentleman returning from the toilet one morning. He had trapped the end of the toilet roll in the rear of his pyjama trousers and the toilet roll had virtually unrolled behind him. A nurse was following him and trying to step on the stream of paper but she was laughing so much she kept missing it. All the patients were roaring with laughter and this was painful for some of those recovering from operations.

Our main nurse, Sister Beaumont, was always larking about. Some of the patients were passing blood and it showed in their glass urine bottles that were kept under the bed. When Sister Beaumont collected these bottles, he waved them above his head, pretending they were carafes of red wine and sang 'Drink To Me Only With Thine Eyes', the drinking song from 'La Traviata'. I've heard Mario Lanza singing the song in a film. Sister Beaumont had a great sense of humour.

Another resident doctor, Doctor Coleman had hardly played a part in my diagnosis. He was an alcoholic and had performed major operations in his past. His colleagues, whilst respecting his past contributions to the profession, had reduced his duties to no more than extracting blood specimens from patients' arms. The patients however, dreaded the sound of his approach. He was often given the task of draining our blood unnecessarily, merely because he was in the way of the other doctors daily running of the sanatorium (or so we thought!) This earned him the nickname of 'The Vampire'!

His approach was always signalled well in advance by the loud click of his steel heels on his shoes, which echoed loudly, warning us of the impending onslaught.

Grown men hid in the nooks and crannies of the wards and corridors at the sound of his approach, trembling with bloodcurdling thoughts of his bumbling butchery. He was not too clever with the needle, especially if he was suffering from withdrawal symptoms.

I happened to have a pair of steel-heeled shoes and I was often mistaken for the approaching Angel of Darkness. Anxious patients often greeted me by saying, "Oh God, it's only you, get rid of those shoes!"

Doctor Coleman was the object of attention of a charming nurse, who to me gave the appearance of someone who had led a sheltered life. To my rough background, her accent suggested a refined education; it sounded a little soppy to me.

I later became aware of her engagement to the doctor and considered she was no fool. She was a spinster and no longer young. The doctor was quite a few years her senior. Her association with the good doctor seemed a fitting match, with the potential of mutual fulfilment, I thought.

At night, the duty nurse conducted the rounds of the wards, inspecting the patients by shining a torch in their faces to see if they were awake and still in the land of the living. The charming nurse was on duty one night, which was unusual. She generally worked the day shift. I had received a minor operation and I assumed as a matter of priority, she would take particular care to check me out. I really liked this nurse with her harmless charm and when she approached me in the middle of the night, shining her torch in my face, I hissed a murmur in the form of a plea, just in earshot.

She drew closer and she whispered softly, "Are you all right, Robert?"

I croaked and she leant me her ear, drawing her ever closer to my face. At the last moment, I raised my head and kissed her on the cheek.

"Robert!" she hushed. "You are naughty!" She spoke softly and drew away. I could sense her warm red blush even in the dimly lit ward.

In the morning as she completed her shift of night duty, she told me, "Robert, you must not tease the nurses." She had a point. A Filipino nurse who I often flirted with had broken down in tears after realising I was only teasing her.

I found it beyond my ability at times to grasp the transformation from life outside the sanatorium to the stark reality of gloom all around me, in my new home of little joy.

By this time it was mid-November and I had received the awesome news from Doctor Trowbridge regarding my future prospects and was on my way to the surgical ward. What next? I thought 'Do I live or die? Will I ever get to the top of Sputum Hill? At best I shall never be as able as I once was, but I'll be over the moon if I live.'

On my last night in West Block A, I saw the most wonderful sky I had ever seen in my life. The skyline out over the moors on a calm autumn evening was generally beautiful with red and yellow colours but this night I saw a dark patch of green in the centre. It was a beautiful, rich green, that I had never seen before or since. 'Could that be an omen?' I thought. 'That's what people in biblical times would have thought was a message from God.' I didn't have that faith.

CHAPTER 10

THE GREAT ESCAPE

My accommodation in New Block was a private room with a single bed. There was no lunch or dinner for me on my first day as I was in preparation for my op the next day. Having settled in, I came into contact with a strange phenomenon in the form of a female staff nurse named Kimble, who was unique in her ability to create an ambience of terror. Like anyone of notoriety, her reputation preceded her.

She was very abrupt with all of the patients with her seemingly uncaring attitude, whilst undoubtedly having credible nursing ability. I personally found her fascinating. I could not believe anyone could be so disagreeable. It was an uncanny "turn on" for me. I had assumed on my experience to date, founded on my rock band exploits that girls generally liked me, but this one was the opposite of everything that I had conceived as logical.

I considered that it could be allied to the fact that I generally chatted up every pretty young nurse in the sanatorium and they responded with the same responsive patter. 'Maybe this one was jealous,' I thought. But no, she viewed me with antipathy equally as much as she perceived all the other patients to be repugnant. She positively bowled me over with what I would describe as a childish, spoilt, selfish, bullying nature and to add to that, she was corpulent and frumpy, and I simply adored her.

To this day, I think of another female nurse who I met in New Block for the first time. She came to my bedside just before my lung operation to administer a pre-med injection. I am pretty sure that anyone who is awaiting major surgery feels anxiety just prior to the op and I am no exception. This pre-med was meant to relax me, to settle me down and allay my fear before being taken to the operating theatre. The nurse informed me that she was running late with her duties and requested my co-operation in a cover story.

Whispering, she requested, "If anyone asks you when you received this injection, tell them you received it an hour earlier or I will get into trouble." She was of Indian origin and I felt sympathetic towards her, so I agreed. I must be truthful in stating that if this were to happen to me again nowadays I would definitely react differently.

As I was wheeled into the operating theatre on a flat trolley, the theatre Sister asked me if I felt sleepy. I was wide awake and told her so. I thought for a moment that they were going to operate on me just as I was, in a state of wide alert!

I anxiously inquired, "Are you going to give me something besides the pre-med, Sister?"

She laughed and assured me that she would. Thank God for that I thought. As they raised me off the trolley and onto the operating table, I spotted the implements that were laid out on a table for my operation. A massive pair of bolt croppers especially caught my eye.

"Are they for me, Sister?" I inquired, whilst raising my head off of the table and pointing at the croppers.

"Don't worry!" she replied and shielded the implements from my view, covering them with a surgical cloth. The tools looked more suited to a garage workshop than an operating theatre. I learnt at a later stage that the bolt-croppers were used to cut out five inches of my fifth rib to enable them to insert a tool that resembled a car jack between my ribs to jack my ribs apart.

The Sister administered the general anaesthetic and the next thing I knew I was laying on an operating table, having just had half my left lung removed and they had not as yet completed their intrusion to my torso.

They were cleaning me up, removing blood and protective garments from my body. I tried to attract their attention to my state of consciousness by screaming abuse at them but all I could say over and over again without any control was: "Oh my God, oh my God." This only added to the confusion.

From a cautious apprehension prior to the operation of impending pain or the finality of death, I had made a transition. In what seemed to me to be a moment of inconsequential time, I had transversed into an uncertain world of never-ending incomprehensible madness and terror.

131

I suppose these things happen now and again. There must have been a miscalculation by the anaesthetist. I remember how uncaring they all seemed, dressed in their green masks and gowns as they went about their bloody business. Not one of them seemed to even look at me let alone speak to me. They rolled me over on my side whilst mopping blood from my body and I felt a terrible sensation, as my body seemed to twist. I felt like I was cut in half, as my body seemed to slew awkwardly on my wound like a half cut loin of meat on a butcher's slab. I felt sick and blacked out for a moment only to return to the madness moments later. I awoke in time to see two of the theatre assistants slide wooden poles down two sleeves in a canvas sheet that I was lying on and then lift me off the operating table and back onto the trolley.

I felt an awful pain inside me as they raised me off the operating table. I found out later that this was due to a half-inch wide rubber drainpipe they had inserted into my back. My weight on the canvas stretcher had forced the pipe up into my chest like an impaling weapon. It was then that I must have blacked out again. I have thought about this fiasco since then and I mostly remember the fear I had of the unknown. What future lay in my path, what was my destiny?

I had borne witness to a future of unbearable anguish and pain, the most awful wretchedness and suffering imaginable. The only way to avoid it was to fight back, to regain my life. It looked to me like eternal torture, terrifying beyond imagination.

When I think of the most painful thing I have ever seen, I think of a newborn baby, straight from the mother's womb. Its little body red raw as if being stung for the first time by the atmosphere that surrounds it. It's little virgin lungs shocked by the intrusion of air, its little muscles stressed under the forces of gravity. Was this the pain I saw on that operating table? Was this the thing I feared? If it were so, one could say there's great joy that comes out of pain!

Maybe it was reincarnation that I saw; many religions believe this to be so. It's not a bad philosophy; after all, each person would be partially responsible for the state of the world they are about to inherit.

I often think it may have been due to the Indian nurse not giving me my pre-medication on time. Perhaps that's why I came around so early during the operation, but who cares after the event? So I kept my word to her, I had more pressing things on my mind than blame.

It was early December when this operation took place. I had entered the operating theatre at twelve o'clock noon, and it was dark when I awoke. I learnt later that I was in the operating room for four and a half hours and Doctor Griffith (of the Griffith Split fame) had not performed the operation. It was an American surgeon named Patterson who had completed the operation on his own. I understood that he was present to only observe my operation but he had conducted it in the absence of the senior surgeon.

When I awoke, I found myself in the intensive care recovery room lying in bed. The rubber pipe in my back lead to a big glass bottle the size of a demijohn, standing on the floor beneath my bed. A glass plasma bottle hung from a tall stand that terminated above my head and a tube lead from it into my arm.

Doctor Patterson came into the room with a bounding gait, wearing a big smile and rubbing his hands together. This was the first time I had set eyes on him. He was a very big man. He came to a halt at my bedside, clapped his hands together loudly in front of him and then adopted a pugilistic stance.

Jokingly, he remarked, "Feel like doing a couple of rounds, son?"

I told him bluntly to FUCK OFF! Just behind him the Matron entered the room. I told her to FUCK OFF too! I was fuming. I told the Matron, "If you ever try to involve me in a barbaric episode like that operation again, I'll throw myself off of a cliff first."

Prior to the operation, I was told that a small segment of my lung was to be removed but a lobe was removed instead.

My father was permitted to observe me in the intensive care recovery room through a glass porthole in a door whilst my mother remained in the car waiting for news of my condition. The doctor thought the sight of me at that time might upset her and told my father to come alone. This was my lowest ebb; I was very thin by this time and looked really ill.

"He looks bad," my father reported to my mother, "I don't think he will last the night," he concluded with remorse. (My mother told me of this later.)

From the moment that I had gained consciousness from the operation, I was continuously parched with thirst. This was normal dehydration, which occurs after being under a general anaesthetic in major surgery. The advantages of the saline drip procedure (adopted today after major surgery) were yet to be discovered. I was not permitted to drink water; to do so would promote the possibility of vomiting. All I wanted was a drink of water and I was going to do anything to get it. I concentrated my appeal for a drink on a male nurse, a stranger to me. Desperately I pleaded with him for the tiniest drop.

After a while, I managed to coax him into filling a vessel resembling a china teapot with ice cubes and ice-cold water. He was taking a risk to his job and made me swear not to drink the water but to just swill it around my mouth, enough to wet the larynx and then spit it out.

After convincing the nurse with all the skills of a determined addict that I would comply, he held the teapot in both hands and gently offered the tiny spout trustingly to my lips. I could smell the ice-cold elixir. I moved my head slightly forward and like a panther wildly snatched the teapot spout in my canines, sucking every drop of liquid into my mouth. I swallowed the lot, whilst the nurse pulled and tussled with the teapot.

"Done it," I said, as I lay on my back in the bed, grinning like a devious Cheshire cat in sheer relief. To my horror, I then noticed Staff Nurse Kimble standing in the doorway. She had witnessed the whole event. The male nurse left the room at nurse Kimble's request. I learned later that she dropped the other nurse and me in it, by reporting the incident to the Principal Doctor Midgley. She was a snitch just like my sister Jean. Being on the carpet I didn't mind but it was bad for the other nurse and, to cap it all, I was not sick after the event!

The next moment Ruby the tramp (less his bag of knives) made an uninvited intrusion into the intensive care room. He must have been sent to New Block and was waiting for a lung operation himself. I was rather surprised to see him and threatened to wallop him with my plasma bottle if he approached any closer to me. Other patients were not allowed entry into the recovery room and the security was virtually non-existent at times. He was meek in manner and he assured me he was only there however to inquire of my well-being, and I believed him. He was probably just a misunderstood enigmatic character.

The voluptuous Staff Nurse Kimble returned the room to check my charts after Ruby had left. She was one of the senior nurses charged with my care and we immediately engaged in the banter of one of our many trivial disputes. First I would say something nice to her that she would immediately take the wrong way and retort with a sarcastic remark. Next I took the piss out of her and she suddenly lashed out at me and punched me with her fist, right in the hole in my side! (The five inches of rib removed for the operation is not replaced, apparently the fifth rib grows again to heal the wound.) You can imagine the shock her punch aroused in me but I managed to keep my composure. I maintained my adoring gaze upon her, and told her that she really turned me on when she was angry! She turned red with rage and stormed out of the room.

I was even permitted to smoke two cigars in the intensive care recovery room the day after my op. Can you imagine that today?

My next dilemma came the same day when I was dying to go to the toilet. Having somehow become infected with a bug, I was suffering from diarrhoea. The nurse on surveillance duty had once more left me alone for a brief moment and I decided to attempt a trip to the toilet. I was a bit shy about using the bedpan. I'd never used one before and I did not intend to start using one now.

With my bottles, pipes and plasma stand gathered around my body, I headed for the toilet. As I staggered down the corridor I must have had the appearance of a cybernetic hybrid! By the time I had travelled no more than ten paces, I realised I had made a big mistake. I really felt ill but I was caught between the urge to go on or give in. I was in no-man's-land so I decided I might as well bat on to the loo.

It was a long distance down a corridor to the toilet but I thought it was worth it on finally reaching my destination. I had turned what I thought was an impossible mission, into a successful motion!

Along the way, other patients were watching my efforts, both men and women mixed (this was not a segregated ward). This was the only surgical ward in the sanatorium and had limited accommodation. They were calling out in alarm to the nursing staff to assist me, knowing that it was not long since that I had come out of the operating theatre. The next thing I knew, a nurse was standing in front of me in the toilet. It was the male nurse, the water boy, who had turned up to wheel me back to my bed.

In the next half-hour I repeated everything I had just done. The nurse decided to isolate me from the other patients and moved me into a secure room. The room was no bigger than a medium sized bathroom. A rope hung from the ceiling above my bed, to help me to pull myself out of bed unaided. A commode was put in the corner of the room and the door was locked. I was now a prisoner.

In my isolated room I had a strange nightmare. I dreamt that I was in West Block A, and calling out for the matron's attention. She was walking past me very fast and took no notice of my call, so I followed her. She was walking too fast for me to catch her and as I walked down the two adjoining wards I noticed that the curtains were drawn around all the beds. The matron was walking into a dark room and I lost sight of her completely but still followed her into the room. I suddenly realised that I was in total darkness and that I was in the mortuary. I now realised that I had been in the coffin in which all the dead bodies were removed from the wards. I was having an out-of-body dream inside my coffin, and floating just above my coffin so that I could see all around me. I was dead!

I looked around the morgue and saw all the other coffins lined up on either side of me. The coffins were distinctive, as they had pointed lids. Suddenly white, wispy images of ghosts started to rise out of all the coffins and at that point I awoke freezing cold and covered in goose pimples. I remained in that frozen state for about a minute and was terrified!

Strangely, I immediately tried to go back to sleep so that I might continue with my dream. Why? It was terrifying!

This dream and the fact that I had wanted to continue the dream was in my mind for the whole of the next day. I can only think it was because I wanted to face the very thing that I feared most, the uncertainty of what was to happen next, and I wanted to face that fear in my dream.

After four days locked in the isolation room and having had all my pipes removed, I decided I did not want to die in the sanatorium and was going home to die. My diarrhoea had weakened my already weak body even further and I was getting dispirited. Escape was my only option.

A sidewall window, which opened onto a field, was my only means of escape. After the morning visit by the doctor and nurses I put my plan into operation. Climbing through the window, I found myself perched on the outside window ledge. I didn't like what I saw. It was a drop of some five feet into a three-foot deep snowdrift. It was now mid-December and a hard winter had set in. I had lived in the sanatorium for approximately six months and had experienced three seasons by now.

I launched myself off of the window ledge and crashed into the snowdrift. I felt as if my lungs were going to spill out through my wound onto the snow.

Later I learned the procedure of my operation when watching a lung operation similar to mine on a documentary program on television. The operation had required over three hundred and fifty stitches and ties. It seemed only the stainless steel stitches on the outside of my chest were holding my lungs intact but I had to go on. I crossed a small, snow-filled field to a wall, which I climbed over and dropped into another snowdrift with the same sickly effect.

By now I was on an internal road, one way leading to the main road and home, the other back to the complex that was the sanatorium. I decided I was too weak at this stage to make it home and so I dragged my emaciated body back to the complex and reached the restaurant.

Harry (the café manager) greeted me as I entered the café with a look of shock on his face. I ordered a cup of tea from Harry and he sat me at a table with a cup and then called the nursing staff who carried me back to my lock-up. I repeated this escape attempt once more the next day, after which they secured my window. If I had made it to the main road, I doubt if the one bus service was able to operate in the bad weather, and I would have probably died out on the moor.

Fit prisoners at Dartmoor Prison could not escape off the moor. What chance did I have? The only person I had known to discharge himself from Hawkmoor was a farmer. He was a TB patient. He made it all the way to his farm where he was discovered lying in the farmyard in a pool of his own blood. He was brought back to the sanatorium and died four days later.

I became aware that Staff Nurse Kimble had been allocated the job of removing my stainless steel stitches. They extended all around the side of my chest. I was a little apprehensive on hearing this because of her violent gesture in the intensive care room. It's odd but when the time came, she was as gentle as a lamb. She turned hostile again just after this, and reported me to Doctor Midgley, falsely implying to him that I was ungrateful for my treatment. I had probably bitched a bit about being locked in my room, but nothing more than that. It was just a part of our normal it-for-tat repartee. I was summoned to the head office to apologise for something very different to what I had said.

I did not inform the Principal about her unorthodox manner. I considered he had enough on his plate in running the sanatorium and, unlike her, I wasn't a grass.

Can you imagine how I felt at that moment, being castigated in the state I was in, standing before the Principal, looking as skinny as a bean pole, with more scars on me than Moby Dick? That was all I needed!

When the time came for me to leave the surgical ward, I was under the impression that I was going home. I was therefore surprised when Staff Nurse Kimble ordered me to pack my suitcase and wait for a porter to carry it back to West Block A.

My temper was high at realising my ordeal in the sanatorium was going to continue. With suitcase in hand I walked to the exit with the intention of walking all the way across the complex to West Block A.

I was so weak by now, my body weight had dropped down below ten stone, and I paused for a rest at the exit door.

Staff Nurse Kimble spotted me and demanded, "You wait for a porter."

With a look of contempt I emphasised, "I'd carry ten of these to get away from you." I then carried the suitcase all the way, non-stop, to my destination. When I arrived I felt really ill and had to go to bed. This time, I received a telling-off from Mr Beaumont the Sister in charge of the ward.

I was surprised to see Mr Pitman, the ward bore, was back in West Block A. He had returned to the sanatorium from the mental home. He seemed like a new man and was eager to help everyone, explaining to me that he was now going to adopt my attitude and try to give his attention to others whilst he was fit enough.

"I heard that you had the Griffith Split, Bob, what was it like?" he asked.

I couldn't possible tell him what I had gone through, so I just said, "It was a lot easier than I had anticipated, Mr Pitman." He had been persuaded by the mental institution psychiatrist to have the operation that he had so feared, which, unlike his wartime battle, was unavoidable.

Having settled in my old ward I started receiving treatment for my diagnosed ailment. I had a disease known as sarcoidosis, which must have been well advanced for them to decide to remove half my left lung, in fact, it was not until they removed my half lung that they diagnosed the disorder.

The treatment I received was a steroid drug, namely Prednisolone, which I believe was frontier medicine in 1963. There were many side affects to be suffered from taking this drug but it did the trick and I am still here, forty years on, to prove it!

From being a finicky eater, I now became a ravenous predator. At meal times I ate everything that was put on my plate. I could eat carrots, cabbage and onions, all the things my teacher Mr Sanders had prejudiced me against when I ate the vomit off my plate as a child. Anything put before me I really enjoyed. I ate as many as three roast dinners one after the other and still chased the food trolley to see if there was any food left over.

The strange thing about this disease is the fact that I have never found anyone who could describe the cause of the illness. The only description I received from the specialist at the time was that I had probably been in contact with a tuberculosis carrier and instead of contracting the tuberculosis my lungs had formed a protective skin, which stopped oxygen from entering my blood stream. This was a very rare disorder.

One of the patients named Bill Crook, who worked on the dustcarts, had a lung removed at the same time as me. Bill put me to shame when doing the exercises that were essential after an operation. He even made a concerted effort at climbing Sputum Hill and got halfway up. I could not even think of attempting the hill at this stage.

The purpose of these exercises was to get our muscles back in trim and to prevent adhesions.

These exercises were very painful and Bill was determined to get well. He had a nice family whom I got to know during their visits and he gave me his address. He lived at twenty-three Kingsway Road, South Molton. I memorised this in order that I might visit him when our ordeal in the sanatorium was over, and recall it to this day.

Two nurses, when dispensing drugs from the mobile drug cabinet, were arguing over the dosage of my medicine. For some reason I called out, "Five milligrams," jokingly in the middle of their discussion. I had no idea why I said it, but they had to retire to their office to find out the correct dose and it was five milligrams! This caused some alarm and I was accused of going through the files in the office because of my remark but it was a purely chance remark, it was as if I was psychic.

Christmas was drawing near and I wanted to go home. I had had enough of this place. Not one person I knew had survived cancer in the ward from the day of my arrival.

New faces surrounded me since my trip to the operation block, endless new faces. Every day I searched the obituary column in the local newspaper and noted those who had gone home to die. It was time to leave this place.

I begged the doctors to let me go for Christmas and on the morning of Christmas Eve I was permitted to telephone my parents to pick me up at six o'clock in the evening and take me home.

For the first time since entering the sanatorium I was permitted entry into the TB ward, where the remaining patients were treated to music played by the Salvation Army band. One of the young men that I had seen in the TB ward that I had waved to when I arrived in the summer was still a patient there. His name was Wes Hall and he told me that he had heard all the stories about me since my arrival. I learned that Wes was a Torquay chap and I often see him to this day. He made a full recovery.

(Hawkmoor Sanatorium has since been demolished and the estate now exists as Hawkmoor Park.)

CHAPTER 11

WHEN KINGS AND KAISERS MEET

In preparation for my homecoming, my father had holed the ceiling above my bed and secured a rope to a ceiling rafter. When I awoke in my own bed on Christmas morning in 1963, I thought it was a great notion on his part as my bed was lower and more difficult to rise from than hospital beds, "At home at last and free," I rejoiced and pulled myself out of bed to greet the day. After the morning rope trick, and the opening of Christmas presents, a traditional home-cooked English fry-up prepared by my mother awaited me, and so my recovery began. This was to be the first day of my new life; I was born again on Christmas Day 1963. I thought of Jesus Christ resurrected from the dead.

Every week I had to visit the local hospital for X-rays and a doctor's examination. The side effects from the treatment were taking effect, resulting in more unwelcome visits to the doctor.

Gaining weight was one appreciated side effect, which was a good sign but other side effects were confusing my state of health. Feeling depressed, I noted from the obituary column of the local newspaper that my close friend Clifford Everly had died on Boxing Day. (Peace to you, Clifford, your memory lives.)

Everyone seemed to be dead by now. All my mates in the band were in Germany on their six-month tour, and my parents were still arguing day and night.

Unfit for work and still unsure of the prospects of my future, my plans to go abroad or to London to work were scuppered.

After a while The Vampire Rock Band returned to England after their Germany tour. To welcome them home and have a chat, I called in at our old headquarters in Newton Abbot where we always practiced. Our headquarters was a hall we hired over the top of a social club. They were just leaving the headquarters to go to the manager's parents' home when I met them. I accompanied them and enjoyed hearing the news of their tour. Our drummer Fego had brought a German girl home with him and was transformed into a Cannabis smoking Hippy!

John, the lead guitarist who had caused the split-up of my first band The Strangers, had accompanied them to Germany as the rhythm guitarist (my old job). They had been working for eight-hour shifts on stage every day near American Army camps and were glad to be home for a rest.

We arrived at the manager's parents' home and walked down the driveway to the front door. I was trailing behind as the elderly parents appeared at the door. I was quite shocked at their menacing stance.

They were waving their arms and shouting, "He can't come in."

All the band members and the manager turned around and looked at me! To my horror, I realised that the old people were referring to me! They were frantic and full of fear. Many times before entering the sanatorium, I had sat with the band in that house sharing a pot of tea and biscuits with the old folks, but now I had to be segregated from the rest of the band and stand out in the road, waiting for them to reappear. Luckily two of the band members came out early to keep me company.

I don't blame the old people. Something that people today might not realise about that era is that many older people were frightened of catching the Consumption. Even though I had been free from tuberculosis, people in those days were more afraid of the Consumption than they are of AIDS today.

Their attitude did not help my depression and the following day I read in the obituary column that old Bill Crook had died. In desperation I drove sixty miles to Bill Crook's house in South Molton, even though he was already dead. I thought that I would get more sanity from Bill's family than I was getting from the people around me. Sat in my van outside of his house, I decided not to go in. It was me who was depressed. Who knows? Bill's family might have been trying to put the tragedy of their loss behind them and my turning up would have been of no help to them, so I drove home.

Anxious to return to work, I pressed my doctor to give me the all clear as soon as possible but it seemed my doctor wanted me to stay at home forever. No inkling of an apology did I receive for her stupid lack of concern prior to my entering the sanatorium. She had actually ridiculed me during my illness. "No more than a smoker's cough," she reported to my parents, and offered me red or green medicine. I only stayed with the "Colourful Medicine Dispenser" for my mother's sake.

Many of the old men in the sanatorium who had been saving all their working lives for their retirement, told me stories about how they wished they had done this and that when young. They advised me should I live, not to miss opportunities and I intended to take their advice.

Through being brought up in a world of rationing and long working hours with low wages, all I could see was the fast life of cars and extravagance depicted in all the American films. This world full of greed shaped the very essence of our society, and was promoted by their indoctrinated manikins of the media, and was advocated by their educational institutions. Even the rich wanted more. Everyone from the less opulent side of society longed for a piece of that misguided folly, which was imposed on us all by the legacy of our Imperialist Ancestors. (Me included I'm sad to say.)

I called on my old partner Brian Kneil and asked him how he was progressing with the business.

"I'm doing well, Bob," he replied.

"What do you think of the idea of renewing our partnership?" I asked.

"You're more than welcome, Bob," he replied.

After again being refused the all clear from my doctor, I told her the news from my old partner. I suggested to her that it would be OK as I was self-employed and my partner was willing, if things got too much for me at work, for me to return home. To this arrangement, she agreed.

My out-of-body experiences still persisted and in desperation brought on by fear I mentioned it to my father. He was reading one of the broadsheet newspapers at the time and as I told him the story, his eyes never left the page. I thought he wasn't paying attention to me (as usual). When I had finished telling him the story, he casually stated, "I get that."

"What?" I replied, shocked by the fact that his vocabulary included words as well as grunts.

"I get that," he repeated. His eyes were still fixed to his newspaper as if he was concentrating on what he was reading. "You're not ready to wake up," he said, pausing for a while whilst he turned the page. "The next time it happens go back to sleep," he suggested. That was his final word; he hadn't looked at me once during the whole conversation.

That's about the only useful information my father ever gave to me and he was right. I have endured out-of-body experiences all my life, and I do exactly as he stated. I just go back to sleep and it works; it helps to overcome the fear and settle my nerves. I often wonder how my father came to terms with the out-of-body experience. I never asked him when it occurred in his life. I imagine he was on his own. My father had not found faith, he believed that there is nothing after death and yet he found the perfect answer to my dilemma. I guess he always approached life in a pragmatic way.

Don't misunderstand my father, he was a good father and I love him but if there is something to be said, in truth, it must be said. To put you in the picture with my image of my father, he was born in 1904 and died in 1972. He was a labourer and had worked on various jobs.

All my childhood friends were too afraid of him to enter our house. I must admit that I was at the time a little jealous of my friends' fathers. My earliest friends Jack Barnett and John Low's fathers were always even-tempered and talked to me whereas my father was to be approached with caution.

Throughout my childhood, my father worked seven days per week apart from one or two days in all. I suppose that's what made him so grumpy, but I admire him for many reasons. After the sanatorium, I had no means of support. The social services do not support offsprings who are living with their families; my father never mentioned the fact. He truly supported me in my hour of need.

As a teenager, my father assisted his own father in the business of tree felling. Every day of the week throughout all the hours of daylight, they pulled and pushed a six-foot long, two-handled saw, man and boy at either end.

In the evening twilight of each day, my father could do no more than ride to and fro on the swaying motion of the saw. He lay exhausted across the saw handle, vaguely hearing the serrated teeth buzzing their seesaw serenade. His father, on the blind side of the tree, kept on pulling and pushing his limp body, as if he was not there.

When my grandfather was very young he joined the army, serving twenty-two years before deserting whilst serving in India. By one boat or another, he made his way home, eventually ending up in Cornwall where he went into hiding. The King eventually gave amnesty to the deserters (there must have been a lot of deserters). Granddad then came home to Devon.

My granddad owned his own horse and cart and besides felling trees, he employed many men to unload coal by shovel from the cargo holds of small ships and barges in Torquay harbour.

Sporting a large, bushy moustache and topped with a bowler hat, my grandfather was known locally for his quick temper and incredible strength. With one punch and in view of many onlookers, he had once knocked his horse unconscious whilst the horse was still in harness in the cart stocks. With brute strength, he then raised the horse out of the stocks onto his shoulders and carried it clear of the cart.

Disputes with his casual labour force over wages and bonuses were a common occurrence as my granddad was a hard taskmaster. Many scuffles took place when doling out their earnings in a local inn. On one occasion, my granddad was warned by one of his associates of a gang of scurrilous men who, unhappy with their tariff, were scheming to waylay him. These men were armed with wooden pick handles and were lying in ambush at a harbour-side pub. Instantly on hearing of the threat, the hairs on granddad's moustache stiffened like the mane of a rabid dog. Without hesitation, he pulled his bowler hat down tightly on his head and marched off down to the harbour.

He cleared the pub of his would-be assailants and threw them into the harbour. He then returned to the pub and put his shoulder under the bar and turned it over, leaving the bushwhackers' chosen alehouse virtually wrecked.

My grandfather offered my father a shilling if he worked extra hard one day and at the end of the day, my father dared to ask for the shilling. As my grandfather stopped the cart outside of a pub, he hit my father with the back of his hand, causing my father to somersault backwards over the cart landing in the road. He lay unconscious in the road while my granddad downed his drink in the pub. I guess he must have had a bad day?

To his dying day, my father still had a large lump on the back of his head where he hit the road. This was noticeable because my father always shaved all the hair off of his head.

Granddad, together with a business colleague, hired a taxicab for a journey to a farm in Exeter. He took my father along for the ride.. The purpose of the trip was to discuss a business arrangement with the farmer, and my father played on the farm during the discussions. When the business dealings were complete, everyone went to the cider barn for a drink of cider and a farmer's lunch comprising of bread, cheese and pickled onions. They sat on a pile of cider apples supping cider and jawing until they were quite pissed. As the day wore on, my father was thoroughly enjoying himself playing in the barn, until all the men decided to pelt him with apples. It was so painful and frightening that my father ran the whole of the twenty miles back home.

Before I was born, my granddad died of cancer of the hip brought on when he fell out of a tree and landed astride a wall breaking his hip. My mother told me he was administered with enough morphine to kill ten men, just to calm him down. The hospital staff could not control his strength when he was under the influence of morphine and he was strapped into his bed. I spoke to old men that knew my grandfather and the stories they told me confirmed the image that I had perceived.

I've heard my mother talking about my father's family having once had the hyphenated name of Sangster-Shears! She told me that there was five generations of his family buried in a communal grave in Brixham. They were all teachers and headmasters of schools. I think I'm the only family dyslexic but there must have been a black sheep in the family, to revert our name back to plain Shears. Perhaps there was another like me?

I actually saw my grandmother (on my father's side). I was very young and she was a sight never to be forgotten. She looked like something out of a Charles Dickens novel! Queen Victoria in mourning comes to mind. Her large frame was dressed entirely in black. A veil hung over her wide-rimmed hat covering her face and a dress covered her ankles.

She sat on a chair in my front room filling the air with a sinister silence. I knew that now was not the time to utter a sound. I was sat on the floor and could study her from that all-encompassing view. Her shoes were black leather with a buckle and had wide heels slightly raised. She wore them over black woollen stockings that could be seen as her dress raised a little as she sat. She never raised her veil or removed the shawl draped over the shoulders of her coat. Her name Rose was never, ever mentioned by my parents after that day and I never found out anything about her.

In 1921, at the age of seventeen, my father had run away from home never to return. Over a period of two weeks, he walked two hundred miles to Birmingham, living on turnips and swedes foraged from fields. He spent time living with gypsies and walked with tramps who were drifting from John O'Groats in Scotland to Lands End in Cornwall. He eventually spent two weeks in a Birmingham jail before returning to Torquay. He had tried to sell a ring in a pawnbroker shop unaware that the ring was stolen. A gypsy had sent him into the pawnbrokers on his own to sell the ring. My father was not streetwise like the gypsy and was arrested. Fortunately my father, unlike me, could spell. All the years I knew my father he was an ardent reader. He would collect a pile of books every week from the library. His handwriting was way above any I had seen, and he was permitted by his jailer to write a letter to his doctor who vouched for him. If it were not for that, my father would have rotted in jail.

On his release from jail, he and another young ex-con were told by the police to get out of town. On reaching the outskirts of the next town, the local police were waiting for them and they were told to keep walking. This happened in every town they came upon. One policeman took pity on them and gave them a shilling to obtain a place to sleep for the evening. A landlady at a roadside inn accommodated them with a double bed for one night. After a couple of minutes they had had to get out of bed, it was full of lice and fleas. They complained and were thrown out and on the road again without the shilling. My father and his companion eventually split up and went their separate ways. The police kept moving my father on towards Torquay. He finally secured a job in a quarry in Torquay, drilling holes in the rock face whilst hanging from the cliffs on a rope.

It was at this time he met and married my mother. She told me how his hands were red with blood, where all his skin had been rubbed off through using the hand drill all day. He described the hand drill to me as a six-foot metal bar, one and a half inches in diameter. It had a bulbous-shaped swelling halfway down the shank to serve as extra weight. My father used this drill for ten hours a day, repeatedly lifting the drill and twisting it as it dropped back into the drill hole.

It took him one hour and fifteen minutes to drill a three-foot hole, which was faster than anyone else did and he was rewarded for this with an extra farthing an hour. Sometimes the hole was packed with dynamite and other times the hole was used to feather and tar. Feather and tar was used mainly to split large rocks in two. The drill-hole was filled with water and two curved, wooden stakes were driven into the hole and left overnight. The wood would swell and crack the rock apart. My mother delivered a hot meal wrapped in cloth to my father at the quarry at midday, to make sure he kept his strength up. After many years in the quarry he was promoted to an explosive expert.

He was called upon to blast out the rock for the organ in the local Regal Cinema! This allowed the organ to rise out of the floor to be played in the film interlude. The cinema was almost completed with its roof intact when my father blasted the rock.

Engineers instructed labourers to load the balcony with several tons of cement contained in one-hundredweight bags, to test the balcony for stress damage after the blasting was complete.

After a few years, he was involved in an accident at the quarry. One of the charges failed to explode and as he walked into the quarry to check the dynamite fuses, he was blown up. He suffered from shellshock for two years after this and could not work. The family lived on the produce from his allotment and rabbits that he snared; he also kept chickens in the garden. My mother told me that at the height of his illness, he used to wake up in the middle of the night and run down the street in his pyjamas in total shock!

Eventually he found employment with the South-western Gas Board as a labourer, using a pneumatic drill to dig trenches. He told me that this job shook all the shakes out of him and he was totally cured. Whilst working for the gas board, he learnt to drive, and worked on building the local gasometer. He knew every rivet and bolt on that gasometer. The bottom metal plates were one and one-eighth of an inch thick and became thinner on every lift as they neared the top stage. The plates covering the top were one eighth of an inch thick and buckled under your weight when you walked over them. (That's how I knew my father could better Doctor Trowbridge's homemade gasometer contraption that I had toppled during my tests in his Hawkmoor laboratory.) In later years, my father painted the holder whilst hanging down the sides suspended on a bosun's chair.

Maintenance of all the governors that kept the pressure of gas supply to the consumers at an even pressure was one of my father's responsibilities. The massive gas governors floated on mercury and my father kept the mercury wells topped up. This gave him access to the mercury, which was kept under lock and key. Mercury fetched a high price in the scrap yard and my father pilfered the odd drop now and then. Everybody saved scrap of one sort or another for his or her Christmas outlay. The mercury was kept in milk bottles under our stairs and I was allowed to play with the droplets on our linoleum floor covering in our lounge.

All this knowledge of the gasometer construction and its workings were to prepare him for the events to come. During the war, the gasometer came under fire from a German warplane and was hit many times by cannon shells and bullets. The whole gasometer was engulfed in flames. My mother told me the roar of the flames sounded like a thousand bombers flying overhead. Our family only lived one hundred yards from the gas works, and we had to be evacuated from our home.

Four gate valves with wheel handles the size of bicycle wheels made of heavy steel controlled the flow of gas to and from the holder. They were situated at the base right next to the holder. The handles became too hot to hold with bare hands. It was my father who alone ran under the roaring flames to turn all the valves off to render it safe.

When the flames were extinguished, my father and one of his workmates were assigned the task of going inside the gasometer to check for damage. The procedure for entering the holder was to bolt an airtight cabin on the top of the gasholder to form an air lock. When my father and his mate were secure inside the airtight cabin, they were instructed to unbolt a steel plate from the holder to gain access. At this point, the pressure in the cabin rose to equal that inside the holder. With no escape route, they were now trapped inside the airtight cabin and suffering under the extreme pressure change, screaming in agony from the pain in their ears. After adjusting to the extreme pain, they proceeded down a long rope ladder descending to a raft at the base of the holder. A million gallons of water lay at the base of the holder and the whole steel structure above the first lift floated upon it. They drifted around the structure perimeter on their raft inspecting for leaks.

After completing their task, my father had a burst eardrum and was permanently deaf in one ear but he never complained to his boss, for the fear of losing his job.

I was puzzled by an incident that happened when I was very young. My father came down our stairs one morning with his shirt covered in blood and a towel covering his face. He raced passed me in our hallway and jumped into an awaiting ambulance. My mother had just attempted to cut his throat with a cut-throat razor and missed. She cut the end of his nose off in her attempt, giving my father a flat face like a boxer dog. This made him appear even more ferocious. My mother explained to me at the time that my father had fallen over and hurt his nose; I did not discover the truth for many years.

It was Bill Parsons, a friend of my father's, who disclosed the full story to me whilst we were having a drink in a pub. This almost caused a punch-up between Bill and me because I disputed Bill's account of the incident. I naturally leant towards my mother's version of the story. My mother later confirmed Bill's story as being true.

At the time, my father was having an affair with another woman. My mother, who was a gentle soul, beat up the other woman, punching her face so hard with her fist that she broke the woman's cheekbone. The police arrested my mother on a charge of committing grievous bodily harm but later dropped the charges. Women sure did fight for their men in those days.

My father was a clever man. He excelled in anything he undertook. He bred Canaries and crossbred them with Bullfinches and Gold Finches, which he trapped from the wild. His hobby culminated in his greatest achievement, winning the prize for the best Border Canary in Great Britain. The competition was held at the Olympia Stadium in London and his picture was displayed in our local newspaper on the front page. He won a big silver salver and a big cup for this and over the years our home was packed with similar awards. I often had the job of cleaning them. All this was achieved in his little garden shed after the age of fifty, when he had given up drinking. He later became an official judge at bird shows.

A competition was held on our council estate for the best flower garden and my father won first prize. He specialised in roses, wining prizes for this, and was adept at grafting one rose bud onto another bush, using raffia to bind the bud onto the stem.

He laid a gift in my memory of the meadow behind the gas works. I can see him now as he grafted different coloured roses on all the wild rose bushes around the meadow. Some of the bushes had three different coloured roses on the same bush. The meadow was even more beautiful than it ever was, and as a child it was magical to me.

My mother was born in Birmingham in 1902; she came to Devon when she was sixteen years of age and found employment in a large house, working in service to a wealthy family. The year was 1918 and all her family, except for one sister, were dead. Her three brothers had taken the King's shilling. This meant they were all volunteers in the Army. They were killed in the trenches in France during in The Great War.

Her father was conscripted into the Army at the late age of fifty. Being a vet, he was much in demand because of all the carnage among the horses on and around the battlefield. He died when a traumatised horse kicked him in the chest. After this, my grandmother lay down and died of a broken heart. All this was reported in the Birmingham newspapers with the headlines: 'Whole Family Wiped Out'.

The eldest brother, who was the first to volunteer, came home on a short leave from the battlefield. He arrived in the back yard of the house covered in mud, blood and lice. Removing his clothes, he told my mother to stay away from him and tell his younger brother, who had not yet joined up, to bring the tin bath out into the yard so he could have a scrub down. He then learnt that the youngest brother was volunteering for the army and my mother and grandmother had to stop him from putting a bullet in his head. He did not want his younger brother to witness the carnage of war!

The second eldest brother was so pleased because he was promoted to a bomb-thrower. Everyone was happy and proud for him being so special. He had played football for Birmingham's Aston Villa in peacetime, which was at the top of Division One, the then English Premier League. How cruel it was to be denied the education to see the folly of such pride. Being so close to the enemy in such a mess of unutterable war was tantamount to volunteering for almost certain death. How cruel it was that these strong oaks gave their lives to a society that cared so little in

153

return. Bow your heads, you Kings and Kaisers, to my uncles and granddad.

Her father had become a vet after starting out as a jockey; he was drummed off the racecourse for doping horses and then became a vet.

When my mother arrived in Devon, she possessed her memories and four copper death plaques, bestowed on the family by the King. They resembled large pennies. I played with these as a child, rolling them along the guttering beside the road until eventually; they all disappeared down the gutter drains. The King's bounties laid to rest like the King's men!

My mother always annoyed me when the woman who had employed her when she was in service paid an occasional visit to Torquay. She would stay in the best suite in the Grand Hotel and off my mother would go, straight to the hotel to grovel to this pompous bitch. Anything that woman wanted from my mother she got. This arrogant woman rewarded my mother with old tea that had to be reheated and the fat and rind off the bacon discarded by the woman's own family. This happened seven days a week, year after year, and yet my mother worshipped the woman. I assume she regarded her as a sort of foster mother after the tragedy she had left behind in Birmingham.

I can only say of my mother she was like a pebble on the beach. For all the storms a pebble must endure, when the storm abates, the pebble emerges, ever more beautiful.

CHAPTER 12

A PSYCHEDELIC ADVENTURE

During the first few months of my recovery, I launched myself out of my depression with the aid of alcohol. For the first time in my life, I met and began to associate with a new breed of merry men. To begin with, two or three pints would always make me sick but I was improving in leaps and bounds in my newfound pastime. Having regained enough fitness and strength of mind to attempt a return to work after such a long illness, I felt the need to celebrate. It was to be my last fling before attempting to get back to the seriousness of launching a business enterprise.

I decided to go out on the town the night before my working début with John Low, my old lead guitarist from my first group. Like me, John was a novice when it came to drink. His experience was lacking, apart from a tot of sherry at weddings or funerals.

Our immature minds concocted a plan for the evening that bears no resemblance to reality. Although we lived inside the bodies of grown men, our minds languished in the psychedelic world of pop music. Initially, John intended to drive my hire purchase, recently acquired Vauxhall Cresta car in a sober state. I was to indulge in as much drink as I could consume until I became inebriated. John was to deliver me to a dance hall in this state. Phase two of the plan was then to come into effect. Miraculously I was to become sober whilst he became drunk at the dance. The evening was to conclude with me safely driving John home. The reality of our ill-planned evening however was to be a little more terrestrial.

From what I can remember, I drank thirty-two rum and blacks in one hour in The Castle pub and was OK. That was the bit I remember, which was correct. I remember this because I attracted the attention of other young drinkers who began cheering me on to consume one full bottle of rum, which equalled thirty-two tots. A game machine on the wall of the pub tested the driving ability of potentially inebriated drivers to stop a car in an emergency. A threepenny bit was placed in the top of the machine. The coin was released by pressing a green button and a red button stopped the coin falling on a measured scale of braking ability. After completing the bottle of rum to a standing ovation from everyone in the bar, I was still the fastest braking contestant on the machine in the bar. After that my friend's memory is all I've have to go on.

The Castle pub is sited on the corner of Factory Lane and Union Street, the main street in Torquay. Apparently a trench ran alongside the pavement in Factory Lane and around the corner into Union Street. According to John I fell in it in Factory Lane! It was pouring with rain at the time and I crawled all the way along the trench into Union Street. I crawled out at the end of the trench as the trench became shallow and then rolled over and over sideways into the middle of the main road.

John became troubled as I began to vomit red rum and black all over my muddy suit. It had the appearance of a haemorrhage! The scars on my chest were still red and John, who knew my father from childhood, did not welcome the prospect of dumping me on my doorstep. He decided to drive me to his girlfriend Elisabeth's house in Teignmouth, to ask her for advice.

The trip to Teignmouth was not the smoothest of rides. The six-mile coastal path is continuously twisting and turning on one hill after another. John has told me many times since that night how he sat me bolt upright on the back seat of the car and how I vomited several times down my white shirt. Most of all, John tells me how I repeatedly spat gob on the back of his head for the whole of the journey.

When we arrived at Elisabeth's, she wouldn't allow me into her house until I was cleaned up. John and Elisabeth's brother threw buckets of water all over me in their garden and then lay me on the floor in her home. They considered keeping me there for the night. Liz thought my parents would be worried considering my state of health and eventually they decided to take me back to my home.

I had to postpone my working début for another week; I still couldn't stand on my feet the next morning and felt awful. The smell of rum as I cleaned that car a few days later still lingers in my mind. I was sick at every attempt. In the end, I had to use strong-smelling disinfectant that left a toxic bouquet to one's nose that lingered for weeks. Never have I drunk rum since that day. What a start to my new business venture!

As I acclimatised myself to working again, it soon became apparent that my partner Brian did not have enough work in hand for the two of us. It was an uphill struggle to get established but we did! Brian actually loved the physical side of plumbing and I hated physical work. I was so desperately tired at the time but keen to get on. At the end of each day I typed the bills and estimates on a second-hand typewriter, and struggled to accomplish a reasonable standard. I had to hold one eye open with my thumb and forefinger to see; I was so exhausted my eyes were closing. Later I learned that the effect on my eyes was a side effect from the drug I was taking.

My sister Jean was no help to me despite all I had done for her before and during my illness. As a top class personal assistant to an executive, having qualified to a high degree in typing and shorthand, she was ideally suited to help me.

Jean had been the top girl in her Secondary Modern School. (She attributed her failure to pass her eleven plus examination to two of the examination pages being stuck together.) She wanted to re-sit the exam and in my opinion should have, but the teachers (who probably thought she was cheating) would not accept her excuse.

Given the second chance, I believe she would have passed and the very fact that she became the top girl at her Secondary Modern School, surpassing over seven hundred other girls, vindicated my sister's assertion.

The difference between us as children continued into our adult lives and this again presented a problem to me. If I wanted to keep the peace in the family, I would have to endure her mental insults in my adulthood.

Just before I entered the sanatorium, Jean got engaged to be married to Tony. She had put a deposit on a house jointly with him, her fiancé. I was working on the house every evening and weekend, installing plumbing, central heating, a new kitchen, and a new roof, and plastering the whole building free of charge. I even supplied the materials free. It took me a whole year to complete the work, during which time Jean and Tony lived with their parents. I went into the sanatorium before completing the building work and secured a weekend rest break to complete it. It wasn't easy in my state of health.

My sister wrote a few business letters for me but she always waited until after I had spent hours trying to write them myself. She just wanted to show my parents how clever she was compared to me, and would hold up my letter and hers in front of my parents. She was the same old Jean as she had been in childhood. Imagine how I felt, straining to keep my eyes open and tolerating her unceasing selfish meanness towards me. I had volunteered to her all that I possessed unequivocally, as a brother should. My education had greatly improved in the technical college throughout my apprenticeship, but I was still being treated as the dunce that I had been in my childhood.

I left the sanatorium in pain to attend her wedding. From the day she met me, until the day she died, I was that other unwanted member of the family that she relegated to doormat. I found it even harder to bear because my in-laws, including some of their children, cast aspersions about me. 'Battle on,' I thought. If I kept trying, I would survive their defamation.

As the business expanded Brian and I started to employ men. I learned the rudiments of the PAYE tables for the employees' tax contributions, and all the things to do with employing people. It was very difficult with my dyslexia, especially as we were working long hours on the building sites by day. I felt no shame in asking the tax office for advice on PAYE or anyone else that I questioned to do with business matters. After all, how could a dyslexic fool know anything outside of his trade? I found that people were ready to ridicule me for my lack of knowledge but willing to pass on their knowledge to me. Being humble became a gateway to understanding.

My parents urged me to give my brother Brian a job. He was married and lived in his own house in Bristol. My father told me how he once laid pipes for the Gas Board and in his opinion;

Brian would soon learn the plumbing trade. I was reluctant to employ anyone other than first class tradesmen, which is what the business required. I had not known my brother well because of the age gap between us. He had left home to do his National Service when I was young and then moved to live in Bristol. He told me how he hated his job in Bristol working for MAC building merchants and engineering firm. His job entailed spot welding fabricated parts for metal barns for storing hay on farms. In the winter time he road his motorbike to work in the dark and rode home at night in the dark having been indoors all day, he longed to come back to Torquay. My parents naturally sung his praises and I was in awe of him. I loved my brother so I gave him a job.

My two elder brothers were some fourteen to fifteen years my senior and by the time I was eight years old, they had both completed their National Service in the army and had married their girlfriends.

Strewn around the walls of my new bedroom, which had previously been their bedroom, were the framed photographs of them dressed in their army uniforms in various locations in the world. I was of the opinion at that age that my two brothers were very special people, my heroes.

Brian was stationed most of the time in Malta. He was in the military police. His photographs were mainly of him sat on a motorbike with his army friends or competing in trials over rough terrain, or through deep water.

My other brother Ron was a motor mechanic in the REME, attached to the paratroopers. He proudly wore his wings on his arm. He was stationed mostly in Palestine and then in Cyprus during the time of the EOKA terrorism. His photographs always depicted him with his jeep with the most beautiful scenery in the background.

My brother Brian was earning better wages in prosperous Bristol than people in my area, and I had to agree to pay him more than the top quality tradesmen that we employed whilst teaching him a trade. My partner Brian never quibbled at this, even when we paid for all my brothers' tools and taught him, in the firm's time, to drive our van until he passed his driving test. Instead of being grateful for the chance to leave Bristol and train to be a tradesman and driver with all the other privileges we afforded him, he now complained about me. He hated the way his younger brother suddenly knew so much more than he did; after all, I was the expert in plumbing and driving but I was still the dunce in his eyes.

Brian was living free of any charge for food or accommodation whilst earning his high wage for several months in my parents' council house, whilst his own house in Bristol was up for sale. He obviously missed his wife and it showed in his temperament. I put his ill manner and lack of gratitude down to this at the time but my youthful perception of my brothers as heroes was weakening as I got to know them better. The large age gap between us contributed towards this. No brother could live up to the image I had built up in my mind. I suppose it's only natural that my perspective of them should wane a little as I matured.

By this time I had built up a circle of friends in my age group who worked in the building trade and we enjoyed Friday and Saturday nights out for a drinking session. We behaved like young people do today, drinking and dancing in pubs and clubs. My brother Ron tagged along sometimes and my mates complained to me because he was always scrounging drinks. I always paid for all his drinks without question and I gave him money to play the fruit machine but he made derogatory remarks about me to my friends behind my back. They resented this and complained because he tried to scrounge from them too. Eventually I had to tell my brother he wasn't welcome.

One evening, my mates and I were in a members only nightclub early in the evening when my pals brought my attention to a beautiful young blonde lady on the opposite side of the room. I was playing on a one-arm bandit machine, and listening to the Beatles record 'A Hard Day's Night' on the jukebox. I turned to look over my shoulder at the blonde, but she had her back to me so I carried on playing the machine. Suddenly I had a tap on my shoulder and turned around to face the blonde lady, it was

Corrine, my first steady girlfriend. She was even more beautiful than when she was a teenager, as my mates had spotted. We had a nice chat and she told me that she was married with three children and lived in Bristol. It was great meeting her again but I felt that I had done the right thing when we broke up.

John Low had married his girlfriend Liz by now and my other childhood friend Jack Barnet had married a girl named Beatrice. I remembered seeing Beatrice at the gigs when I was in the band, and had kidded Jack that she was one of my groupies. Jack had left the railway due to the Doctor Beeching railway cuts and the change over from coal to diesel engines; firemen were not required nowadays. Jack moved up north and worked in mining after this and his family kept me in touch with his progress in life. I felt very strongly that they had chosen a life in marriage that was not suited to me.

I was enjoying my life of occasional boozy evenings and weekends but at the same time it was not an easy task to establish myself as a businessman. My partner Brian was the easiest man going, sure he would like to be rich but only if it happened that way and if it did not, he didn't care. He simply had no head for business but he was as honest as the day is long, and we became great pals. I found that my age, my lack of business knowledge, my dyslexia and the location of my home and office address were stacked against me as the business picked up. Being located on the notorious Hele Village council estates, in a town split noticeably between the haves and have-nots did not help.

Fortunately, there was a modicum of understanding people who followed the strategy to live and let live. As time went by, I was able to sort out the wheat from the chaff but this did not influence my bank manager who had Victorian attitudes toward people of my station. Privileged serf no doubt, was the manager's categorisation of me. One who was given his freedom, by a weak Act of Parliament.

I had the additional misfortune of suffering from adhesions after starting back to work. They were very painful. Often I thought of my friend in the sanatorium Bill Crook, vigorously engaging in his exercises and wished that I had applied myself to the task a little more aggressively.

Fortunately, I no longer suffer from them. If you are unfamiliar with the term adhesions as a medical word, I can only explain the way adhesions affected me.

I was working on a contract for the South-Western Gas Board, installing copper pipes on a building site. These pipes had to be buried in the brick walls, which entailed cutting a channel in the bricks. No mechanisation was available to form the channel; it was done the hard way, by hammering a cold steel chisel into the wall with a four-pound lump hammer.

I was holding the chisel in my left hand above my head for long periods, causing the muscles under my left arm to become tense. These muscles had been severed in my lung operation and blood had congealed between the muscles, causing them to adhere to each other. The affect this had on me was a sudden shock of pain that resembled an explosion going off under my arm. The muscles had been stuck together and suddenly parted. The result of this was to render my left arm and shoulder virtually useless. On these occasions I stopped working and drove home, using my right arm to steer the van and change gear.

The effects of this took days to wear off. I may have suffered more because I had returned to work sooner than my doctor had thought advisable, but I had felt obligated to try and repay my parents for my upkeep during my long illness. All three of us had been living on my father's meagre wages as a labourer during my illness.

Our business began to expand too fast; we were building up a good reputation as contractors. I had recently acquired a large Gas Board contract and they only settled their accounts every three months, which meant that I had to finance the workforce for that time. To meet the needs of my ambitions, I needed financial help. I arranged a meeting with my bank manager with the intention of introducing myself as a hardworking, trustworthy man with an expanding business that he could assist financially for our mutual gain in the years to come.

It transpired however to run less smoothly. This banking business was a different ball game to me.

On the day of my appointment, I walked into his office wearing my working garb. My thoughts were focused on the workforce I had just left and how quickly could I expect to rejoin them.

The manager's first words to me as I entered his office were, "Have you got a cold in your head?"

I had forgotten to remove my hat. Protocol was the last thing on my mind, having just left the squalor of a building site. I was not versed in the conduct of banking. I did not apologise for my simple-mindedness, as he had himself lacked candour in his remark, I chose to ignore his less than wholesome greeting. I took my hat off and got straight to the point of my visit. He got straight to the point of rewarding me with a swift return to the squalor from whence I came, with the added knowledge of my need for a different strategy. He was an old man in my eyes, intent on maintaining me in my station. I had at least learnt to respect my elders but I now perceive him as a stuck up Victorian asshole steeped in his own standing. On reflection, it's clear to me now that he had no intentions of helping me as soon as he had noted my home address and my age.

I struggled on for a while with financial problems. Basically, I could not turn my limited financial assets over quickly enough to settle my monthly accounts. At this time, I received a call from my biggest customer requesting a meeting to discuss a private building venture. Two brothers owned this multimillion-pound consortium. Their interest included a large building firm, a farm, a garage, a hotel and the largest of the local building merchants (with whom I was mostly in arrears).

One brother was the man who had given me my start as an apprentice plumber on their building site. The other brother was an ardent follower of a Christian satellite faith and it was he who needed my help. He had purchased a church building for the Sect. The building needed extensive renovation including the installation of a new central heating system.

He had personally estimated the cost of installing the central heating system at four hundred pounds and later realised that this amount didn't even cover the cost of the boiler. It was a substantial job, which included installing twenty-two large radiators. I suppose that having his own builders' merchants business, he thought he would purchase the materials from it and cut the cost. Having realised his mistake he was anxious for me to help him find a way out of his dilemma. The true cost of the installation was two thousand four hundred pounds. I suggested he leave the matter in my hands and without further consultation proceeded to install the system.

On completing the contract, I presented him with a bill for the total cost of four hundred pounds. He looked surprised and was very grateful for my help. He inquired if there was any way that he could help me. This is what I was gambling on; I could not afford to give away two thousand pounds. I poured out to him the obstacles preventing me from promoting my business ambitions. I suggested that extended credit facilities would permit growth in my business. My hands were temporarily tied by a lack of ready cash or credit facilities. He was the main shareholder and the premier director of the builders' merchants. I knew that some customers gained preferential treatment by receiving extended credit facilities. I suggested it might be of benefit to me if he mentioned at his next board meeting the credibility of my business as a worthy applicant for these facilities. He assured me he would raise the matter at the next board meeting.

I received a letter in the next few days, informing me that I had three months to settle what was previously a monthly account, and the prices of goods I purchased were slashed. This was the equivalent of securing a free overdraft of thirty thousand pounds and I no longer needed the bank's assistance.

CHAPTER 13

THE PARTING OF THE WAVES

To regain my strength during the first two years of my working recovery required a lot of therapy. A lot of my previous strength was related to the type of physical effort required in my work. In my late teens I played about with my pals, arm wrestling and would take on two at the same time, or there was no contest. The steroid drugs prescribed to assist in speeding my recovery were now enhancing my strength to a point unrecognisable at times. I felt a little more than fully fit.

Two of my employees were assisting me in carrying a cast iron bath up a flight of stairs. It was a four-man job normally but I held one end of the bath and they held the opposite end. We had reached a point at the top of the stairs where I, being at the top end, was able to come around the side of the landing, above my two helpers and hold the bath upright. I had my first two index fingers poking through the waste hole of the bath, taking the full weight of my end. Suddenly, my two helpers stumbled and released the bath to my sole control. With hardly any effort, I held the bath in mid-air with my arm outstretched. It was amazing; the bath was gently swinging on my two fingers!

My two helpers were on their backs gawking in amazement at the sight. They rushed back to assist me to complete the job and, on reaching the top of the stairs, they asked, "How did you do that?"

To this day I really don't know. I must have experienced a strange metamorphosis, like the Incredible Hulk. I think the steroid treatment had something to do with it.

The threat of an early death hung over my head for years after leaving the sanatorium. I persistently tried to obtain a life endowment policy to check on my life expectancy but even though I felt so fit, all the doctors gave me the same answer, "Come back in ten years and try again!" My lifestyle was all drinking, gambling and loose women. I didn't want to form any lasting relationship with any woman; after all, with my life expectancy, it would have been unfair in my opinion to let her down by dying on her. I still thought that I was looking at a short life.

My association with the sanatorium as a patient had ended, but I returned several times with some of my friends to attend the Tuesday evening dances. Harry, the sanatorium café and bar manager took me out in his pink Rolls Royce car to look at some of his properties that he rented out. Brian my partner and I did a lot of building work for Harry, and Harry advised me to invest in property. Whilst his advice was sound, with my life still in the balance that was the last thing that I wanted.

Mary Tickle the longest live in-patient, I also visited several times; she's sadly no longer with us but her legend never fades. When listening to Mary, I began to understand some of the thoughts that lay in the back of my mind. Long-stay patients like Mary elected to remain in the sanatorium. It was a way of life to them. They had adopted the complex as their home.

On entering the sanatorium, they never expected to leave. The cure for tuberculosis was discovered and used to redeem their lives. Why should they want to leave?

I remembered the different societies within the complex. There were those who had been given this new lease of life? Can you imagine the comradeship that they felt after being reprieved of the terrible fate that they all expected? They were living in a beautiful private domain, amongst their friends, on the edge of Dartmoor, with all the facilities of a holiday village. Outside the security of this sanctuary, they were treated like members of a leper colony.

In my half of the society, in West Block A, we were still experiencing the original thoughts of dying within the complex and not by choice. The only people left in the sanatorium that I knew were staff and long-term patients. The young nurses I had known were replenished with a new batch of eager angels. I was surprised to see three young African nurses from Kenya. They wore three horizontal scars on their cheeks that resembled the mark of the Mau Mau terrorists in Kenya, which had risen up against the British Empire in the 1950s. I spoke to them but their

English seemed to be very poor, or perhaps they were shy? I bet they had a story to tell!

For the nurses, I organised a bottle party in the private reception hall of their living quarters. Young guests were invited from my home town and young officer cadets from HMS Britannia, Dartmouth Royal Naval College. I thought that they would like that. The party was well organised with Harry, the bar manager, providing a barrel of beer, paid for by my friends.

I also organised darts matches between my local pub darts team and the sanatorium staff team, who played return matches in my local pub The Union. It was great to have a proper drink with Yorkie the cleaner and Jim the stoker who had really, for the first time, introduced me to drink during my stay at the sanatorium. One of the members of the sanatorium darts team was none other than Staff Nurse Kimble. She had married an older, rich farmer from a local farm. I thought that lifestyle would suit her; being in the company of all the other mammals in the milking parlour.

Whilst attending the dances I courted resident nurses. I never wanted a lasting relationship and I thought going out with the nurses was not so bad because they would understand my predicament. The problem that I found with these dates was the fact that I was doing all the talking. Having travelled around in the band meeting pop stars I felt as if I was a chat show guest. The girls in general played host by asking questions like: 'and what did you do then?' and 'what happened next?' I was just singing the same old song, and got tired of assignations. After pampering customers all day, I felt I was doing the same for the girls in the evenings. I wanted to relax, and that meant getting pissed with my mates.

Eventually, the sanatorium facilities were incorporated into other hospitals, and the place was gradually run down, so my association with it petered out. I read in the local paper later that poor old Yorkie the sanatorium cleaner got killed in a road accident when leaving his local pub The Clay Cutter's Arms.

In 1965, I met the guitarist Derrick Luscombe, whom I had replaced in The Vampires. Derrick had contracted the very same lung disease that I had. This was most strange because this ailment was quite rare.

Derrick was lucky in one way, as I had been the guinea pig who was experimented on, and he was able to forgo any biopsies and operations, probably because of the experiments that I had endured.

He also had a decent doctor, instead of a quack. Derrick often got in touch with me because he was worried about the side effects of the treatment, but I was able to console him, as the effects, whilst being very uncomfortable, were only temporary. The side effects from the treatment went on for two years and were serious enough to require two further visits to hospital.

On the first occasion I thought I had a fish bone lodged in my throat but there was no bone! It was found to be my throat that was just raw and bleeding. The second time was because my nose was permanently blocked and this affected my speech, which was embarrassing when I spoke to my customers. Each side affect lasted for a period of three months and then disappeared. I became temporarily impotent for three months. Derek was really concerned at this stage of his recovery because he was contemplating marriage and fathering children. I had one more side effect yet to come at this stage, which were gallstones.

During this time I had to visit the local hospital every two weeks for a chest X-ray and medical examination. I was beginning to think this would never end, until one day an old man, who was sitting in the waiting room of the radiography department, asked me how I was coping with my recovery.

I told him exactly how I felt and inquired, "Does it ever end and how long have you been coming here?"

He replied to the second part of my question by saying that he had been attending the hospital for six years since his operation and asked me, "How long have you been attending since your op?"

"Two years." I replied.

"Don't worry," he said, "it takes about two years for your body to adjust. The side effects will stop and you should start to feel better soon." I am glad to say he was right, and thought how lucky we both were to still be alive and kicking.

At the age of twenty-three I met John Kay, a businessman who had inherited a fortune from his father; he was the same age as me. John had a public school education specialising in business studies. On leaving school, he controlled a chain of grocery stores he had inherited from his late father's estate; he also inherited a very large property company and owned a builder's merchants business. I came into contact with John through the builder's merchants business and had a substantial account with him. He supplied various brands of merchandise that were not available in other merchants' stores and I needed this specialised stock on various contracts.

John and I had a sound business relationship, which became stressed after two years, when I became bedridden through my recurring ailments. He was pressing me for settlement of my monthly account and even though he was aware of my plight, he threatened ruination for me, unless I found the means to meet my monthly deadline. He was a typical businessman, trained to be ruthless; all that mattered was profit and making money. That's not a criticism; he was what I would have expected from a professionally trained businessman. I was the novice and had an awful time.

I had contracted yellow jaundice due to my gallstones, brought on by the steroid treatment for my lung disorder. I pleaded with John to give me a little time to recover but to no avail. He kept the pressure up and his letters became more and more threatening.

At the time this was happening, my only chance of collecting debts from most of the builders I contracted work from was to send my partner Brian. My normal routine for collecting debts was to visit the builders on the site. This gave us the chance to discuss other business matters regarding the workforce or financial matters like short-term credit or interim payments of their account. Builders sometimes had their own financial problems and the need to be flexible with money matters was paramount.

My partner was a good friend and colloquially one of the boys; he had no interest in running the business. Brian did not care if we expanded the business, or just carried on with the two of us. He had a childish side to his nature and could not take anything seriously. He was certainly not subtle enough to deal with major business clients. Brian had perfected a method of shocking people using a floorboard as a theatrical slapstick. Holding the board upright he would release it, allowing it to topple like a falling tree and at the last moment he'd stamp his foot on the board helping it on its way. This created a resounding crash as it made contact with the floor.

He called on one of our clients to collect a substantial amount of money. The client, Cyril Mitchell, was recovering from a heart attack. Brian crept up behind him in an acoustically resounding room and stamped his foot on the slapstick, nearly killing poor Cyril with shock. Cyril never wanted him on his building site again and of course, the money was delayed until I apologised to Cyril in person for my partner's irresponsible behaviour.

On another occasion I asked Brian to call on a very important client, Mr Fairman, who owned the prestige building site in our town. Mr Fairman maintained a very high standard of craftsmanship and was the only builder that I knew who would shine a torch parallel to a wall that had just been plastered, to see if any shadows highlighted any uneven spots on the surface of the wall. If there was a shadow, the whole wall had to be stripped and re-plastered.

The word was that Mr Fairman had acquired his wealth dealing in South African diamonds. His workforce felt that he held himself aloof from them with his refined and gentlemanly approach to disputes, and this earned him the nickname of 'Bwana'.

A young apprentice was traipsing around behind Brian whilst he looked for Bwana. He was searching the rooms of a large luxury dwelling under construction. As he walked down a long corridor and thinking the apprentice was walking behind him, he grabbed the boy's hand and held it next to his buttocks.

He then broke wind with a resounding abandonment into the hand, only to turn around a see Bwana standing where he thought the apprentice should be. Bwana's eyes were fixed firmly on his cupped hand; Bwana just turned without uttering a word with his hand still cupped and went home. I received no money from that soiled hand for a while!

Eventually, I managed to settle my account. I did not bear malice toward John Kay the impetuous merchant's behaviour. In business the rules for the majorities are win at any cost, there are no scruples.

In 1966 I managed to acquire a mortgage from the same builder that had given me my start as an apprentice. He had lots of properties that he rented out, and could afford to extend a mortgage to anyone he pleased. He knew I was unable to pass a fitness examination for a building society mortgage, but he was prepared to extend the same facilities as the building society to me, using the house as collateral. If I had failed to pay the mortgage he would simply have one more house to let for rent.

At the time, I was still living in a council house with my parents; the house I was born in. I wanted my new house to be registered entirely in my father's name, even though I was to pay all the cost of the property myself. I wanted my father to be respected in his rightful role as the head of the family. I had at times helped my family members in various ways and felt by owning our house myself I might encroach on the respect my father truly deserved.

This house would give him and my mother the security of the property, should I not survive. I had to settle eventually with half the house in his name and half in mine.

I believe the wily old solicitor thought my father was taking advantage of his stupid son (everyone still thought that I was stupid). This was my way of showing my parents respect for bringing me up and supporting me in the true sense of parenthood.

After settling in our new home my father acquired a kitten and we called him Timmy. We always had a cat in our family.

Timmy, to begin with, was kept in the integral garage of our home, whilst he became house-trained.

My father (who always treated a cat as a working pet) walked through the kitchen door that led to the garage and saw a small pool of water in the centre of the floor! Timmy was sat at its edge, looking innocent. My father grabbed the kitten and rubbed its nose in the pool to teach it a lesson. This happened three days in a row until my father discovered that the pool was due to a leak from a water main under the garage. Poor little Timmy!

Moving into our new home with (for the first time) modern amenities of fitted carpets, central heating, and a garage, etc, was great for my father and for me, but I learned that it was not altogether good for my mother.

The one thing that I had failed to realise when changing homes was that you leave your friends behind. This was no problem to my father and me, as we were mobile but my mother, on the other hand, was now suffering from arthritis and finding it difficult to walk. I was to learn the effect of this on my mother, through a conversation in a pub many years later.

Our new house was situated beside a school sports field. Unbeknown to me, our old neighbour (who was a child when I left the council house and attended the adjacent school) regularly climbed over our garden fence to talk to my mother. She gave him cigarettes to coax him into giving her all the latest gossip that she missed so much.

Until my neighbour (who was now an adult) and I had a conversation in the pub, I hadn't realised her plight. My mother had lived in our old house through the best years of her life and it's only natural she missed the news and the gossip with her old friends.

When I was thirteen, my father had caught me in the act of smoking and severely punished me. My mother never smoked and agreed with my father's views that, as a child, I should not smoke. So it came as a shock to me in the pub, when my neighbour told me this story about my mother in her new home.

Fancy being so hard on me smoking and giving another schoolchild fags.

After I bought my house my partner Brian did the same on the same estate. We had acquired two warehouses during our expansion and built an office in one of them, and we now employed a full time secretary. I was generally involved with the running of the office and dealt with company representatives touting their wares. One such was an agent selling Kalamazoo office equipment. I spent about an hour discussing the merchandise in his portfolio and made a purchase.

Suddenly, without any inclination of what I was about to say I bluntly asked the representative if he was a relative of Clifford Everly, who had been my best friend and fellow patient in the sanatorium to which he replied, "I know a man of that name but he is dead." We compared facts and it turned out it was the same Clifford Everly he knew. The rep told me that they were best pals as children and grew up together in Manchester, 300 miles away from where I lived. They did not look alike and I was puzzled by the fact that I had some how unconsciously made the connection between them.

I have thought about the phenomena many times and I believe, as they were close friends; he probably picked up Clifford's mannerisms. It was possibly this that I subconsciously noticed.

The fact is it shows the strength of my feelings, to be aware of those mannerisms. Men believing they were dying of the same ailment develop a close bond. If only everyone had that bond. The meeting with this representative left me with a feeling of well-being; it was as if my friend Clifford had returned to bid his last farewell.

In 1969, a local builder approached me with an offer of a merger between his building firm and my plumbing firm. This interested me because the business was still expanding and the pressure of running the business on my own was committing me to working morning, noon and night. The builder was not interested in including my partner Brian in the merger, which was understandable, so I approached Brian and made an offer to purchase his half of the business. Brian wanted the business to stay as it was, and could not make a decision to save his life. He had the best of both worlds. He consulted with his wife and friends and came up with a demand for his share of money that was out of proportion with what I could afford to pay. Our assets were stock and you can't pay bills with stock.

This left me in a dilemma. I was not prepared to continue working myself into the grave, but there was no way of making the merger in the situation I found myself. So we parted company after being together for six years and divided the firm up.

We were and still are the greatest of friends. I gave him the first choice of our customers to take with him to set up a business of his own. I gave my brother, who had worked for us for the last three years, the chance to set up his own plumbing subcontracting business with the choice of the remaining customers, leaving myself with the residue.

My partner and I entered into a deed of arrangement with our creditors, whereby we handed over the two warehouse properties we had acquired and all our stock, to clear our accounts. There was an imbalance, a shortcoming on our side at the final tally, which led to our bankruptcy. This was a great shock to me. I was so worried about my parents and our home. Imagine if I should lose the house after moving my parents out of their council house. Believe me when I say that bankruptcy can be a very worrying affair.

However, the deed of arrangement agreement with our creditors that I had fought so hard for kept our homes intact and we were permitted to carry on trading. It was like starting all over again, without the need to buy homes or to find contracts. It was now up to us individually to continue on our way.

An amazing incident occurred at the meeting between my creditors and me that beggars belief. It was my wish that this deed of arrangement could be secured between my firm, consisting of myself and my partner, who at the request of all the other parties had no need to attend the meeting. I was recognised as the only member of the partnership who dealt with business matters.

My partner, with all due respects, would have been better off penned up in a play school for half an hour whilst I secured the best deal in both our interests. Brian didn't even know that we had gone bankrupt. He is doing well by the way; he eventually included his son in his business and the two of them work together to this day.

My plan had been to settle the accounts of all the small creditors, which I was sure I had achieved, leaving only the four big creditors to enter into a deed of arrangement. My accountant, through me, had arranged this meeting with them. I had obviously earned a lot of money for them in the past and I thought that at my age they must have been pretty sure that I would continue to do so, so why bankrupt me? This agreement had been aired prior to the official meeting.

On the day of the meeting however, the builder, whom I had helped in the church, turned up with a small bill amounting to four pounds. My accountant read out the list of four creditors and the builder stood up and stated in a booming voice, "That list is incorrect, I have an unpaid bill in my possession that is not on that list." He said this whilst dramatically waving the bill in the air above his head. He further stated, "How many other unpaid bills are there? It could be any amount, we have no way of knowing." I had wondered what he was doing at the meeting.

I was very shocked; I couldn't believe this man was stabbing me in the back. He had known me through my apprenticeship and as long again in business, it was a joke! I explained to the creditors how that I had called into this man's garage as they were on the list of creditors and asked for all my bills in order that I may settle them, which I did. His garage obviously mislaid this tiny account or perhaps held it back for this reason. He shouldn't have even attended the meeting. He was rich, powerful and well connected and had the means to procure details of the meeting. He obviously wanted me cut down to size.

I rose to my feet to address everyone in the room, and stated, "This meeting is being held for interested parties who are here in the hope of a constructive meeting to determine the future activities of all our mutual business interests. I am dismayed that someone amid us in this room should deviate in showing respect to its members." That said, the agreement I was pursuing was signed. I was fighting for my life. If he had wrecked the meeting as he obviously intended to do, I would have lost my future in business and my house, no doubt.

This man was vexed because I was considering merging with another builder instead of approaching him first to give him the opportunity of merging with me. As he hadn't approached me himself with an offer, I had no idea that he was interested. On reflection, I believe he thought I had been dishonest in seeking a merger behind his back, but it was the other builder that had approached me with the offer.

He had helped me with the extended credit facilities with his builder's merchants business in exchange for my help in his church and thought that a merger with anyone other than him would create a conflict of interest. In other words, I would be a spy for the other builder on any future building contract tenders. Instead of approaching me to tell me of his concern at the time that I was contemplating the merger, he had waited and made this approach at the meeting.

I am still shocked to think I had thought that we were friends. This was a dispute that should have been aired long before this stage of my affairs. There was no conflict of interest in anyone else's mind. On the whole it was a bit of a mess.

After this upheaval I struggled for a while. The builder who had put up the idea of a merger was not interested in the business of a bankrupt, so I had to carry on on my own. I had been obliged by the indentures of three apprentices to maintain their craft instruction. This entailed keeping three extra employees to train them that I did not require. The best contracts I had released to my partner and my brother. The fact of the matter was that I was in a desperate situation and was worried about my home. I had accumulated a debt of eight hundred pounds in National Health stamps and was threatened with another personal bankruptcy.

I decided to call on my brother Brian; I knew he had that sort of money in the bank. I had given him a readymade business of his choice on a plate and felt sure he would want to help me. I offered to repay the loan in one year and to give him my half of my house, which I never wanted anyway. I promised to pay for the house mortgage as I had been doing as long as my parents and I could live there for as long as my parents lived.

What his wife said to me when I called at their house to ask for their help I couldn't repeat. It shocked my memory to silence forever. It was all take and no give with my relatives. After the shock of her reply, I drove home thinking, 'What did she say?' My mind was a blank.

Needless to say, after the shock I pulled myself together, stopped drinking with my pals on weekends; went on a diet and went to the business of sorting things out.

CHAPTER 14

STARTING ANEW AND GROWING UP

A short time after I had commenced trading on my own, the builder's merchants (owned by the builder of my recent dispute) that had previously provided my partnership with extended credit, was taken over by a larger corporation. My ex-partner Brian had been awarded trading facilities with this firm immediately after our separation. Our deed of arrangement secured at our creditor's meeting allowed us both to trade legally after our bankruptcy. I had not as yet arranged credit facilities with them, and therefore approached them cautiously carrying cash.

This merchant was the only local stockist of a particular brand of plastic rainwater guttering and downpipes that I required, amounting to five hundred pounds in value. As I approached the counter to place my order, the floor manager, who had worked for the previous owners, intervened and refused my order. He was boisterous and contemptuous in his manner and drew the attention of other customers to our controversy.

I was astonished, especially when he refused me access to see the general manager. Considering that it would take me several days to get the goods from out of town, and that men's jobs were at stake, I ignored him. Sweeping him to one side, I approached the general manager's office. His secretary stood in front of his office door with her arms outstretched barring my way. She too had a contemptuous disposition.

I explained to her that I had urgent need for these supplies and that I would pay cash but she wouldn't budge. She, like the floor manager, was being faithful to my previous adversary and biased against me. So I gently eased her to one side and pushed the door open.

Feeling irked by now, I approached the general manager with a serious intent. With my hands placed on his desk, I leaned over him in an intimidating manner and said, "I have men with wives and their children to feed and they're waiting on site for materials with which to earn their livings." I spoke bluntly; pausing for a moment to give him time to answer and then I cut him off as he began to utter his first word. With three short bursts I declared:

"I have the cash!
You have the materials!
Let's trade!"

He got the message and introduced himself to me and then assisted me to collect what I required. He even helped me to load the goods onto my van. After this, he accompanied me to the cash register. He watched me pay for the goods, but did not offer me the same credit facilities that my partner Brian had secured. He just thanked me for my business and then returned to his office. In his absence, I requested a receipt from the girl on the till and said, "You will deliver these goods to the building site for me," and she agreed. I drove out of their yard loaded down with all the rainwater goods and the next day, a duplicate load was delivered on site free of charge. Two for the price of one, I thought, that would cover me for the time wasted.

The same millionaire, who was at my creditor's meeting, was trying to put me out of business. Although he had left the merchant company, he still had sway with the floor manager and his faithful secretary, but he had no sway with the new general manager.

I never again traded with this company; my business expanded way beyond the need to squabble with any company. I learned the difference between money and power in my new approach to business. The shock of almost losing my home and the reaction of people around me had hardened my business attitude. The millionaire builder had made a feeble attempt to end my career but his influence was ebbing, and mine was beginning to flourish.

For months after my partnership had failed, I had not socialised with anyone, due both to my diet and the effort needed to establish my new business. It did me no harm in the long run; I lost four stone in weight (only temporarily though) gave up smoking and managed to secure even more lucrative contracts than before. I was becoming quite successful.

My two brothers offered me a place in their pub darts team. I thought this might be a chance to show there was no malice between us and accepted their kind offer. At the match, I drank orange juice and allowed myself one half-corona cigar, which unfortunately gradually started my smoking habit all over again. Things were going OK until I joined company with two of my brother's mates.

They were sat at a table and as I sat down, one of them remarked, "Are you a brother of Ron and Brian?"

"Yes," I replied.

"Not like that other big fat lazy bastard, are you? The big-headed one with the briefcase that calls on the building sites?" He was talking about me; I had lost so much weight he failed to recognise me.

"Oh," I replied. "Do you know him?" making out that I was not quite sure of their drift.

"We don't know him personally but your brothers have told us all about him. We didn't know there was a fourth brother!"

With my brothers I just couldn't win. Their moral status I had taken too critically perhaps. My nature to keep my own counsel kept me from losing control of my temper.

Being the youngest and poorest achiever in the family meant that any comment from me was met with ridicule and in later years when I became more successful, the ridicule became enhanced with jealousy and disdain.

On adjusting my image of my brothers, I found we were of two different eras that were not compatible. They were "short back and sides" army smart. I was a Teddy Boy who was well dipped into rock and roll. To meet their criteria, I would have to be married with two children and struggling to pay the mortgage on a house and the hire purchase payments on a car. Most people from our background had that qualifying criteria. They had met all these obligations of society. I, on the other hand, had been a teenage Teddy Boy, suffered critical illness and become a successful businessman, even employing one of them for many years and set him up in his own business.

My family could have anything they wanted from me but it seemed the more successful I became, the more we grew apart. Instead of binding the family closer together, I was creating a greater conflict between us. I had always had my place as the dummy of the family, the dunce and a weirdo, who dressed in funny clothes and liked funny music. I was nothing like a member of the family unit. I was more a threat to their ideals and yet my success created something that I had not understood. Jealousy had reared its ugly head. Something in all of us but up until then, I believed this only existed towards people outside the family, towards the privileged society, specifically the upper classes that still maintained their Victorian principles.

This rift between us I never mastered. I had to live with it. Their ridicule of me did not change or intensify, but it began to hurt. My buried feelings were disclosed only to my mother, who always came to their defence. She was the peacekeeper, the linchpin of the family, holding it together.

My mother passed on a strange story to me regarding my youngest sister Jean. As children, Jean and I fought like cat and dog. She not only told fibs to our parents about me but also greedily grabbed anything that was going. She sat next to my mother in the cinema between my mum and me to gain first choice of popcorn or ice cream, or sweets if there were any. She consequently became fat, whereas I was not. That constituted my only retort when she told a fib. I called her Fatso! My father was not slow in handing out punishment and I, being the less promising child intellectually, faired less favourably in disputes. Consequently, I tired of punishment. I inquired of my mother, the wisdom of her deliberation as to the cause of our discord. My mother beseeched me to indulge in tolerance towards Jean, believing she was troubled from birth with a special problem.

Jean was born in the middle of a bombing raid and my mother had been terrified whilst in the act of giving birth. As Jean developed, she experienced a recurring nightmare. Jean awoke crying and when my mother asked her what was troubling her, Jean would hold out her hands saying, "Stones," as if she was buried in rubble and pushing the stones off of her body. My mother emphasised her story to me, holding out her own hands with upturned clenched fists. This was the fear my mother experienced whilst giving birth to her, and my mother developed a special bond with my sister. I believe my mother's story; her fears in the bombing raid were passed on to Jean.

Like many people, I had experiences in my early years of familiarity with my surroundings, knowing it was impossible for me ever to have visited the location in my lifetime. Many religions associate these phenomena with reincarnation. That may be so but there are other considerations such as, it's possible your mother visited the site, whilst carrying your embryo in pregnancy. How much closer can a bond between two people be than this? Arguments like these are inconclusive but that's not to say they always will be.

My mother always protected every wrongdoing my kin perpetrated with some excuse. I always respected her every wish toward all my family. This made the rift even greater because if they wanted anything from me, they would get my mother to approach me, knowing I could not refuse our matriarch. My mother met their every need at my expense without question.

This picture I saw of the family union was completely out of my hands. The job of holding the family together became entirely that of our mother. In conducting this role she truly became the matriarch, although understandably, she was unable to improve the overall difference in our psychology (to do that would have required a miracle).

When I reflect on that situation today, I realise that I was fully absorbed in my own life and was unaware of the fact that their lives were so mundane. (I was there to be castigated, like a tiresome family pet.)

My mother told me she once saw Jesus at the end of her bed when she was ill. I would imagine she was suffering through one of her births. My mother had a string of nine miscarriages and was told by her doctor not to fall pregnant again. She then gave birth to my sister and finally me. I have often wondered when her vision occurred. I have called out for God when I was in a desperate situation. I have thought about this on many occasions and decided it was because of the fear of God installed in me as a child at Sunday School. I listened to a radio news broadcast of an aircraft pilot speaking as he fell victim to a hijacker's bullet. The last words he spoke on his microphone were, "I've been shot, oh my God, oh my God!" This was exactly the way I spoke the very same words on the operating table, with no control over my choice of words.

As a child, you are unable to form an opinion on such matters. It's difficult enough when you're an adult. It's true we are all entitled to faith but the different sects should respect our right to choose between them. A biased opinion can be indoctrinated into children and encourage a discrimination that's hard to reason with when the child reaches maturity.

It's funny but when my sister Jean had her first baby she became and remained slim for the rest of her life. After my experience in Hawkmoor, I became fat from the drug treatment and remain fat to this day. Perhaps that's karma? I'm the fatso now! Lots of people in jest call me fatso but I'm also alive and that's good enough for me.

After my father's retirement from the Gas Company, he asked me for a job. I had established myself in my new business well enough to afford this, and was happy to oblige. It had taken me just over a year to become solvent and in profit. He still maintained his hobby of breeding canaries, but wanted a part-time occupation because he was not the sort of man to sit around. I gave him a job driving a brand new van when it suited him. He'd rather drive that van than his old Austin car. There was always someone on the building sites who wanted materials delivered and I left it to his own convenience to decide when and where he worked.

I'd tell my father constantly how well that I was doing. After all my troubles with my bankruptcy I felt I had to reassure him at every opportunity. He always belittled whatever I told him as if I was exaggerating. I wasn't showing off, my concern for my parents was genuine. I had been driving around in an old Rover car, and as I was doing well with every month that went by, I decided to purchase a better car.

My father drove me to a garage so that I might drive my new car home if I made a purchase. He thought that I was going to buy another old Rover but I asked the sales rep if I could test-drive an almost new BMW saloon. This shook my father as he thought I was taking the piss out of the rep. The car cost four thousand pounds. This was over one thousand pounds more than I had paid for our house. I told my dad to drive. He looked at me as if looks could kill. He felt sure I was going to get us both into trouble.

After the test drive I said to the rep, "I'll take it, will you take a cheque?" My father was dressed in his Gas Company overalls and I was dressed in old working clothes. The rep was showing a hint of apprehension at this point, and asked if he could ring my bank, "By all means," I said. I paid the full amount for the car and my father drove it home. I told my father to sell his car as he could drive my BMW from now on. After two years of my new business, I had about ten thousand pounds in my bank account and I left bank statements lying around the house knowing that my dad and mum would peek at them. I would do anything to keep their minds at rest.

I hired a builder to build an extension onto my sister's house at my expense in case anything happened to me. It had its own toilet and basin en suite and central heating. I now felt more secure in my own actions should I fail, knowing that my sister was in a position to help either of my parents in old age should anything befall me. I was planning for their future but not mine.

Employing my father led to our first eyeball-to-eyeball confrontation. I was driving around building sites generally taking stock of my business and on returning home, I saw a number of central heating boilers stacked in my driveway. I had noticed a spot of rain on my windscreen and thought the boilers needed putting under cover immediately. I started to put them in my garage and as I was carrying them in, my father was carrying them back out!

I said to him, "What are you doing?"

He said, "I'll put them under cover later." (I suppose he wanted to place them more tidily than I was.) I told him I had just driven through some rain and was worried about the electrical connections on the boilers getting wet. (They came to a considerable sum.)

My father looked up at the sky and then at me and said as if I was still his stupid child, "It's not going to rain!" And my father continued to carry the boilers outside. I tore into him just like I would any employee who disobeyed an order. I had respect from all my employees and was in no mood for his lack of understanding. (In other words I lost my temper with my dad.)

It was face-to-face aggression, like looking in a mirror. My father backed down and got into the car and drove away. I have no idea where he went.

We did not speak again for two weeks. This was driving my mother nuts.

She said to me, "Bob, please just say something to him!" I was not the kind of person to carry on this childish sulk but I had seen my father do this before with my mother, and my brother Brian had the same way about him.

In the end I simply said to my father, "Do you fancy a cup of tea?" I got a grunt in response and the feud was over. It was not the nicest experience having to confront my dad in that way but I know things changed a little for the better.

CHAPTER 15

SUCCESS

Whilst building up a first class business, I was perplexed at times at the level of my success. My accountant confided to me that my strength was in my negotiating ability. As a young man because of my lack of achievement at school, I considered myself to be wanting when dealing with educated people. By now, I was beginning to think my dyslexia kept me on my toes and I believe it was beginning to give me the edge in my negotiating. I became more careful and precise. I spent much more time in preparing my strategy before the negotiations than my counterparts.

Three different figure estimates were prepared for each contract in advance of negotiations. This was arduous and time consuming but I persevered. I'd submit the highest tender and be ready to drop my price progressively down to the lowest tender after a long battle of wits. I secured the middle tender more often than not, which was always a bonus because the lower price was acceptable. These tenders comprehended quantities of all labour and materials down to the last nut and bolt. Each tender amounted to a dossier of information. I always investigated the background of my negotiating opponent before every encounter; I became a predator!

My perception of my opposite negotiator was that he knew nothing of my trade and dealt mainly with the end figure. I was the master and had to assure him that my quantities were accurate and that I welcomed any dispute over the details of my estimate.

These contracts ran into millions of pounds at times, and the negotiations would go on for weeks. I remembered one of the most lucrative contracts I had secured. The negotiator played cat and mouse with me, assuring me at one time that he had other tenders submitted to him that were forty percent lower than mine. He wanted me to lower my highest estimate by forty percent and another two and a half percent. This was well inside the scope of my lowest pre-prepared tender.

I suggested I would better the offer and drop my price by twenty percent plus a further twenty-five percent. He mistook this as a total of forty-five percent. He had not realised that my offer equalled forty percent and he signed the contract on that offer. This was my most lucrative contract, sealed because of his lack of simple arithmetic.

I became aware that having purchasing power was more powerful than wealth. Having secured the large contracts in my area, the merchants flocked to me, showering me with credit facilities and deals on merchandise. It's being in demand that creates power. It's the difference between being someone instead of a has-been. It's generally the same for film stars, sports personalities, politicians or the like. When you're in demand, then, you command!

I had built up a great workforce with whom I shared information concerning future projects. It was important for them to know that their jobs were secure, and before contracts were signed for large building projects, I would call them into my office to see if they agreed with their wage structure for each contract. They knew my door was always open to them for help in any way.

A situation arose concerning an old plumber Tom Hardy, who had been in my employment for some time. One morning, Tom called into my office to inform me of his wife's sudden illness. She had been taken into hospital over the weekend, whilst they were visiting in-laws in Tiverton, a town sixty miles away from his home. He requested I listen out for telephone messages regarding his wife's well-being, to which I agreed. He then continued on his way to a building site at Dawlish several miles away, where I had several other men working.

Later that day, I received a telephone call from his traumatised brother, who simply stated, "I'm Tom's brother, tell Tom the wife's dead." He then put the receiver down. That was it! End of message! I thought, I couldn't telephone the site with a message like that; I'll have to deliver it in person.

Whilst driving to the site, I was cogitating on my line of approach, 'How should I deliver the message, should I sit him down first? Should I engage in light conversation to assess his mood?' I was not looking forward to the task.

In the end, I came right out with it and told him bluntly, "Tom, your wife's dead!" I thought, 'It's going to be a shock, no matter how I tell him.'

"Oh no!" said Tom, and began to collect his tools together, in order to leave the site and go to the hospital. I intervened to say I would take care of his tools. "Just go, and I'll see you when I see you," I urged. I didn't expect to see him again for a week or two.

The next day I visited the building site, to see if the other plumbers were coping with being one man short. To my surprise, there was Tom, working away as if nothing had happened. I explained to Tom, "I didn't expect to see you for a while."

He replied, "My wife's not dead, it was my brother's wife that my brother was telephoning about, and my wife's home, and she's made a full recovery." Apparently, she had merely fainted over the weekend and was only being held in the hospital for observation.

All my employees on the site were in accord when they instructed me, "If you get any messages for us, KEEP THEM TO YOURSELF."

My new contracting business was very efficient. My working hours reduced to an average of ten flexible hours per week. I owned a half share in a boat and found lots of time to go fishing. I started to live a life of leisure and did whatever took my fancy.

I passed a fitness examination when applying for a life endowment policy in my late twenties. It's hard to express how happy this made me feel, after living on the brink of death for so many years. It presented me with the opportunity to adopt a normal socially balanced approach to life but I had got used to the way I was living. I enjoyed the lifestyle I had adopted and could not imagine being married and tied down. In the back of my mind was the evidence of the battles between my parents and all the squabbles among my kith and kin!

'Imagine,' I mused, 'if I had children and they all turned out like them and had no respect for me whatsoever. Oh no, I decided. I respect the person I have found in me.' I concluded in my thoughts, 'If I gather a measure of respect in the people around me, I could survive or even thrive. I am of the opinion that I have no need to pass on my genes. The evolution of my species is secure enough without any propagation of mine joining this overpopulated planet.'

A remark made by a teacher in my school, proclaiming that soon there wouldn't be enough food in the world to feed all the children, registered in me. I was brought up in a world of rationing, and this has always played on my subconscious mind. Perhaps a dyslexic brain picks up the spoken word more than the literal mind does? It has influenced me against having children of my own.

It's strange how people differ. I had witnessed a situation in the Surgical Block at Hawkmoor just after my lung operation. A man in his early twenties was screaming the building down as he was wheeled past my door. I asked the other patients what he had been through, thinking he had just gone through hell. It turned out he had just had a bronchoscope inspection of his lung under a general anaesthetic. This was normally done under a sedative and I asked, "Why all the screaming?"

It was the terror in his mind. Apparently he had gone through four lung operations leaving him with one lobe of lung, which was diseased and he was to die very soon. All the previous operations and the general anaesthetic sent his mind a false message, hence the screaming. He wanted to have a child before he died. I later saw him masturbating into a sample bottle. Being a bit green, I asked the men around me why he was doing this? He wanted to see if his illness would pass on to his children. I could not understand his need to have children but respected him.

I suppose you could say that this was the most stable time in my life, even my parents seemed to be at peace. We had a comfortable life, our health was intact and we had no money problems. These were undoubtedly the halcyon days of my life, and then, DISASTER! My sister Sheila turned up.

Sheila who was thirteen years my senior, lived in Salisbury, Wiltshire with Roy, a garage mechanic. They had lived together for nine years and often visited and stayed in my home.

Roy seemed to have a stabilising effect on Sheila and my parents and I liked Roy a lot.

Roy had suffered when young from TB and spent eighteen months in a sanatorium. He had made a full recovery and we got on well because of our previous experiences. We chatted endlessly about our respective ailments and I believe he had suffered an ordeal worse than mine. It entailed having seven ribs chopped out of his chest with a bolt cropper while he was fully conscious. He was sat naked on a chair with an electric current running through a wet rubber pad under his buttocks when this happened. He said he felt sick with every jolt of the cropper. He had a two-inch diameter pipe inserted in his back and played tennis in this state whilst recovering.

Sheila had decided to leave Roy, and asked for my parents' permission to stay with us. My parents and I discussed this and although I was against it because of Sheila's drug addiction and my concern for my parents' well-being, I accepted their wish. This was the very reason for my concern, when I initially wanted my house registered in my father's name. I wished my parents to retain their just title as heads of the family, and to retain their dignity in such matters as these. I had no right to take them from their council house into my home and deny their right to care for all their children equally.

Sheila became addicted when her doctor prescribed a drug (which has since been banned from prescription) to treat depression. The strength of the addiction to that drug was said, by investigative specialists, to be worse than heroin, and when the drug was withdrawn from public use Sheila seemed to live on a cocktail of alternative drugs. She was hooked!

Unfortunately Sheila made my life in my home impossible to bear. I knew she was very fond of me but there is a saying, 'you always hurt the one you love', and she seemed hell bent on driving me out of my head.

She sat in my lounge late at night, dressed in her nightdress and dressing gown, waiting for me to return home after I had spent an evening relaxing with my friends. It was like an evil presence in my home. It was like a Doctor Jekyll and Mr Hyde scenario; from now on I never saw Doctor Jekyll, I only met Mr Hyde. As soon as I arrived home, she greeted me with a scowl on her face, cursing me for being out so late, and threatening me as though she hated me. This was probably the way she had been treating Roy, her boyfriend. I began to understand why Roy never again came to our home to try and win her back. She was truly in a terrible state.

It was the effect of the drugs causing this madness, and no matter how much I tried to dissuade her from obtaining these drugs from her doctor (who incidentally was my "quack" doctor) she always managed to acquire a supply. I'd search her room and the whole house for drugs but I could never find a thing and yet she always had them concealed somehow. If you had never had a drug addict in your house it would be hard for you to understand how clever and devious they can be. After she had lived in my home for eighteen months, spending every day lounging around in her dressing gown in a dazed stupor, I knew I had to do something. If I didn't get out of my own home, my business and my own health would suffer.

I couldn't have a decent nights sleep with her in my home. We had no locks on our bedroom doors and at times, I thought she would sneak into my bedroom whilst I was asleep and knife me! My sister loved me more than anyone on this earth, and I her, but I thought she would kill me given the chance. In her mind I had replaced her boyfriend Roy as her adversary. How could I go on living like this?

Desperate for a solution, I spoke to a business colleague Ron Sheen, whom I had recently got to know through work. Ron had purchased the local disused YMCA building, and converted it into a hotel named The Paradise Castle. I had just completed the plumbing and central heating contract on the hotel for Ron. The hotel promoted a very modern discotheque and I made many new friends there. Although the discotheque had been up and running for a couple of months the hotel had only just been furbished and was about to open. Ron suggested that I stay at The Paradise as his guest for as long as I wanted. I insisted on paying for my stay and Ron said he would take a token payment of five pounds per week. I agreed to this and moved out of my home and into the hotel. I had been a good spender in the hotel bar and dining room and tried to make up for Ron's kindness by continuing to be so.

Ron Sheen had a son Roy who was the DJ in the disco bar. Roy told me he was once a roadie for the pop group The Bee Gees, and he was in his element in the disco bar. He had lots of American friends that regularly visited The Paradise. They were stationed at an American Air Force base in Cornwall. As I had already met the Americans in the disco bar previously, before moving into the hotel, they had become my beverage buddies during the evenings. There were quite a few of them but the main core amounted to six or seven. They drove from their base to Torquay in a large American car, which was always well stocked with booze.

On the day that I moved into the hotel, I met up with the Americans and joined them in an enormous drinking spree. I was drinking more than usual as a result of my home troubles, trying to put them out of my mind. Two newcomers among the Americans were black men and they told me that they were special weapons technicians. One of them had a gold front tooth with a diamond set in it. I had not seen anyone embellished with this spectacle before. His bejewelled golden incisor became the object of my humorous banter during our drinking festivity.

I was really drunk come the evening; so much so, I began to stagger. The Americans (who I believe were aware of my home troubles through Ron or his son Roy) decided to help me to my room and grabbed hold of me, picking me up bodily by my arms and legs. The black man, who had born the brunt of my humour, unfastened the front of my trouser braces and stretched them out behind me until they were about ten feet long. He was using them like a set of reins on a stagecoach. Before carrying me to my bed, they decided to do a circuit of the dancehall. They ran around the dance floor carrying me, whilst the black guy hailed, "Yippee! Giddy-up, man! You've been riding me all day man and now I'm gawna ride you! Yahoo!" It took three attempts for them to carry me up the stairs to my bed. After that day we were the best of pals.

The hotel wasn't equipped for early risers like me, so regularly I had to leave the hotel using a fire escape at seven o'clock in the morning to attend to the needs of my employees. I generally returned entering the main door at nine o'clock for my breakfast and ordered something exotic like scallops or crayfish, which was added to my weekly account. At weekends I'd have champagne with my breakfast.

Ron allowed me to sit in the disco in the afternoons to do my office work when necessary. With a bottle of scotch on the table, I'd sit at a window estimating contracts with my building plans, to maintain my workforce by continuing work. This did not have to happen every day as my business was very efficient, but business is nonetheless relentless in its demands. Regularly representatives from merchants called at the hotel for orders so that the supplies of materials for my workforce were maintained. I had never drunk alcohol at my home before and never have to this day, but I took on a different personality at the hotel to suit my surroundings.

Daily I called into my home and witnessed no change in the situation. My parents were upset at my leaving and repeatedly asked me to return home to live but I was adamant about my decision. I still paid all the bills at home and looked after the family's needs. I could do no more under the circumstances.

My spare time was spent in the usual way when living in a holiday town in the summer. Regularly I towed the Americans around the bay on water skis behind Roy's speedboat; they were dead keen on skiing. They decided they would like me to take them out fishing on my boat, so I arranged to meet them on the jetty one morning.

They arrived on time in their big car stacked with crates of beer and bottles of spirits. It took several trips to and from the car to load the boat. I had a twenty-foot, carvel-built boat with a deep keel, and by the time all the booze was loaded and all six of them were on board, the boat was almost sinking!

We set off around the bay cruising into a slow swell. The kind of sea not suited to landlubbers. They were all in high spirits singing sea shanties and laughing and joking when one of them turned green. In the end they were all seasick and I dropped them off one by one in various outcrops of rock around Torbay. I came back on my own with a boat full of booze. God knows how they got home but they certainly helped to ease the pressure on my mind at the time of my troubles.

Always expecting the worst when visiting my home however, I became worried to the point of exhaustion. 'What if she turns on my parents while I am not there to take the brunt of her attack?' She chain-smoked cigarettes, 'What if she burned the building down in the middle of the night?' These were some of the thoughts that plagued my mind. Both my parents adopted the same stance as they had pursued all my life; my needs were sacrificed for the others again and again. It was a true dilemma for them; they must have looked upon me as the stronger at this time. They coped with the situation with a strength I have never found.

Ron Sheen also owned the Talk of the West nightclub in St Agnes, a small town in Cornwall, and had world famous stars appearing in cabaret regularly. The nightclub was situated on a holiday camp that Ron owned and Ron suggested that I stayed there as his guest for two weeks, so I accepted his offer.

Ron regularly employed entertainment staff at his holiday camp. The camp was established long before he owned The Paradise Castle. Donald Swan, a comedian and Connie, who was a real old time thespian, were regulars, doing the rounds of holiday camps in the summer and theatre pantomime in the winter. Their duties included shows at The Paradise Castle with old time music and comedy nights.

One of the friends I met in The Paradise Castle was a man named Jack Lee from Blackpool. Jack was a guest at the hotel all summer and initially was cruising by Torquay in his boat named Zingara on his way to the Mediterranean.

Jack had received a radio message from friends anchored in Torquay harbour aboard the Bacardi (the boat used on the TV advert, advertising the drink of the same name). He stayed in the Imperial Hotel for one night and met the DJ son of Ron Sheen there. Roy was a very keen water skier and this is how he made the acquaintance of Jack Lee. Jack moved into The Paradise Castle for the whole summer season. I spent a lot of time socialising with Jack and often accompanied him on the Zingara.

Zingara was an eight-berth cabin cruiser built for the Round Britain Power Boat Race and originally had petrol engines that provided a speed of over forty knots. She was very impressive in style.

Jack had since had the engines replaced with two one hundred and sixty-shaft horsepower Perkin's diesel engines. The petrol engine used up forty gallons of fuel an hour and limited the boat's range. The diesel engines were more economical and extended their range for cruising but they were still very powerful. We managed to pull sixteen skiers out of the water from a dead start on one occasion and it was really funny to watch them emerging out of the smoke from the labouring engines. Jack and I often dropped anchor just off the beach used by the water skiers and shared a bottle of scotch. We would sit at a table talking and watching the little boats pull the skiers around the Zingara. Torbay's a beautiful place in the summer.

Home life was getting worse and the worry on my parents' faces was very noticeable to me. This came to a climax when one day I could hear my sister from outside of the house screaming abuse at my mother. They were in my mother's bedroom and as I entered the room my mother was cowering down from my sister, who had adopted a threatening stance with her arm raised as if to strike her. I grabbed my sister and pulled her away from my mother.

"Pack your gear and get out," I growled and took her by the arm into her bedroom. I grabbed her clothes and started to throw them into her suitcase. I escorted her down the stairs and out of our house. As I got outside I heard my mother screaming, "It's all over, I'm going!" I raced back up the stairs to see her lying on her bed with pills all over the floor. She had taken an overdose. Picking her up by the ankles, I shook her until she brought up the

195

pills. My sister was strutting up and down the road outside of the house looking like thunder. After calming my mother down I called Sheila back into the house. My mother said that Sheila must stay. What the hell could I do now? I had to devise a way out of this dilemma, as everything pointed to disaster. What should I do? My life was under threat every time I entered my home; my parents' lives were under constant threat. I had pleaded in vain with her stupid doctor for help. Then it came to me like a bolt of lightening. SORORICIDE! I would have to kill her!

Night after night I thought about this, how could I achieve the perfect murder and get away with it? There was no use in going to prison for life. I wanted things as they were, a happy family. All I wanted was to get rid of the threat to my family and me, and the only thing I could see was life without my sister. I set about concocting a plan of murder!

My chosen method would have to blend in with my routine lifestyle, so as not to arouse suspicion. About ten miles offshore, near enough in the middle of the English Channel, I often fished from my boat over a wreck. This was far enough out for the coast guard lookouts to have to strain to see me even with high-powered binoculars.

Knowing she could not swim, I could devise a plan to lure my sister aboard my boat. When approaching the wreck, I would nudge her overboard, keep the engine running so the boat was still in motion. I would wait until the boat was fifty yards away from her and jump in myself, as if I was trying to save her. The boat would carry on with the engine still driving it forward. That should work, I thought.

It would be a very risky operation with great danger to my life. I would be left with a less than an even chance of being found alive before I died from hypothermia or drowning. My sister would drown. It would look like a tragic accident if I were saved under these circumstances. I was desperate enough to wager my life on the outcome.

The matter was resolved, thank God, when my sister found herself another boyfriend. My parents had supplied her with money and talked her into going out for a meal now and then and, being so attractive, she soon hooked another sucker.

She had attracted the attention of a group of waiters from a local hotel who invited her to a party. They were all either drunk or drugged and became involved in a car accident late at night. Sheila suffered a whiplash injury and as an innocent passenger received over four thousand pounds in compensation from the car insurers. She offered to give me the money for her keep but I suggested she found herself somewhere to live. A chef at the hotel became attracted to her when visiting her during her recovery and they became an item.

He was a Frenchman named Victor. She moved out of my house and they settled in the south of France. I was very pleased to return home. My two-year ordeal was over. I had spent the last six months of the ordeal in the hotel. Perhaps that was a good time to leave home for good and buy another house of my own. My business was going from strength to strength and money was no problem. I think I saw the vulnerability of my parents and over the two years of this ordeal I had felt very protective towards them. They registered in my mind as two frail old people.

My sister later married Victor and we were at peace once more. He was an alcoholic who had taken the pledge, abstaining from alcohol. Perhaps this gave him the quality of experience to help my sister in turn with her addiction. We fished from my boat and he told me how the French fishermen had trawled up everything around their shore. There were no fish left in French waters worth catching. When he and my sister returned to France they filled their car with tins of food, like ham and corned beef because it was so much cheaper in England, we had not joined the Common Market at that time.

Victor often visited us after they were married and he was a nice man. Don't get me wrong; if it were not for the fact that I was worried about my parents' welfare, I would have willingly looked after my sister until her dying day. If forced to choose between her and my parents however, my parents would come out on top.

After the dust had settled from this awful affair, my mother often upset me when I was at home in the evening after being out all day. I had had enough of nightlife whilst living in a hotel over a disco bar and enjoyed staying in at home and watching the telly now and then.

My mother would say to me, "Are you going out tonight?"

"No," I'd say, and that was that, but she would ask me the same question over and over, until she would be begging me not to go out, even though I had made it clear that I was staying in! Even my father would butt in and say to her, "Leave him alone, Kid," (Kid is what he affectionately called my mother) and in the end I would get fed up with her constant jibe and go out to get away from her nagging. It seemed that this was a side effect from my leaving home for six months that had brought on this sort of insecurity in my mother, as if every time I went out I would not return. It was something that never got any better.

Ever since I began socialising in pubs, people that had associated with my father in his drinking days would tell me that my father was a happy man. They all indicated that he was the life and soul of the party and always laughing. I had rarely seen my father smile and nor had my brothers and sisters. He always had a scowl on his face at home. It would seem to me now that as he had worked so hard, he expected to be able to drink with his mates, and this was the cause of contention between my mother and him in those early days, and the contention between them had become a private ritual. Would it ever end? I thought.

I often saw older men being bawled out of the pub by their wives, and once saw a housewife throw her husband's dinner over his head. It would seem that this contention was not uncommon, or not so in working class families at least. No marriage for me, I thought!

I often reflect on my thoughts of sororicide and now realise, that if my parents had discovered that I perpetrated such a deed, no matter what the circumstances, they would have disowned me.

Such desperation, I never want to see it again. Don't think I am unaware of my parents' strength and my weakness.

CHAPTER 16

THE HEALTH FARM

The rewards of my business enterprises expanded my leisurely pursuits beyond the provincial comforts. Rather than globe trotting, I preferred ten-day excursions to a health farm. Living in a holiday town like Torquay and taking holidays in similar locations was like taking a busman's holiday to me. I found travelling tiresome and boring. A good cross-section of people visited the health farm. The facility was exactly the change of environment I sought.

Actors, titled people, television personalities, judges, even people similar to myself, who had accumulated enough wealth to have a peek, visited the health farm. Seldom had I mingled with the like before. To me it was enlightening.

When I first arrived at the vast estate I felt a little overwhelmed. A large imposing gate was my first sight. I hesitated and queried my mind, have I got the right address? I drove through the gates and on up to the main building. It seemed rather impressive in a grand sort of way. My anxiety urged me to turn away and go home. This can't be right, I thought.

As I entered the building, a long stairway leading up to the heavens beckoned me. Portraits of family ancestors on either side of the stairs peered down at me one after the other as I ascended. When I reached the reception desk at the summit of the stairway, the convivial staff soon suppressed my misgivings.

Over the next few years I frequented the health farm and met some really interesting characters. One of who was George Harrison-Marks. George introduced himself to me as a film director. We struck up a great friendship on the day we met. Way into the night we talked about comical situations and both had tales to tell about our different lifestyles.

George was into his fifth marriage and I'm single, you can't get more diverse than that. On the whole, we had a great holiday. When I first met him, I was sat alone at a table in a botanical garden housed in an extension to the main building. He inquired if I would mind his company at my table, and I welcomed his request. As we got to know each other, I noticed a peculiarity; he kept instinctively extending his hand towards the table; reaching for a non-existent glass. He was aware of my curiosity and explained that he normally drank from a glass of brandy whilst working on the film set. I knew at this stage we were going to get along!

He owned a Rolls Royce, and at the time I owned a new BMW. We swapped vehicles for the holiday just for a lark, and both decided that we were more at home in our own cars, but that it was an interesting experience. I had a reservation at the health farm for the following month and George said, "I'll ring you then, Bob. I can't return here myself. I'm about to start a new film in Norway. I'll ring you from there."

On returning home, I was telling my pals about George and his promise to ring me and found that two of my friends knew of George and had met him personally. I'd never heard of him.

Sure enough, one month later as promised, he did telephone me. "I'd rather be in the health farm than over here, Bob," he said. "Look out for my wife and her friend, they're arriving in the health farm shortly. They're looking forward to meeting you. Good luck," he said cheerfully. I wished him well too after a brief chat and hung up.

During our telephone conversation I had asked George for a description of his wife and her friend, so that I might meet them on arrival. Being used to the place I could familiarise them with the daily procedure.

"Look for the two most beautiful women imaginable," he said and when I first set eyes on them, I knew what he meant. We met in reception.

"You're Bob," they said. They knew me right away. They were dressed in kaftans and having already settled themselves into their rooms, they were now about to have their introductory medical. I suggested that I call in at their room in half an hour.

Half an hour quickly passed and as I knocked at their bedroom door, his wife called out, "Come in" and I entered, only to be confronted by the two of them, stark naked! I turned immediately to leave, exclaiming my apologies, but she called out

"Oh don't take any notice of us, were always like this, we're models!" Well, I was a little shocked but not upset; we had a whale of a time during the next ten days.

George's wife Toni joined me in the swimming pool the next morning and our paths crossed as we were swimming. Suddenly, she wrapped her arms and legs around me, gave me a big slobbery kiss on the lips and scratched me all down my back with her fingernails. People all around the pool were watching this. She then got out of the pool, leaving me with a metamorphic change in my anatomy that seldom happens to me nowadays. For at least half an hour I had to remain in that pool, waiting for the metamorphosis to wear off.

I met Consuela Semprini, the wife of the famous pianist, at the health farm. I had seen Semprini the pianist on television many times. Consuela was a regular visitor. She told me of her intention to introduce her husband to the health farm at some time in the future and sure enough Consuela brought him along on her next visit. We were to meet on a few occasions. I purchased all his long-playing records whilst on a shopping spree in a nearby town. There must have been at least eight of them and he signed them all. My mother was over the moon, as she was one of his greatest admirers.

We talked for hours and I mentioned that I had once been declared bankrupt. He told me that he had failed more than once in his lifetime and that the spice of life was to experience it from many angles. He was a very understanding and interesting man.

Consuela was Spanish and she told me they owned three boats. She amused me when she tried to pronounce the type of one of the boats they sailed in, which was a 'Pinnace'. She always confused the pronunciation of the word with a similar sounding male anatomical word. The couple sailed around the coast of France, anchoring in small inlets and bays near to wherever Semprini was appearing in concert.

One evening, whilst relaxing at my home, a friend telephoned me to tell me to switch on the television. I complied and there was my pianist friend with all of his family whom I had also previously met, appearing on 'This Is Your Life'.

Semprini told me of a funny incident that had happened to him in the sauna bath. We were kept separate from the women when using the sauna and the women usually used the facility before the men. On this occasion, Semprini had confused his appointment times with the women's and entered the treatment room with them.

Semprini wore thick spectacles and these had to be removed in the sauna because of the steam. He told me he was most embarrassed when they told him of his error. He said to me, "I wondered why they wore their towels so high up on their body!"

Barbara Shelley, whom I had seen on television when I was a young teenager, was there. She had starred in the Quatermass films as the gorgeous blonde assistant to Professor Quatermass. It took me back to when I travelled on a bus seven miles to Newton Abbot to my pal Tony Crane's house just to watch the film that was serialised on television. Tony lived in a terraced house at the far end of a long road leading from the bus stop.

In the last episode of the series, Professor Quatermass had infiltrated a chemical factory run by aliens. Everyone in the room was on the edge of their seats when he discovered dead human bodies stuffed in a pipe. Quatermass was fearful of an eerie, white, steamy, gaseous cloud, creeping towards him over the factory wall. We were all chilled into silence.

To catch the bus home, I had to walk the full length of that road in the dark. There was lamppost every so often emitting a dim light. On the opposite side of the road running parallel to the houses was a lofty wall concealing the railway maintenance yards. Steam from the trains crept over the railway yard wall just like the gaseous cloud in the film. I remember being terrified every step of the way!

Barbara had changed her hair to auburn and was even more beautiful in real life. A daughter of two famous television personalities was also a guest, and used her mother's title name as a Christian name, as though she wanted recognition. I felt a little compassion for her, as it must be hard to follow in the steps of two famous parents. She appeared to act like a spoilt child, which seemed to create an ambience of unease amongst the guests. From some of the guests she had borrowed money, including me. Barbara, who was acquainted with the young lady's family and knew of her traits, took control. I believe she gave the young lady a pep talk in private whilst recovering the money, and then returned the money to the guests.

A rather elegant lady whom I had assumed was another actress accompanied Barbara. I had met many people in show business for whom gender was never a point of disparity and a thought presented itself in my mind; (perhaps they are more than friends are, perhaps Barbara had matured from a swan into a beautiful dykling?) The years had been kind to Barbara and it made no difference to me. To me, she was simply a charming person.

Among the people I met at the health farm was a teenage gardener. The first time we met, he had served two weeks of his employment and was cleaning small items of flotsam from a pond in the botanical garden. I introduced myself briefly, summing up my familiarity with the estate and other members of staff, and enquired as to the nature of his employment.

He informed me of his deed of apprenticeship as a gardener and how his family had lived in a tied cottage on the estate for generations. It was a foregone conclusion that he would follow in his family's tradition as estate gardeners. Apparently, the estate had employed forty gardeners at one time but since mechanisation, this number had reduced to four. The young gardener seemed pretty contented with his prospects.

Following introduction, some of the guests had a sad habit of asking, "What do you do?" I found this question unpalatable. Snobbery peeking comes to mind. The question is all right in the right context but not immediately after introduction. Its intimidating connotation is unintentional or unnoticed perhaps, by people a little tranquil after a sauna or steam bath. If anyone asked me what I did for a living, I unashamedly replied, "I am a plumber." On one such occasion, Consuela jumped in quickly as if to defend my statement and said, "Oh, in a very big way." (As if it mattered.) Bless her intention anyway.

I was upset on one occasion, by a young secretary in our company who seemed embarrassed when stating her occupation, as if she was a lowly person in distinguished company. I thought the question was so unnecessary. Who cares what you do? It's not that important. Perhaps it's just me being paranoid. Nosy noses are for smacking where I come from. Who one is, is a matter to be volunteered by oneself at the correct time, if at all.

Some of the guests informed me they were receiving therapy from her Ladyship. Apparently she was a psychoanalyst, I can't think of a better place to relax or convalesce than the health farm. One of the reasons for visiting the health farm was to lose weight. There was a choice of diets and exercises, including fasting for set periods.

On one occasion, I had chosen to fast for several days but was not in the psychological mood to achieve my goal. Whilst browsing the shops in a nearby town, something small caught my eye. It was a winkle; I am crazy about winkles. I have relished these tiny little molluscs since my childhood. They were displayed on a cold slab in a fishmonger's shop window, screaming out for my attention. I considered, should I break my fast?

The powers of my resolve cracked. I was craving for the little leg-less crustaceans, like a pregnant woman craves for a pickled gherkin. I pounced on the chance and purchased a one-pint pot of winkles. Where to eat them? I thought. I jumped into my car and was off out into the countryside. Finding a secluded spot in a quiet country lane, I parked the car and eagerly unfolded the paper wrapping. Damn it! I thought. What do I do now? I haven't got a pin! How do I get them out of the shells? I need a pin!

Now this was a problem. Being a man, I have never purchased a pin in my life. Where does one buy a pin? There I was, in the middle of the countryside with a pot with no pin to pick in!

Cogitating over the question I drove back to the town. Where do I get this pin? It suddenly dawned on me to buy a shirt! There are always pins in a new shirt.

Stopping at the first tailor's shop I came across, I purchased a shirt and was off again, out into the countryside. I unravelled the wrapping around the shirt and sure enough, there was the pin. And there went the diet! I discarded the shirt and tucked into my winkles.

On two occasions whilst visiting the health farm I met a wonderful titled lady named Lady Roy. She introduced me to her family on her second visit as they escorted her to the farm. She often accompanied me on shopping sprees in a nearby town. Her knowledge of architecture and history fascinated me. It was like being escorted on a conducted tutorial whilst walking around the town. She was an octogenarian and born a Lady, rather than acquiring the title. She told me stories of her youth that are only dreamed of nowadays. As a young lady, she toured Europe in a chauffeur-driven Rolls Royce car, stopping off at small inns and hostelries along the way. The inhabitants welcomed them with refreshments free of charge because of her family nobility.

She was about the most interesting lady I have ever had the pleasure of knowing.

We were perusing the shops in a town on one occasion and were about to cross a busy road. She suddenly stepped off the pavement and into the path of an oncoming juggernaut. I ran into the road between the lady and the juggernaut and facing the juggernaut waved my arms above my head shouting, "STOP!" It shuddered to a halt about an inch from my nose.

The lady didn't bat an eyelid, her gait never faltered and she kept her dignified graceful walk all the way to the opposite pavement. Feeling positively traumatised, I ran to the lady's side and said to her, "You were nearly run over then, my dear."

She replied with majesty, "I refuse to be run over by anything barring a Rolls Royce." I shall never meet her equal.

Lady Roy and I were accompanying the daughter of an ambassador from a South American country with whom I had become acquainted whilst in the health farm. We were browsing through the bookshops in a nearby town, looking for a book written by Sigmund Freud. It was the young lady's intention to purchase the book as a gift for me; she was under the impression that I was in need of psychiatric awareness. She had referred to Freud in a conversation prior to our trip and seemed surprised when I told her that I had never heard of him.

The ambassador's daughter, having been unsuccessful in locating the book she sought, purchased a book of Shakespeare. I thanked her for the book and was observing its cover when Lady Roy inquired, "What have you there?"

Without speaking, I showed her the book. "Good God!" she remarked. "What on earth did she buy you that for? It's of no use to you!" She was right, to this day I have never read the book but I have been aware of some of the contents. If only I could have been involved in its treasures as a student but as a dyslexic, I might as well be the rear end of a theatrical horse!

Meeting people like these broadened my insight of life in many ways, making me aware of some of my shortcomings and some of theirs.

I was in the company of an earl and a high court judge who had just retired. The judge's retirement was reported in all the newspapers and he was portrayed as a very lenient judge. In our conversation, the earl had mentioned the press's view of his career and I gave my view. I remarked that there still existed a law for the rich and a law for the poor.

They both disagreed and I pointed out the then recent widely publicised case of Sir Gerald Nabarro, a Member of Parliament. He had been charged with drinking and driving and after retrial after retrial costing a quarter of a million pounds, had eventually reversed the verdict.

No working class person could have found that sort of money or gained legal aid to support him or her for such a trivial case and even though the taxpayer paid the bill in the end for Sir Gerald, he would have had to pay the bill if he had lost. I believed that to be conclusive evidence backing my assertion but they stuck to their guns and disagreed.

One man in the health farm told me he was once the High Commissioner of Hong Kong Police. He had also at one time been the Mayor of Norwich. At the time he was employed as a Bursar in a private school. I asked him if he knew Godber, the policeman who was found guilty of extortion and corruption on a big scale in Hong Kong. He told me he had written a thesis on Godber stating his quality as an outstanding officer just before Godber was exposed.

I thought it was quite comical when he had his car pinched from the health farm car park. It was later found abandoned in Ipswich. I asked him if he locked the car as I always locked my car even in my own driveway. He said he thought it would be safe on such a large private estate. I could see his point but the health farm had lots of young female staff living on the estate. They brought back young men from the local area at night. There was no public transport and open cars with the keys in the dashboard must have presented a temptation in the middle of the night. I still chuckle when I think about it. I bet the opportunist had no idea whose car it was.

I learned the meaning of the 'royal we' in the health farm. The daily living procedure began with a limited breakfast served at your bedside, along with a timetable of your daytime treatments. The treatment generally consisted of a sauna bath and massage or steam bath and water massage. Sometimes there was a sits bath, where you sat alternately in cold water and then hot water. I assumed this was exercise for the wedding tackle? One morning I noticed a change to my agenda, I was due for irrigation. Now I had been visiting the health farm on many occasions and never heard of irrigation before. I thought, what can it be? Oh well, I might as well see what it is, after all, it's all paid for, it'll be a new experience.

Boy, was I shocked! I lay on my side naked and unsuspecting when the masseur crept up behind me. In no time at all he was inside of my anus with a hosepipe filling me up with water. My stomach was swelling up like a balloon.

"Tell me if it starts to hurt you and I'll stop," said the masseuse.

"STOP!" I yelled.

An apparatus on the wall that looked like a common or garden water heater (a geyser, like an Ascot) supplied the warm water. The masseuse grabbed the tap valve to shut off the water supply and the tap handle came off in his hand.

As he battled to refit the tap handle, I called out to him desperately, "UNPLUG ME!" He turned his attention to me as the machine suddenly malfunctioned and water started to shoot out of the top of the machine, hitting the ceiling spraying everywhere. He was torn between the machine and me. As this was happening, my belly was getting bigger and bigger, swelling to an enormous size, I was beginning to panic. This was a plumber's nightmare!

Eventually I was set free like a balloon at a fairground and ran for the nearest toilet. Talk about gaining experience! I never saw this in a plumbing manual!

On my next visit to the health farm, I was sat in the blue room with Her Ladyship. We were having a routine introductory chat to prepare my treatment schedule. Her Ladyship remarked whilst she perused through my file, "Oh, I see. 'WE' do not wish to have irrigation." I thought, they didn't tell me in the Ag class at school about irrigating people!

I had a relationship that turned very passionate with a lady visitor at the health farm. After I had spent three nights with her in succession she told me that she was married. Our affair carried on for the full ten-day holiday. She was two years my senior and the full ten days were spent either having sex or arguing. I had never known anyone like her. She was the sexiest woman I have ever known and the most argumentative. She would always storm off after an argument and then turn up at my bedroom for sex. She told me that she wanted to leave her husband and live with me. She gave me her home address and her work address to contact her, but I avoided giving her my address. I imagined my mother and father at a similar age to ours, and realised that I was not even born then. My mother was also two years older than my father was and they too had argued like us. I wonder if they were as mad sexually as we were. My sister Jean and I were both terrified when we heard our parents raising the roof in arguments at night when we were tucked up in bed. Imagine if we two turned out to be just like them if we lived together. Not likely, I thought, and I made sure that she did not get my address.

CHAPTER 17

THE LAST TREE

Whilst attending a local boxing tournament held at the Imperial Hotel in Torquay, I met Chay Blyth. He was famous at the time for, among other things, having rowed across the Atlantic Ocean with his Army captain in a small boat. My father and I had read about the adventure, as it was serialised in a Sunday newspaper. I knew my father admired Chay Blyth very much because of the nature of his achievement. I had a good drinking session and chat with Chay, which ended with an invitation for me to sail on his yacht. Apparently he ran a company named Supersail that offered excursions on his yacht for a fee of eighty-seven pounds per week. He wrote a Dartmouth town address on the back of my private address card (I always carried a personal card instead of a business card when hobnobbing at functions, as touting for business whilst socialising could offend one's company). On the night, I had really meant to take up his kind offer soon but after sobering up the next day I thought better of it. I considered that he might have assumed a different disposition aboard the yacht, probably that of a hard taskmaster. I told my father about my pleasant encounter the following morning and showed him the card. My father was as proud as punch when he later told his workmates the story. After our meeting, Chay sailed around the world backwards in a yacht (I bet that took some doing!)

The serious side of this story however, is how sad it is that you can't show your parents your achievements when they are gone. So much of ones life is spent being nurtured by them and when the time comes for you to take the helm, there is so little time left to give in return. As I grew older and wiser, my parents (now old people) were becoming my very best friends. I encouraged my father to drive my BMW car as much as possible because he had never owned a decent car. Clothed in his best bib and tucker, and flat cap, he drove my mother on jaunts. He'd roll up beside his mates working in trenches along the roads and play the toff.

In 1974, I was still visiting the health farm and meeting people, who like myself, were regular visitors. Some of them travelled from one health farm to another, as though it was included in their social calendar, it probably was. Until I met the landed gentry, I never realised there was such a thing. Their existence was brought home to me in a pub near the health farm one evening, when socialising with two of the health farm guests. One of the guests (a solicitor of some repute) I had met previously.

My day had begun with a grave message from home concerning my father's health. On the day I was leaving home for the health farm, my father had suffered pains in his stomach and was subsequently admitted into Torbay hospital for test. It was suggested by our family doctor that he was suffering from gallstones. Specialists at the hospital had since diagnosed his ailment as a tumour situated in his pancreas and confided to my family their prognosis of terminal cancer. It had been agreed among our family in my absence, that my father should be kept in the dark about his terminal condition and I was therefore remaining in the health farm, so as not to alert my father's suspicions by returning home early.

In the morning, distraught by the news, I had confided my grief-laden predicament to the solicitor whom I was now drinking with. As we stood in the bar socialising, I asked of the solicitor's friend the very question I detested, "What do you do?" (My mind was elsewhere.)

The solicitor leaped to my rescue and apologised to his friend, who unbeknown to me had been informed of my traumatic news by the solicitor earlier that day, "He's gentry, Bob," the solicitor whispered to me. I apologised for my ignorance but they understood my stress. The solicitor then surprised me by revealing their sentiments to me. "We are very respectful of you, Bob, we admire your strength under duress." They had obviously discussed my predicament with compassion. This eased my embarrassment considerably.

Whilst returning home from the health farm, traffic police stopped me for speeding. My driving was so fast that the Jaguar motorway patrol car had not been able to keep up with me. They finally caught up through roadworks that had created traffic congestion. I had no idea that I was speeding through my preoccupation of my father's demise. I had cried most of the way home.

On reaching home, the first person to greet me was my eldest sister Sheila. She approached me in my driveway when I was removing my suitcase from the boot of my car. She was dressed in her nightgown.

Her arms were outstretched towards me in a plea-full manner and she dramatically kept repeating, "Oh, Bob. Oh, Bob. This is terrible. This is terrible!" This sent a chill down my spine; it was blatantly obvious to me that she was as high as a kite on drugs. She was in her fantasy world. This was all I needed at that time.

"All right, Sheila," I said, consoling her with a cuddle like you would a little girl. "Just give me a chance to move my stuff into the house." My mother or other sister Jean must have rang Sheila at her home in France. She had come on her own without her husband who generally kept her mentally intact. As she was staying in my home, you would think my family would have at least informed me of her intentions to visit me, but it came as a complete surprise to me.

The next day, I managed to get her into a fit state to see her father in the hospital. My main concern now, was would she keep his terminal illness a secret?

Her visit to my father went off free of incident and I persuaded her to go back to France within the next few days. My mother was wracked into frailness by the event and was prescribed a sedative by the family doctor for a suspected weak heart; she was confined to her bed. Sheila presented more of a problem to me than caring for both my parents.

The saddest torment of anyone's life is that of a family bereavement. There is no deeper lasting wound than this. It became apparent to me for my mother's sake that my father should reside in a nursing home after leaving the hospital. He remained unaware of his terminal state and living at home with my mother in her tranquillised state would have warned him that something was up. I therefore looked for a suitable place for him to spend his last days. There was no hospice in those days and the places recommended to me by the authorities were, to say the least, disgusting. I wouldn't let a dog die in those places, never mind my father.

After racing around for a couple of days, I found a private nursing home run by two caring retired hospital Sisters who agreed to keep our family trust. They duped my father into thinking that he was being nursed in a private extension to the hospital. Thank goodness I was financially sound to afford the care I wanted for my father.

On the day that my father was transferred to the nursing home, I accompanied him in the ambulance. As we approached the nursing home gate, my father who was able to sit in the ambulance pointed to a large stump of a fir tree in the park that was facing the entrance to the home. It must have been a massive tree; the stump looked about five feet in diameter.

"Us cut e down, me dad en me, when us wuz a boy," said my father, in his rich Devon dialect. He told me that it was the last tree that he had helped his father to cut down whilst he was working for him. My father was later to die within fifty yards of that tree stump.

Having settled my father into the home and having sent Sheila off in a taxi to Heathrow airport for her flight home, I prepared to call on my father every day. I'd take him out in the car whilst he was fit enough, or sit by his bedside to comfort him.

The day after Sheila left my home I received a telephone message from a nurse. She told me that Sheila had fallen down a flight of stairs at Heathrow airport and spent the night in hospital. The following day, I received a telephone call from France. It was a hotel owner and neighbour of my sister. He was a friend of Sheila's husband Victor and was an Englishman. He said that Sheila had arrived in his hotel that day and was drinking very heavily. She had upset Victor in the hotel bar and gone home. When Victor returned home later, he discovered Sheila's dead body lying at the foot of their integral stone stairs. She had fallen down the stairs and broken her neck.

You can imagine the pressure that had started to build up in me; I couldn't leave my mother in my home sedated, or neglect my father's needs.

My sister's husband Victor, whom our family had got to know and like, had broken his abstinence from drink because of this catastrophe. The French police had arrested him on suspicion of committing murder, as this was a matter of procedure in French law. Although he was later released, we never heard from him again. I believe he had turned permanently to alcohol. I was tortured by the fact that I could not go to France and represent my family in my sister's affairs.

My family doctor suggested that I drop everything and go to France. If I had disappeared from my father for one day, he would have rumbled that something was wrong. My brother Brian or my sister Jean always sat with my mother when I was with my father; it was impossible for me to be everywhere at once. My brother Ron took no part in helping the situation. I explained to the doctor that I had asked my other sister and my brothers to go to France. My sister Jean and her husband had recently been to Paris on holiday and told me how they loved everything that was French. Their holiday had cost them a few hundred pounds, as that was what the considered they could afford. I had offered any one of them, accompanied with their spouse, one thousand pounds plus all expenses, to finance their trip to France to tend to our sister's affairs. They had declined my offer because in their opinion my sister had always brought disgrace to the family.

My father died three weeks after this, and on the day he died he swore Sheila was present in the room. He knew nothing of her death, as this information had been kept from him. I found this most strange. My brother Brian was with my father the moment he died; I was there up to a few minutes before and arrived back a few minutes afterwards.

I had left my father's side briefly to visit my solicitor. I had been summoned to appear at Bridgwater Magistrates Court the following morning, to account for my driving misdemeanour when returning from the health farm. I arranged with my solicitor to have the hearing adjourned until a later date, so that I might be with my father in his last hour. My solicitor had previously advised me to appear in court in person, believing that my driving licence could be forfeit. It was unfortunate but at the time it seemed everything was happening at once and I just failed to get back to my father at his last moment of life. I kissed my father on the forehead as he lay there in peace; this was the first and last time I had ever kissed him.

My father was under the usual morphine sedative administered to cancer patients when they are nearing their final moment. My brother described to me how my father awoke at the last moment of his life. He opened his eyes wide and sat upright in bed. He looked shocked and then he dropped back on the bed released from his trauma and at peace at last. I regret not being with my father in his last moment of life. My father had a hard life; he had worked hard from the day he was born until his death. I believe my father deserves a place at the table of his maker.

My father told me he did not believe in God. I also have no religion but I have a firm belief in our creation as a body of intelligence, with a single aim and purpose in life. I respect all religions as the industries of faith, a meaningful necessity for many people. The last thing in Pandora 's Box was hope. To me that hope is akin to faith. If asked about my faith, so as not to offend any of the religious denominations, I submit that the instigator of our being is worthy of the highest reverence.

I have never felt so drained of energy since that experience.

After my father's death I wound up my contracting business and took an early retirement. I couldn't find the time to run the business and look after my mother. For about a year I nursed my mother, devoting every day to taking her out in the car and being by her side. There are many beautiful locations around Torquay worth visiting and her favourite location was undoubtedly the reservoir at Henock on the edge of Dartmoor. It was the spot that she had mostly visited with my father when he was driving her around. Early June was her favourite time for visiting the reservoir as the water is surrounded by rhododendrons in bloom. Thankfully she picked up her strength and the will to live, which left me free to continue my normal lifestyle. As for my sister Sheila and the effect on me not being able to represent our family at her funeral, or for me, to not be there for her in her hour of need, is still a pain to this day. It is my belief that a man who affords no dignity to the dying or dead, is without dignity in life.

CHAPTER 18

THE CASINO KILLING

As things gradually settled down at home, I found myself enjoying the company of a variety of successful business friends that enjoyed the convivial atmosphere of the cocktail bar. A tryst was held at The Palm Court Hotel each Thursday that my friends and I designated as the Wednesday club gathering. At the meeting we drank at the bar and indulged in congenial repartee, before taking luncheon in the dining room. Sociable local trawler men gave support to our luncheon by supplying us with a variety of seafood free of charge. It might be scallops one week, sprats another, it varied as the seasons would allow. The hotel chef was requested to use his culinary prowess to cook whatever seafood there was available in as many variations as possible. The meal was presented before us on a long banqueting table during the afternoon.

Invitations were extended to the trawler men and the chef, to join us at our table and some of the people in the hotel were also invited. Up to fifty guests were accommodated at the luncheon.

The arrangement for settling the bill was left to one of the Wednesday club members. The bill was limited to drinks only (drinks consisting of full bottles of wine or spirit of the guest's choice and laid out on the banqueting table) as the hotel owner donated the services of the chef, and the trawler men the repast. One member of the club always settled the beverage bill voluntarily and there was never a dispute over the privilege to pay, it was a happy club.

Our Wednesday club was always held when the licensing laws outlawed drinking after two-thirty in the afternoon. We overcame this law by booking the venue for the event in a licensed hotel. The proprietor was treated as an honorary member of the club, who indulged in all the club privileges free in exchange for his application for an extension to his liquor licence on the day of our meeting.

After the meal, we resumed our social gathering in the cocktail bar during normal licensing hours and the day ran into evening.

Another charitable organisation commenced their weekly get together in the cocktail bar as ours waned. Attending this meeting was my dentist David Hawksby-Mullins who, like me, enjoyed a tipple. David reserved Fridays for treating his private clientele at his dental clinic which I currently attended. I was midway into a substantial course of private dental care involving the capping of several teeth.

On the morning after the festivities, I met David for my regular weekly dental appointment.

"Good morning, Bob, did you enjoy your evening?" he said whilst introducing me to the chair gesturing with his hand.

"Very pleasurable, David," I replied and opened my mouth wide for his recognisance.

"Your Friday morning Molar Mauler am I!" he recalled, holding the steel toothpick in one hand and grinning with an impish smirk, Oh no! I thought, as I lay at his mercy and recollected our evening. In a moment of poetic stupor, I had expressed the cognomen of David to my drinking confederates in the cocktail bar. Fortunately, David took it in the right context and it has always remained as a standing joke between us.

The variety of guests staying at the Palm Court was generally a social delight. I found most people on holiday had no inhibitions. They were there specifically to let their hair down. The Palm Court cocktail bar was the happiest haunt in my drinking diary.

One of our Wednesday club members was the chairman of the Licensed Victuallers Association. Regularly I was invited to attend the LVA annual dinner, followed the next day by a private luncheon with the LVA committee.

Gambling in casinos had also become a regular pastime for me. I enjoyed unwinding after an evening socialising and drinking with my pals. In Torquay, I was a member of four casinos but mostly frequented the Carlton Casino. I had also acquired an Ace of Clubs membership card, which allowed me to enter many of the clubs in London that I frequently visited. The Royal Bath Hotel casino in Bournemouth was another of my favourite haunts.

John Tsigarides, the proprietor of the Carlton Club, introduced me to Paul King who was to become my sidekick for the next ten years. Paul is an ex-professional boxer and John employed Paul as one of his persuasive ushers at the Carlton Club, which incorporated the Carlton Gambling Casino. Paul had the appearance of a two fisted fighter who led with his nose, which was an added attribute in his new found profession. He has an excellent sense of humour and being ten years my senior, had led an interesting life prior to my meeting him. My father often spoke of his exploits, which transcended far beyond his boxing career.

My routine visit to the club usually commenced in the disco bar and later moved on to the casino before retiring to my home. During the evening of my first meeting with Paul, he bore witness to my less than fortunate wager at the wheel. As the evening drew to a close, he offered me a lift to my home, believing me to be broke. I accepted his kind offer; perchance to chat en route. He had a carefree manner that I liked and our childhood backgrounds were similar. He offered me a lift at any time in the future should I be broke and was surprised when I popped a ten pound note into his top pocket whilst thanking him for the lift. That was my normal tip to taxi drivers.

One of Paul's attributes was an incredible ability to communicate with mentally handicapped children. He applied to a local mental hospital for a job, which entailed helping to improve the children's fitness. Paul believed that with the right method of improving their physical ability, it would enhance their mental ability.

He offered his services to the hospital free for two days every week, which the hospital accepted. As time passed, his work was proving to have a positive effect on the children's mental health. The specialist in the hospital noticed the effects of his contribution on the children and he was offered a part-time job. As time moved on, his method became an accepted part of the children's therapy and he was instated as a full time member of the hospital staff.

Eventually he was promoted to the status of a lecturer and toured mental institutions, lecturing to the staff on his own method of therapy. Paul once confided to me that if they didn't offer him the paid job at the hospital he would continue working free of charge for as long as permitted. I often accompanied Paul to the hospital to watch him go about his job and I found it to be therapeutic for myself, watching these, who I would describe as 'little characters' taking part in their exercises. It was unfortunate when Paul received partial incapacitating injuries when he was involved in a motorcar accident and was forced to take an early retirement.

In November 1977 a friend Dave Stacy approached me and asked me outright to be the chairman of the Torbay Amateur Boxing Club. The art of pugilism had evaded me and I was therefore surprised at his request. Dave knew me from school days when he had been a schoolboy champion boxer. 'Why me?' I thought. Although I had attended most of the dinner jacket boxing tournaments and dinners, I knew nothing about the sport or the procedure of committees. On explaining this to David, he assured me that all I had to do was to sit in the chair as a figurehead and virtually nothing more. I could do that, I thought and accepted the position. It did not turn out to be quite that easy however but as the majority of the committee knew me (or knew of me) all my failings were accepted.

The club was established many years before I arrived on the scene and yet never had a gymnasium of its own. It always seemed to be renting ramshackle places for short periods of time, which was sad. It seemed to me, to be a mark of the dedication of its members that it had been around for approximately twenty-five years, without the security of a permanent gymnasium. During the course of my chairmanship, I was proud of the fact that we managed to purchase our own gymnasium. The gym stood within one hundred yards of the house where I was born.

It was an old Baptist Church, outgrown by its followers, who had moved on to a larger Church nearby. We soon renovated the building to suit our purpose and the boxing club is flourishing to this day.

My interest in boxing had brought me many new friends connected with the sport. I attended the Devon Sporting Club annual committee meetings and received invitations to their dinners several times each year. These were formal dinners, requiring formal dress, at which I would secure a private table for my employees and the casual friend or two.

One of the Torbay Amateur Boxing Club committee members, Snip Cornish, was also a sports reporter for the local newspaper. He invited me one evening to meet some of his friends in the Fortunes of War, a local pub. People known to me as ex-professional boxers accompanied Snip, and those with him who were unknown to me turned out to be of the same ilk. He explained how he had organised this reunion of ex-professional boxers for the past thirty years and asked me if, somehow, I could create a charitable association for them and others associated with boxing. It was his wish that they would go on long after his lifetime, meeting together and raising money for charitable needs. I invited everyone present to accept an invitation at my expense to a dinner at the New Grand Hotel. An association named The Square Ring was formed that evening, with me as its first chairman.

Paul King became a Square Ring committee member at that meeting, and is its chairman today. During his boxing career, Paul had fought a twelve-round fight for the European title losing narrowly on points. He had also topped the bill on three occasions at the Royal Albert Hall in London. He introduced me to other professional fighters whenever I needed a guest of honour to attend charitable venues for The Square Ring.

At the first annual reunion of The Square Ring, our guests of honour were Danny Holland (who was Henry Cooper's trainer for fifteen years) and Terry Spinks (an ex-British champion boxer who had won an Olympic gold medal). Sadly, my old reporter friend Snip died unexpectedly before the first annual reunion. His request to me to form the lasting association had been well founded. A memorial fund was set up at the reunion for him and a memorial trophy bearing his name was purchased with the funds.

After the reunion, Paul King and I were returning our two celebrities to London when Terry Spinks offered Paul and me a chance to attend a function in Dereham in Norfolk and we accepted.

Terry was the guest of honour at this function too. We sat together at the top table and the tournament began. These were schoolchildren engaging in the art of pugilism and the preliminary bouts were fought out between the youngest children.

I was surprised when Terry remarked privately to me with a look of concern, "Look at their poor little mouths, they're not wearing gum shields." Imagine, I thought; the gloves of a thousand losers had signed their mark on Terry's face and here he was, feeling compassion for the little children. That's what I call caring.

The three of us stayed the night in Norfolk and returned to London the next day. Back in London we called into the Thomas A'Becket Pub in the Old Kent Road, where the world famous boxing training club is based above the pub. Danny Holland had an office next to the gym where, amongst many, he trained the famous Henry Cooper. Allen Minter was in training just before he won his world title and I had the pleasure of standing beside the ring watching him train. Allen had been a guest of honour at one of our Amateur Boxing Club tournaments in the Grand Hotel in Torquay. We spent the rest of the day meeting Terry's friends in other clubs and bars. It was a bit of a binge and the sort of everyday lifestyle I was used to living at the time.

We stayed the night with one of my London pals Malcolm Hammond and the next day decided we would all go to Suffolk to visit some friends of mine. The problem was, we were all still quite inebriated in the morning and no one wanted to drive. I had just purchased a new 730-range BMW car a few days before and the question was who could we get to drive it? A bright idea then occurred to me! Telephone the hospital and persuade a nurse to drive us. That's what we needed. We telephoned a local hospital and explained the details of our plight to the receptionist and to our amazement, she herself volunteered to drive us there and then.

Sure enough, half an hour later she turned up and off we went to Suffolk. To our surprise, her driving was so bad we all sobered up, we were terrified. She drove like a maniac, hitting the kerb three times and overtook everything in sight. Paul, who was the soberest, had to drive her home from Suffolk.

On our way back to London, we called into a Newmarket horse-training stable, where Terry had once been a stable boy.

Paul and I stayed in London for a few days in my friend's flat. Paul was able to open a lot of doors for me in London to do with the world of professional boxing because of his past achievements in boxing. Amongst other things in those few days, we were invited to the Cunard Hotel in London to a boxing tournament. I met Billy Walker (the ex-professional boxer) at the Cunard, who was to become another guest of honour at one of our local events.

Paul had introduced me to many boxers on that night. It was a dinner jacket only do and I was wearing a lounge suit and trilby hat. Paul was dressed in brightly coloured striped trousers, a chequered jacket and a bowler hat. Paul often donned colourful clothing that his mother sent him from America where she lived. We had attended the function on the spur of the moment as the guests of Danny Holland and Terry Spinks.

Partway through the show, Paul and I left the hotel briefly and returned to face an enormous doorman who asked us to show him our tickets. Paul, noticeable by his colourful clothes walked right past him saying, "We're the cabaret" and the doorman believed him. The real cabaret was the guest of honour, the great Tommy Trinder.

I flew to Jersey not long after with The Torbay Amateur Boxing Club for a boxing tournament against the Jersey club.

Billy Walker (who lived in Jersey) was cutting his garden hedge as I drove by his house with some of our club members. Billy invited us into his home and we were playing darts and drinking for the rest of the afternoon. He said the authorities are very strict on its residents maintaining their hedges and imposed heavy penalties on those in default. Billy jokingly remarked, "You'll have to come back when I have brought back some more duty frees from the plane, you've drunk me dry."

During these years of my success, I had no regard for saving money. The old men in the sanatorium had advised me to take all the opportunities that were presented or I, like them, would feel regret if I should survive to their age. The spice of life is the uncertainty of not knowing what befalls you. They were really saying if they had known then what they knew now, things would have been different. This made sense to me because I had no moral certainty in my life, I was still internally wrestling with the question, 'Why am I here, what is the purpose of all this?'

My years of being refused a life endowment policy had also instilled in me a 'live for today' attitude. Having had my medical application constantly refused in the early years by all the doctors, who always seemed to advise me to try again in ten years, made me think life was an irreversible sequence of terminal opportunities. Each opportunity was a living bonus.

At one of the dinner venues I attended, I won a brand new mini car in a raffle and asked the young lady sitting next to me if she had a car. When she replied, "No," I stated, "You do now," and I gave her the car by simply handing her the keys. I don't know who she was to this day. I would think nothing of losing several thousands of pounds in gambling casinos in a single night. I suppose stories like these were going about the town, and unbeknown to me fuelling jealousy in my sister and brothers. My food bill at home for my mother and me, topped four hundred pounds a week. I never complained, although it was obvious that I was feeding an army. My mother was constantly buying me clothes that I did not need and they were passed on to my brothers. Anything to keep the peace, I thought; I had other things on my mind like a dispute with a friend in a casino.

A private argument blew up one evening between the Carlton Casino manager Leon and me, when John, the owner of the club was on holiday. Leon was a nice enough person and I generally got on with him, so I considered that the argument was better left until a more sober moment, considering that I had been drinking all evening. The following day I had to fly to Spain with my accountant and a few of his friends on a week's boozy holiday and I intended to sort it out with Leon on my return.

I really wanted to sort out my dispute with Leon on the Friday night of my return to England but I was just too tired come the evening and therefore went to bed. I thought another day passing by would not matter.

On Saturday morning I went to see a friend named Cliff whose son was employed as a croupier in another Casino.

"Have you heard the morning news, Bob?" said Cliff.

"What news? I replied.

"It's on the radio," said Cliff looking quite aghast. "There's been a shooting at the Carlton Casino and six people have been shot!" He spoke with his eyes wide open in stir! Cliff was an early riser who routinely listening to the radio whilst having his breakfast.

"You're kidding me?" I questioned, equally shocked but it was true! A policeman in uniform and three others were shot dead, including Leon.

Marty Fenton had done the shooting. He was one of my old customers when I was in partnership with Brian Kneil. Marty owned a catering appliance and refurbishing of clubs and restaurants business. He tendered out the installation contracts for installing his equipment. Brian and I had often contracted work from Marty.

My friendship with Marty had become strained after an incident on one of our contracts. Brian and I had a dispute with Marty over the drawings of the pipe installation. Being an expert at reading drawings, I pointed out an error to Marty and he ignored my advice to his cost and tried in vain to swing the blame onto me after the contract was completed. Marty ended up in a mental home at that time and I was led to believe he had been unable to cope with mental stress. At times, he was a highly intelligent man walking on the boundary of sanity.

Forever after that contract, I would see Marty at various social events and I could hear my name being broadcast in his conversations. I also saw glances in my direction that was annoying for me and heard stories from friends that he was casting aspersions about me.

About three weeks before the shooting, a few days before I left for my holiday in Spain, I had met Marty in passing on the casino stairs. He paused on the stairway and held out his hand to me in friendship.

"Let's bury the hatchet, Bob," he said smiling. I felt annoyed at his suggestion, as I was not the instigator of our conflict. I felt it was he who should be apologising to me, as he was at fault and an apology was in order. I suppose if I had been older, wiser and sober, I would lean to his humble tack but I rejected his offer with ruff arrogance regretfully.

"I'll bury it in your head, Marty," I retorted cockily and ignored his hand. Lucky for me that I failed to keep my appointment with Leon that night of the shooting, or Marty might have buried me!

Paul King too was fortunate not to be shot by Marty Fenton on the night of the casino killings. He wasn't too friendly with Marty. Paul was working in the adjoining disco bar when he heard there was trouble in the casino. He left the disco to enter the casino from the main street and met Marty on the pavement as Marty was leaving. Marty raised his gun and pointed it at Paul's face. He pulled the trigger but the gun was empty. Paul stood still, unsure if Marty was carrying other arms as he made his escape. The police in a country lane finally apprehended Marty, where he tried to take his own life. He had tried unsuccessfully to kill himself by stabbing himself in the chest. He was sentenced to thirty years in imprisonment and later died in jail.

The casino opened for business the next night but was closed not long after the shooting. An accusation was made against its owner, my friend John Tsigarides. He was accused of allowing gambling after hours and bribed someone to falsify evidence at the trial and was subsequently sentenced to two years' imprisonment for attempting to pervert the course of justice.

When my friend John Tsigarides came out of prison, we were having lunch in the Strand Restaurant, Torquay, a place owned by his brother-in-law. John told me that he had lost a fortune when he lost his gambling licence but he picked himself up and went on to become a well-respected millionaire businessman.

CHAPTER 19

THE CASH AND CARRY DRINKER

After a lull in business activity, brought about by my mother's frailness due to our family bereavements, I embarked on a new business venture. Prior to this short interlude I had acquired a large store on the building site at Dawlish and made use of it when offered a transaction from John Kay. John (who had pressed me for money when I was in partnership with Brian Kneil and very ill) retired from his builders' merchant business and wound up the company. He had married and his lifestyle had changed to the pursuit of leisure. Having no use for his stock, it was offered for sale and I struck up a deal with him.

John apologised to me for his unsympathetic behaviour during my illness many years before, saying that we were both too immature at the time to know better. I was appreciative of his apology and thought how time changes us. We are good friends now that we have developed through age and experience.

The stock I had plans to use at some time in the future to open up cash and carry plumbing supplies shops. Becoming a merchant specialising in plumbing and central heating equipment was an old ambition of mine. None existed in the southwest at the time and as my mother was settled now, I felt that the time was right to launch my new business venture.

Brian Caunter was a friend who owned A C Young Builders Ltd of Newton Abbot, and was the builder who offered to show an interest in my plumbing firm in the form of a merger during my partnership with Brian Kneil. He was a more steadfast person than I was, and I believe he would have made that business viable.

As a plumbing contractor, I had kept in touch with Brian Caunter over the years whilst subcontracting from his building firm. Brian had other successful business enterprises and was a friend enough to me to discuss my ambitions in the cash and carry enterprise. He agreed with me on the viability of the business, and suggested a site for my first shop.

Brian owned a successful funeral business, which had expanded and he was compelled to move to larger premises. He suggested that I use his obsolete funeral parlour as a base for my first cash and carry.

Brian owned a substantial plot of land in the centre of town next to the then proposed Newton Abbot General Post Office. It incorporated the main office building for his building firm, and his expanding highly successful leisure business. The whole plot was due for redevelopment and Brian had planned (and since developed) new offices for his business enterprises.

Also incorporated on this plot of land was Brian's builder's yard, which included his old funeral parlour. Brian proposed that I use the funeral parlour for one year as my shop and that I pay him rent for that period only if it were successful. Brian was a true friend. He suggested to me that with the planned future redevelopment of the site, my cash and carry could expand with it. I naturally took up his kind offer and commenced with the setting up of the business.

Having no staff at the start of my new venture, I had to prepare and run the business on my own. It was an experiment, a trial run to see if the business was viable. It was snowing heavily at the time of preparation, and I had to transfer stock to the premises using snow chains on the tyres of my vehicle. This encumbrance slowed down my progress considerably. Refurbishments to the shop were taking longer than I had anticipated and I was not entirely ready to meet my opening deadline.

Fixed to the wall behind my counter stood a large gold coloured cross. It had belonged to the old chapel of rest and I had not had the time to remove it before my opening day. As customers entered the shop, I stood at my counter before the cross, which towered over me and I waved my hand across my chest like the Pope giving a blessing and said to the customer, "Bless you, my child, how may I help you?" The shop was a huge success in the first week; everyone wanted to see the mad holy plumber's merchant!

The business expanded so fast, I found myself working all hours and was glad to pop over to The Swan at lunchtime (the nearest pub) for a pint and a meal. I closed the shop each day for a one-hour lunch break; it was the only break I had.

During one lunch break whilst sat in the pub, one of my regular customers came in for his lunch and sat at my table. We had a good chat about business and some of his friends who were plumbers joined us. Having people of my trade at the table was great and I took the opportunity to socially promote my business by paying for their meals.

We had quite a party and things developed into a full-blown afternoon session. It was market day (legal all day drinking in a market town) and I knew the pub would be busy but this was ridiculous. Everybody I knew seemed to be there.

During the afternoon, I suggested to my friends that this was a great meeting and we should repeat it one day.

"What brought you all here together in this particular pub?" I asked, to which they all resounded, "WE'RE WAITING FOR YOUR SHOP TO OPEN." I had completely forgotten the shop!

After that episode, I took on staff to give myself more leisure time. I made The Swan on market day a regular event. Jim Bonny, an old friend of mine, owned the pub and his sister and her husband ran it. I knew Jim through my association with the LVA. Jim had owned a casino, bingo hall, bookmaker's shop and other business enterprises. He asked me if I could give his son Andrew a job and I did. Andrew had a good nature and proved to be a very capable employee.

The pub on market day was a favourite for musicians, and filled with artistes and their instruments performing all afternoon. Jim sometimes locked the door when he had the right atmosphere to make sure that it remained so.

After the session, Jim and I often went for a meal at another pub named The-Nobody-Inn that was situated in a small village named Doddiscombsleigh. The cuisine was supreme.

My new driver, Eddy Baserrak, often drove me to The-Nobody-Inn after my Wednesday afternoon session at The Swan.

After one year of success in my new business, I paid the years back rent to Brian Caunter and Eddy drove me from The Swan to The-Nobody-Inn. Eddy more or less carried me into the pub, as I was really inebriated.

Keen on celebrating my new business success with my pal Eddy, I was in a happy mood as usual and ordered a bottle of champagne from the wine waiter.

"What champagne would you like, sir?" he asked.

"The best you have," I said. I looked at the wine list and all I could see was the most expensive champagne on it and said, "I'll have that one if I may." It was priced at forty-four pounds and about the dearest single bottle of champagne I had ever purchased. Eddy and the wine waiter tried to dissuade me from buying it. I thought they were trying to prevent me from wasting my own money because I was pissed and celebrating my success, so I insisted.

Halfway through my meal, I noticed this large shadow descending over my plate. I looked up to see this enormous bottle of champagne standing in the middle of the table.

"What's that?" I said with astonishment.

"That's what you ordered, sir," said the waiter smiling. I had ordered a jeroboam of champagne. In my drunken stupor, I had thought jeroboam was the name of the vineyard and not the size of the bottle. No wonder they had tried to dissuade me from buying it! What a chump!

I looked at my little friend Eddy and then looked at the bottle. Eddy looked at me and said, "Oh no, boss, I'm not drinking all that," so I gave everyone in the pub a drink of my champagne and a laugh at my expense; Eddy and I couldn't possibly drink all that but we had our fair share.

CHAPTER 20

BUNGALOW BOB

After my first shop was established, my life expectancy came into question once again. I suffered a multiple pulmonary embolism. It was quite a painful experience capable of commanding one's full attention. It came upon me in a manner resembling heartburn or indigestion. I had a pain in the left side of my chest like trapped wind.

It was painful enough for me to sit bowed in the forward part of an armchair, where I found some relief from the pain. When I attempted to lean back into the chair, the pain would become unmanageable to the point of affecting my breathing. I would gasp in small breaths and each gasp produced a sharp pain limiting the amount of air that I could draw into my lungs. I still thought it would go away on its own accord. I stuck it out throughout the day and all through the night whilst remaining in the forward part of the chair.

By the afternoon of the following day, I was beginning to get exhausted, and telephoned my doctor. My doctor was on holiday and a locum called on me. On examining me, he tried to get a specialist from Torbay Hospital to call to my home but failed. I was therefore admitted to the intensive care unit of Torbay hospital.

Ten days later I was released from the hospital with instructions from the specialist to take it easy. I was prescribed Warfarin tablets and required to register at Torbay hospital's anticoagulation clinic twice a week. On these visits, I received a blood test, followed by an X-ray and finally a medical examination by a specialist.

"Don't lift any heavy weights," said the doctor, but I was about to launch the opening of my second cash and carry shop in Torquay. Having a schedule to keep up, I felt I could not let everyone down. My new shop-opening day was extensively advertised and I was expecting lorry loads of supplies including heavy goods that had to be unloaded. There were displays to assemble and stock to shelve among other tasks.

Ignoring the advice of the specialist and acting like a fool, I charged into the foray of graft as self-employed people do. I attended the clinic for a while and again like a fool, I refused further treatment considering that I was too busy to care for my own well-being.

In business, at times you are driven to think that the need to support those around you is more important than your own life. Business? You can keep it!

It's funny how life turns out sometimes, but I found myself launching my new shop from the site of Moses' old store where I had purchased my tank aerial for my fishing rod and my old bike parts when I was a child. Old Moses must have passed on or retired. I now had two shops, one being a refurbished funeral parlour and the other a refurbished junk shop, but both were very successful. One of my new employees Dave Challis was an old friend of mine who had formerly boxed as a heavyweight for the Torbay Amateur Boxing Club. Dave was a carpenter and I had initially employed him to put up shelving in the shop.

Whilst drilling the concrete floor to gain a fixing for his timberwork, he struck metal just below the surface. He investigated and found an old two-foot square safe just under a shallow screed of cement. The locked door opened upwards from the floor and Dave had to investigate. I suppose it had belonged to old Moses and Dave thought that there would have been a fortune inside. He attacked that safe with every tool in his arsenal intermittently for three days and finally got it open. There wasn't a sausage inside.

Things at home were again worrying since my father's death. My mother's arthritis had deteriorated to a point where she had great difficulty in negotiating stairs. Our stairs had two handrails and my mother held on to both rails to help her to climb them. Every step that she took was accompanied by a loud thwack, like a wet rope striking a stone slab. It was the bones of her hip joint cracking and she winced with every step. I used to cringe when she climbed the stairs. On two separate occasions when my father was alive she had fallen over and each time she had broken her arm. She had also fallen and broken a rib since my father's death. I decided to purchase a bungalow to ease her stress and for her own safety. To find a bungalow in Torquay built on flat ground is difficult as Torquay, like Rome, is built on seven hills. Consequently I took the first bungalow that became available which was far too large for just the two of us.

Two large gardens supported the bungalow front and rear. A majestic oak stood to one side of the front lawn and cherry trees bordered the main driveway. Flowerbeds and a variety of shrubs blended with the bordering hedgerow surrounding the large lawn. Near to the bungalow and just to one side of the front entrance, a palm tree stood at the boarder of a fishpond. All my neighbours wanted me to chop the majestic oak down because its leaves in the autumn drifted onto their lawns and rooftops but I love trees. The oak was in prime condition and towered over the neighbourhood. At the rear of the bungalow an orchard surrounded a secluded lawn with a lily pond as its main feature.

At springtime, a pair of Green Woodpeckers nesting in a nearby wood brought their new young to our commanding oak tree. They used it as an observation perch before landing on our lawn to forage.

My little cat took to the garden. He used to stalk me as I roamed around the flowerbeds and ponds, now and then making a mock attack. I was glad he adjusted to moving home; sometimes they never re-acclimatise to a new habitat. The only downside was his menace to the young birds.

My life was running as usual betwixt business and pleasure and chairing the boxing club meetings. My mother and I were happy and I still took her out in the car now and then. She seemed to enjoy hearing about some of my jovial exploits with my pals in the Wednesday club.

I was looking for my trilby hat one morning and my mother lead me to the front door saying, "There's your hat, up in the tree!" She told me I had arrived home at two o'clock in the morning without my keys. I had probably handed my car keys to the landlord of a pub and left my front door key on the ring.

My mother said she opened the front door for me and stood there, dressed in her nightgown, with her walking frame.

Apparently I had asked her, with a big smile, "Do I live here, madam?" She laughed and said, "Yes, come in, you fool." I then cheered and threw my hat up into the oak tree where it remained until the morning. I had to throw lumps of earth at it to shake it loose. It had been one of those nights when I had been lucky at the casino. She told me I had thrown all the money that I had won up in the air leaving it to settle all over the floor and then went to my bed. Later she told me I always gave her all my money when arriving home at night.

I struck up a friendship with a young lady named Jamie, who was a girlfriend of Jumbus Ali Khan whom I never had the pleasure of meeting. Jumbus was related to the famous Aga Khan. Jamie was the double of Tina Turner, my favourite singer, and was always fun to be with. I met her in the cocktail bar of the Palm Court Hotel in the company of my Wednesday club pals.

The cocktail barman Paul Jones was renowned for his extensive knowledge of the trade and every year entered his own cocktail concoction into a local competition.

On the day I met Jamie, Paul had concocted his entry for the competition and was lost for a name for his cocktail. Jamie suggested Barbarella and it was the way she pronounced it that convinced Paul to adopt the name. Paul won first prize with the Barbarella and the drink was registered in the cocktail manual.

Jamie arranged to pick me up from my home one morning to take me out sightseeing on Dartmoor. She arrived in a broken down old banger of a car and she could have had a choice of good cars from her boyfriend who owned a garage but that was Jamie! I even offered to let her drive my BMW but she just thought it was more fun in the old banger.

Jamie had her long, bushy hair dyed a bright red and I suggested we play a prank on my mother who was very prejudiced. She even disliked the Welsh and her maiden name was Evans, so she probably had Welsh blood in her own veins.

Jamie and I pretended we had become engaged to be married and Jamie, true to form, waltzed over to my mother in our lounge and kissed her on the lips. I have never before known my mother to be speechless!

I took Jamie on a tour of my garden. One lily was in bloom in my rear garden pond and Jamie almost toppled into the pond as she grabbed the flower to put in her hair!

Little did Jamie know that I had a daily routine of showing the lily's progress in bloom to my mother! By removing a large mirror from our lounge wall and taking it into the garden, I could hold it above my head enabling my mother to view the lily's image.

My mother was unable to access the garden and viewed the lily from her bedroom window. Jamie's action really put me in the doghouse but Jamie was worth it. We had a great day out on the moors.

Living in the bungalow however was not my ideal choice of habitat. The natural environment during the day was all right but the animal kingdom gets up so early in the morning. I was used to sleeping in a bedroom situated on the first floor of a house all my life. The dead and stiffened dry leaves on the palm tree just outside of my bedroom window rattled against its trunk like a chorus of slapsticks driven by the wind. The noise that came from that tree was unbelievable. Sleeping on the ground floor next to the palm tree was like sleeping with a thin piece of glass between the jungle and me.

After settling into the bungalow, I decided to go on a diet. My leisurely lifestyle enhanced the weight problem that I had acquired initially from my steroid drug treatment. To suit my needs and raise money in aid of the Torbay Amateur Boxing Club, I had entered into a charity slimming contest. In doing so, I had coerced a business colleague Tommy Diamond into extending his restaurant to accommodate a slimming section to cater for the likes of me. To promote his restaurant, a photograph of me seated at a table eating lunch in his new extension was illustrated in the local newspaper. Unfortunately, the slimming section never caught on, so Tom lost a considerable amount of his investment. To make amends for my uninspired business advice to Tom I invited him, at my expense, to join me for a week's holiday at the health farm.

It was a mistake; I vehemently stressed to Tom the need for him to conduct himself in a sane and befitting manner, as this was not a piss-up in a brewery. Unfortunately, Tom was unable to control his behaviour, at least not enough so as not to be caught whilst misbehaving. This was in February 1978 and everything went all right for the week I had reserved, but we became snowbound due to a very heavy snowstorm that had spread from the southwest, and I had to extend our reservation.

I managed to reserve three more days, which was sufficient for the storm to abate and a thaw to set in. Tom became bored, so we went for a drink with some of the other guests. Instead of returning to the health farm residence we were invited by a lady to her flat in another building that housed the staff and private guests of the management.

The lady just wanted to chat, but Tom thought that there was more on offer and the lady's virtue was at stake. Things got out of hand and Tom and I became embroiled in an argument. The argument culminated in Tom and I vacating the building to do battle for the lady's honour.

We were both really pissed by now and chose a spot to do battle. During the fight, a five-bar gate was breached allowing sheep to escape from a field. I carried the day, but became covered in mud from head to foot as we rolled about in the snow and slush. I claimed my spoils and stayed with the lady at her invitation (I was being chivalrous in my stupor).

On leaving the bedroom in the morning, having donned my muddied trilby and suit, I was confronted by an important female member of the staff who stated, "Mr Shears, you were making an awful noise last night, your language was abominable, your behaviour despicable. You were fighting with a man outside and you let our sheep escape through the gate and they're lambing." She paused for effect and continued; "You have slept with that woman all night and she is a personal guest of the management."

She paused for breath and I interjected, "If you don't mind, madam, I have an appointment," and I tipped my trilby with my forehand and left.

On my way back to the main building, I must have looked a spectacle trudging through the snow on an unfenced path that led across a grass field (which was barely visible). My nice summer suit and trilby hat was plastered in dry mud! En route, I met a shepherd who was stood in the field beside the path and leaning on his crook. He had spent the night gathering in the sheep,

"Good morning," I said, touching my hat and he returned the courtesy acknowledging me by name. I inquired, "Do you know me?"

He replied, "I've never met you but I knew who you were as soon as I saw you, you're a rascal!" He said it with a smile and chuckled as he walked away.

It was still very early in the morning and the main building was locked when I returned, so I reconnoitred to see if there was a way in and found a door to an old coal chute that was open. I slid down the chute into the cellar and found myself covered in coal dust in a pitch-black room. I found my way up to the main floor and returned to my room. I really was a sight, all covered in mud and black dust.

Later, at home, I received a letter from the health farm stating they were unable to accommodate me in the future. Enclosed was a cheque returning my deposit for two further holidays reserved for later that year. I was really pissed off at this, having always enjoying my holidays there, and I felt that I had let them down; after all, I had made many friends among the staff and in the surrounding area to the health farm. I had just buried an era of my life!

CHAPTER 21

THE WRITING ON THE WALL

The atmosphere began to change quite quickly at home because of my mother's health. She refused my offers of excursions in the car to her favourite haunts, "Why?" I asked her but she just said she didn't want to go out. Although her arthritis was bad, she was relatively comfortable once seated in the car. Up until now she had looked forward to our little jaunts out into the surrounding countryside. Her arthritis was worsening however and I put it down to this, but she told me that she had other women's medical problems. This was especially worrying as she would not confide to me the nature of the problem and she refused my offer of employing a home help to ease her burden. I felt that she needed close help at hand because of the previous accidents in our old home.

I lived in constant fear of my mother having another accident. Now that my father was no longer present to absorb my mother's sorrow, I took the full brunt of her despondency. She would beg me not to go out some evenings and often told me that if I did go out that she would be dead when I returned. My mother could crush me with a tear but I had to learn to cope with her tearful pleas. How could I continue in this way? She refused every concept of help I came up with. I suggested paying one of her old friends as a home help just to keep her company. I even suggested employing a gardener in name only. He could muck about in the garden or do odd jobs but mainly to be there just in case of accidents and to keep her company.

On the last occasion that my mother had injuries in my other house, I had arrived home to find her on the floor, unable to get up; she had fallen over outside the home. Now in the bungalow, she began ringing me on the telephone at any time of the day. She left messages everywhere, including my office and all my drinking haunts, that always urged me to contact her, or to return home immediately. I was in fear for her life. I would respond by rushing home to find that there was nothing wrong. She just wanted my continual attention. It was becoming impossible to maintain my business and my social commitments. Nothing was beyond my capabilities, in my mother's eyes, and she demanded accordingly. The stress depressed me, and to compensate, my drinking increased.

Such a large proportion of my adult life had been spent caring for my elderly parents that my sense of purpose was confused. I had no answers to the problem. If I failed, what was the purpose of that for which I had strived? Since my release from Hawkmoor, my parents were half my life and now, what purpose would I serve without them? This lady was my friend, who had suffered the torments of the Great War, the 1930s depression, the Second World War and the hardship of rationing after the war, and who gave me life despite it all. This was my only true friend, this frail old lady in her mid-seventies. I was approaching middle age. I hadn't noticed the part that I had unconsciously played in her life since Hawkmoor. Since my father had passed away I thought that things had panned out quite well, considering. The enigmatic problem now was this shadowy illness, this woman's problem that women never discuss with men. "I can't talk about it," she would say.

Some friends in the boxing world were pressing me to become a boxing promoter for professional tournaments. I tried to tell them that I was under pressure with my social commitments and that I was just too busy. A meeting was arranged with two professional boxing trainers in Western Super Mare that I attended, and I was informed of the rewards for promoting tournaments. Apparently a bond from the British Boxing Board of Control would cover me for any losses at these tournaments and any profits would be mine. It was a great offer that I would have accepted if my trouble at home were not so all consuming. My drinking became excessive with the stress, so much so that I seemed to experience a time of pure plasma, a psychedelic world in which I tried to shut out all my family troubles. It was like living in a fantasy world that switched on one day and lasted for an eternity of uncaring abandonment and synthetic immaterial diversion.

I was losing sense of my own direction. Everything seemed, once again, to be pointless. It seemed everyone around me, especially my family, resented the fool who had made good. Distraught over my situation at home, my flourishing business was next to feel the strain; things were not well at work.

Through the drink and self-pity, I began to lose interest in my business. Gradually the neglect to my business began to tell. Despite many warnings from my bank manager and from my resident accountant I blindly carried on in the wrong direction. Even my suppliers dropped hints like, "Bob, go back into your shops, things are not right." The writing was on the wall of my impending downfall and I was in no way perturbed. I simply wasn't interested anymore.

Unexpectedly, I received a large tax rebate. My accountant informed me of the windfall that he had perceived as good news and asked me to go to the tax office to pick up the cheque. He had informed me this would probably swing the business around but I was still responsible for my mother and my own daily drink dependency and things continued to flow downhill. I knew what was needed to turn things around; I had built the business up from nothing but that spark had gone.

The extension that I had previously had built onto my sister's house came to mind. This could be the answer to these problems if all else fails. My mother would be better cared for at my sister's home.

My sister had left her employment as a secretary when she had her first child. Her husband had a secure job as a school caretaker. From then on, she was a housewife. Jean was perfect for taking care of our mother. She daily visited my home over the years to sit with my mother and tell her all of her troubles. I thought they would continue to be good company for one another.

My drinking had begun to affect my health, I experienced the usual signs of deterioration similar to an addict but I am no addict. I was just burying my deepest feelings and drinking had played its part.

The wildlife in my garden seemed to grow louder and louder with a bizarre effect. Doves that had settled in our oak tree cooed first thing in the morning. In my drunken stupor I felt as though I could interpret their bird chatter. It was generally three evenly spaced coos in a row repeatedly saying, "It's blackmail, it's blackmail." It's as if they knew my family were blackmailing me through my mother and treating me with disrespect.

I was mentally confused with the booze. I found myself walking down streets and somehow conscious of the faces of strangers strolling by. I felt as though all these people had come to see me, just to look at me, to somehow bear witness of my being. I was alone in this strange world. At home, I was so tired when I tried to sleep it didn't matter if my eyes were closed or open, the same people that I had seen in the street kept floating by. They seemed so real. I actually reached out with my hand to touch one of the faces.

These floating faces were somehow different from the ones I had seen by day. They were laughing and some were grotesque. It was as if I was seeing the other side, the inside of all the people I had witnessed that day.

Maybe it was all the passing faces of Hawkmoor that had brought this on. Alcohol can affect the mind so profoundly, promoting the most horrific nightmares. In the end I consumed these nightmares, turning on the monsters as I tired of their constant threat.

This retaliation I believe was the turning point of a near nervous breakdown. It was not a pleasant experience. To relate a few of the nightmares, the most common was a bull chasing me down a lane with no escape on either side because of the high hedgerow. This I attribute to all of my creditors who were beginning to chase me for money as my business faltered. It seemed like everyone was after me at the time. The bull represented my fear as a child in the countryside, when my friends and I would taunt a big Devon Red Bull, by throwing stones at it and running away.

In one dream, I attended my own cremation whilst I was still alive! After receiving a letter from my doctor, informing me of my impending death, I decided to get it over with without to much fuss whilst I was still alive and fit. I rode in the hearse beside my own coffin as far as the crematorium, and on my arrival everyone was shaking my hand and saying their goodbyes. This is what I had planned, a happy send-off. I was about to jump into the coffin and be burned alive! I then received another letter from my doctor. It cancelled the previous letter as a mistake. My family then wanted me to get into the coffin anyway! "You're so unreliable, you always let us down. Get in the coffin," they screamed. Perhaps the dream resembled my reprieve at Hawkmoor and my homecoming?

My father had featured in another dream in which I was driving a lorry with no brakes up a lane inside of a tunnel with a steep incline. Behind me the lane ran down over a cliff into a bottomless pit, in front of me was my father. He was standing in my way, and if I stopped the lorry I would roll back over the cliff to my certain death. To go forward was to run over my father. I called out to my father, "Get out of the way," but he turned his deaf ear towards me and kept repeating, "What?" In the end, I knocked the lorry out of gear to save my father and rolled back down towards the cliff.

My father was watching me as I began to tip backwards over the edge, I saw a look of horror and shock on my father's face as he realised he could have saved me if he had stood aside and let me through. I just shrugged my shoulders and raised my hands at the last moment, as if to say to him, "So what?" I wonder if that was the face of my father that my brother described to me just before my father died?

Gallstones caused me pain over the years, so much so that I was twice hospitalised for ten days with an enflamed gallbladder. They were quite painful at times and even affected one of my nightmares. In the dream an old gypsy lady was seated on a five-bar gate ahead of me as I walked down a country lane. To pass the time of day I stopped to talk to her and caught a glimpse of three men in the background wearing hoods. They looked like monks. I could not see their faces but I was aware of something sinister.

I had to walk past them when I had finished talking to the old lady, and was apprehensive of their intentions. As I approached them, they crowded around me and one of them drove a knife into my liver; the pain was terrible! I believe this was the point of my rebuttal of these nightmares when I turned on the assassin. I forced my grimacing face into the face of my assailant and holding him close to me cursed aloud, "NOW WATCH ME DIE." I was full of anger when I awoke; it was the pain in my dammed gallstones playing me up. The old woman was my mother and the hooded assassins were probably my family.

Sheila my eldest sister, turned up in a dream. She was ill and I was trying to console her, when all of a sudden, a grotesque monster burst out of her. It was like the demon I always saw in her through her drug addiction.

The obvious answer to most people by now would be to put my mother into a decent nursing home but she had often expressed in the past that she would rather die than live in an old people's home.

I could not bring myself to put her in an old person's home against her will. I approached my sister to explain my difficulties in looking after my mother and posed the question of her keeping her promise to look after my mother if a situation like this arose. My sister reneged on her promise to move my mother into the new extension that I had built onto her home some years before. I was devastated. I had no inclination of my sister's intention. She said, "No, what if my husband's mother should need the room?" Her mother-in-law was in her fifties and fit. Her father-in-law was also fit. They were in the prime of their lives. The extension was built for our mother with my finance. My sister had visited my home every day up until then and I had always been very generous and helpful to her. The only change in circumstances was that of my impending business failure.

After this period of neglect on my part, the business finally crashed. I at least made sure that all the small creditors had their accounts settled in full before the crunch and my employees had their full redundancy entitlements. I was left facing the representatives of the larger companies. The amount of shortfall in monetary terms was very small, considering the amount of business that had passed through my hands over the previous years.

All the local big creditors were allied to multinational conglomerates that mostly wanted my business activities stunted. Prior to my cash and carry business, the builders' merchants in my area had formed a cartel, price fixing their products. This meant they had cornered the market and there was little competition between them. Contractors could not purchase goods from the manufacturers of building products; they had to purchase their wares from these merchants. I had become a thorn in the side of their local outlets, breaching their cartel and under-cutting their prices. I even had one of the local managers of one of their shops escorted out of my shop, for openly complaining whilst in my shop to my customers. He managed a branch of one of the large building merchants near one of my new shops. He was under so much pressure from his company boss to arrest his falling sales that he had lost his cool with me. He later telephoned me to apologise for his behaviour.

My biggest supplier and creditor was a merchant based outside of my area, who had stated that if things came to the worst, they were anxious for me to return to do business with their company when the dust had settled. They told me they would never enter any agreement to bankrupt me but they did not have to, the local cartel would take care of that. It only takes two companies to form a petition of bankruptcy.

All the same, the local merchants had done business with me over the years running into millions of pounds, and they were hedging their bets with soft talk to my face. It was the old story, they knew of my ability when I was in a fit state, and wanted a piece of the action should I start up another business.

I was in a real pickle now, being forced out of my bungalow as I had handed the deeds of the property as security to my bank. With no help from my sister, I was given very little time to find a suitable two-bedroomed flat for myself and my mother.

Another tragedy in our family at the time concerned the death of my cat. He had been a member of my family for many years and at the time of my bankruptcy, losing everything included losing my cat. I had to put my poor, struggling little cat into a cardboard box and cart him off to the vet's to be executed by lethal injection.

I thought Jean would have taken my cat into her home, I begged her to adopt him but to no avail. Her two children were so fond of the cat; they had loved it when they visited my home. Jean had guinea pigs in her garden but she point blank refused to take my cat, employing the excuse that he would bring fleas into the house.

Jean had been brought up with cats. There were no refrigeration units in our childhood; everyone had a larder. People kept a cat as a pet and a working animal. It was a mouse catcher and working class houses were infested with mice. He knew he was being taken to his death, he screamed and whined to the last moment when I handed him over to the vet.

You may think that the plight of my cat was too insignificant at that time to reach through my already tortured mind but let me describe what my cat meant to me. He never hurt me; he was never any less than a pleasure to me. I was always greeted in my driveway by my cat, as I often went fishing and he was always there expecting a small fish. He often climbed into our hedge beside our gate and took a swipe at my trilby hat as I walked by. If my cat could speak he would have been a loyal ally.

In my old home, he one day climbed onto the settee by my side, a thing he would never normally do. He snuggled up to my side; he was telling me there was something wrong.

When I tried to examine him, he kept crying so I put him into a cardboard box to take him to the vet. He did not struggle or whine, like he did on the day of his execution, he knew I was helping him. It turned out he had been involved in an accident; he had a large gash in his belly. The vet revealed the injury to me and prescribed tablets to assist my cat's recovery. Don't ever tell me a pet is not a member of its family.

The same difficulty beset me whilst looking for a flat, as had previously worried me when looking for a bungalow on flat ground to suit my mothers needs. Eventually I found a ground floor flat in nearby Paignton town, and we settled in together.

The flat was situated near a steel railway bridge that spanned the road that we lived in, and the noise of the trains rumbling over the bridge was ten times worse than the jungle din that had troubled me from my bungalow garden. The first time I noticed the noise was when I was awoken from a deep sleep on my first night in the flat. It sounded like a jumbo jet was about to land on the roof of the flat. I had leapt from the frying pan into the fire as far as noise was concerned!

We settled into the flat fairly well and my mother seemed to complain less. Perhaps this was because I was at home in the evenings more often, or perhaps she saw the gravity of our situation.

During the preliminary bankruptcy proceedings, I felt paranoid towards anyone with a different opinion to mine. My fall from grace had not as yet sunk in. After all, this was only at a stage of enquiry into my affairs that were to be later submitted in a court, where I would then and only then be judged. The representatives of authority and some large companies' viewpoints and treatment of me were directed toward me, as a person, I thought. Unlike a criminal who is treated as innocent until proven guilty, I felt I was guilty from the beginning of the full implications of the offence and awaiting my sentence. There was no need to go to court as judgement had already been made at this hearing.

I felt that some of the interested parties exceeded their limits as interrogators, purging their own misgivings upon me (like kicking their own dog!) One such was a Public Examiner official, who on reflection makes me chuckle.

Meetings with an aid to the Public Examiner were arranged for me in Plymouth and I attended them each day for a week. John Tsigarides had given me the use of a car for as long as I needed it during these troubles, as my car had been confiscated. During these meetings I made a statement of my business affairs, dating back over seventeen years. It was difficult without my papers and notes to remember the prices of property that I had purchased over the years, and it always ended up with an argument over the exact price. It seems ridiculous to me that when they had confiscated all my written records, they then asked me for the details contained within them.

The purpose of this statement was to air its contents at a court hearing. I was co-operating in every way, answering his questions to conclude the statement and get on with my life. I had nothing to hide; I had neglected my business and admitted it. He was intimidating and I suspected he was psychoanalysing me personally. He now and then threw in a personal question about my mother and I would snap back at him in temper. What on earth did my mother have to do with any of my business activities? How did he even know anything about my mother and me?

If I had a weakness in his eyes of my love for my mother, he was personally prejudicial against my weakness in conducting his Crown duties. Hence punishing me personally, man to man, inflicting punishment of his own choice and not the business of the Crown.

My threatening retaliation to his personal intrusions prompted a change of tack into a diverse discussion regarding an overflowing toilet in his bungalow. This is what I find so amusing to recall. He would ask my advice on how to repair it and inquire, "Do you think it needs a new washer?" I wanted to throw him through the window; he was testing my flashpoints. He repeatedly inquired if I knew a Torquay man who had gone to prison for bankruptcy (another prod for a reaction). What's someone else's business got to do with me? The purpose of this analysis was to become very clear to me later in court.

En route to one of the meetings, I called into The Queen's Hotel at Newton Abbot for a quick snack. Sat at the bar was Jack Harvey, of Harvey Plant Hire. Jack was an old social friend of mine, who was aware of my predicament. He was a self-made multimillionaire, a well-known eccentric, with whom I had spent a great deal of leisure time. The very day that I had purchased my last new BMW, Jack had purchased a long wheelbase special order Mercedes. It was a very expensive car. He decided that we would swap cars for a while on the day we acquired the cars. That was typical of Jack.

During the Second World War, Jack had risen through the ranks to the rank of Major. He was a very astute, wily character who, after the war ended, had started a small business in plant hire. Eventually he floated the business on the stock market and made his fortune. An insurance agent and friend of Jack's had shared our recreational habits. He was a decoy, Jack used him to discover the nature and worth of every businessman he encountered.

The insurance agent specialised in saving tax expenses through his insurance schemes and whilst he was a genuine agent, the information he gained accessing your internal business affairs was leaked to Jack. Being in the company of a multimillionaire gave the impression he was good at his job. Jack then had the optional advantage of inside information should he be interested in involving himself in your business activities.

Of course I, like many others, fell for it, so on meeting Jack in the course of my bankruptcy, I knew he was fully aware of my business dealings. Jack made an arrangement to meet with me, after I had conducted my business with the Public Examiner, with the intention of proposing a joint involvement in a business venture.

Knowing of his vast fortune and his experience in business, plus the fact that I knew he had insight to all the details of my business career, I thought this was a worthwhile proposition. It would be foolish to ignore such a potential business associate. In the back of my mind I had thought about how I had bounced back after my first business venture with Brian Kneil had failed. I had also started again in a new business venture after my father's death. I would probably start another business of some kind in the future. Jack and I met later in a hotel, to discuss the details of his business proposition, which I thought was an incredible offer.

He had shares in a large chain of outlets that were spread throughout the country in the form of superstores dealing, among other things, in household commodities.

He proposed I secure a section in each of the stores, devoted to the sale of plumbing and central heating products, which was my forte. I would control the whole business, whilst he financed it with his incredible financial resources, a partnership of dreams (I thought).

Having discussed the deal, he invited me back to his home for a little libation and a quiet chat. He had a beautiful home and we settled in his snooker room, which was decorated to resemble a Wild West cowboy saloon, with batwing doors and all.

During the afternoon his wife entered the room, hurling a string of abuse at Jack. He had apparently forgotten an appointment he had made earlier to watch his child competing in a school swimming gala.

He apologised to his wife and stated he would go to the school immediately.

His wife retorted, "You're drunk, don't you dare go to the school in that state," and in the next instant she picked up an open bottle of Guinness and poured it over his head.

Jack sat in his seat with Guinness dripping down over his immaculate fawn suit and on down to a beautiful fawn carpet.

"There you are," he exclaimed, smiling, "You have met my wife, I presume? You see how she treats me!" He continued, "I, on the other hand, am a perfect gentleman." He pointed to the saloon bar and said in an assumed posh voice, "There's plenty more Guinness, my dear, you may continue pouring!" She exploded! She tore off into another room, returning with a long whip and set about whipping him! I thought at this point, it would be in my interest if I respectfully retired. I arranged to meet him at the hotel in the morning and wished him an amicable outcome to his day and left.

The next morning, I met Jack with the intention of continuing the discussion about our plans for the future business venture.

"Good morning, Jack," I said, shaking his hand.

"Ah, good morning, Bob. What are you doing here so early?" he asked.

"I've come to discuss our new venture," I said.

"What venture?" said Jack. He had forgotten everything! I reminded him of our planned venture that we had discussed all the previous day, "Ah," he exclaimed! "I remember!" He then became just as enthusiastic as he was the day before to continue with the plan. It happened all over again the next day. It was Ground Hog Day! I became aware to my dismay, that it was all a fantasy; my friend was just romancing in his drink. He is another old friend who has passed on and I miss his character and eccentricities.

It was then that my next disaster happened. A few months after moving into our new home, I had been out one evening for a few drinks at the local pub just up the road and arrived back home early to hear a weird sound coming from my mother's bedroom. She was normally up when I came home and I sensed something was wrong. I called into her bedroom to check on her well-being and saw she had froth running down her cheek. She seemed to be choking and I could not wake her. I called the local doctor and my mother was rushed into Paignton hospital. She remained in a coma for three days having suffered a blood clot on the brain. The blood clot dissolved and she recovered without any permanent damage.

The doctor at the hospital told me they had thoroughly examined my mother whilst she was in a coma and found she had suffered a prolapse. This was the woman's medical trouble that my mother would not confide to me. This was the reason she stopped wanting to go out in the car with me on our regular outings. At the time, I had been upset with this thinking that she was bored with me, but she had just been uncomfortable sitting in the car. She had not even told her old friendly doctor that had looked after her for years. I suppose this was down to my mother's Victorian upbringing where anything to do with sexual matters was sacred and kept from anyone, even from her doctor. I can't understand that she would have kept this from my sister Jean, but perhaps that's why Jean reneged on her promise to take care of her. The thought of giving my mother the constant care she really needed rather than sitting in my lounge chatting while her kids ran amok around my home eating all the sweets provided by me, was a much different proposition. This was the cause of the change in my mother's attitude that I could not understand.

When the time came for my mother to leave the hospital, she wanted to come home to me but because of her age and the extent of her illness; she was subsequently moved into a nursing home under the doctor's order.

She hated being in the nursing home and complained to me daily. She begged me to take her home but her doctor insisted she needed permanent supervision that I could not give her as I was out tending to my bankruptcy and I had to try and earn some income for our upkeep.

My mother fortunately recovered enough to leave the nursing home and ended up in a warden-controlled flat, run by a marvellous couple, with whom she became very friendly.

My mother seemed quite happy now. I was able to either telephone her each day, or call to see her. My sister Jean lived near her and called in most days. My two brothers however kept their distance and this troubled my mother. Their reason for avoiding her was that the gravy train that I had previously provided for them had naturally stopped and this became so obvious in time even to my mother. I called on my brothers and persuaded them to show a little more interest in their mother. Everybody kept their distance from me and this gave me some relief. I would always call and sit with my mother whilst in town and telephone whilst away. Not one day went by without my contacting her.

After leaving the two-bedroomed flat in Paignton, I temporarily moved into Paul King's home at his invitation. Having relinquished all the material things I had worked so hard for, I now realised they were only shackles and chains. Some of our furniture that had belonged to my mother, I gave to my sister Jean to keep in stock. I felt it was the least that she could do after all she had the extension to her house that I had built for her. I found I had thirty-five suits in my wardrobe when I left the flat, so I selected four of my favourite outfits and took the rest to the local tip. I noticed a council refuse man about my size on the tip and I offered him a couple of suitcases full of suits. He accepted them with gratitude and I often saw him after that day around town, dressed in my two hundred guinea suits. He was the best-dressed dustman in town

When friends of mine ask me if I miss all the trappings of wealth, I tell them, "I felt like a tortoise with a cracked shell, wandering around with all my possessions on my back." You can't move around when you're tied to responsibility and when that entails an impossible situation like the position I had to contend with, you're better off broke and on your own.

I have often thought about that night when I found my mother unconscious with foam running down her cheek. At the time things were very hectic with our change of circumstances, but a thought occurred to me years later when I remembered my mother swallowing pills on the occasion that I threw my sister Sheila out of our home. I think that it's strange that my mother was in bed in our Paignton flat early that night, it's strange how she managed to get to bed if she had had a stroke. Could she have tried to end it all that night by taking pills? How many times had she said when we were living in the bungalow that she would be dead when I returned home? The hospital doctor had insisted that it was a stroke, but I am not sure. I guess that the question will haunt me for the rest of my life.

CHAPTER 22

THE BANKRUPTCY

After the Public Examiner's office had finished taking my statement I was free to continue my life as I pleased until the court hearing. I left Paul King's home and went to the flat of my friend Malcolm Hammond, in the East End of London, looking for plumbing work and secured a contracting job with a London firm working in Chelmsford. I kept in touch with my mother each day by phone, until one day when she told me that two large policemen in uniform had turned up at her flat looking for me. They had told her that they had a warrant for my arrest, and this had unsettled my mother. I returned to Torquay immediately where I was once again welcomed into Paul King's home.

I called into the local police station to clear up any misunderstanding. Later, on the very day of my appointment in court, Paul King and his son Ian accompanied me to The Country House pub. I thought that a good stiff drink of scotch would steady my nerves before I put my bankruptcy troubles behind me. Like most things in my life, the obvious to me was the opposite of fact. The two or three hours of relaxation before the court battle turned into a drinking session! Other old friends turned up on the day and I was receiving drinks from all of my confederates until I was drinking treble scotches. I hadn't drunk any shorts for months and the alcohol had a very strong effect on me. Paul and his son Ian accompanied me as I set off to the court to the cheers of all my other blithe friends.

When we arrived at the court, I asked a man who was scurrying up the main staircase for directions to the courtroom.

"Up this way," he said, pointing to a flight of stairs. "I'm just going there myself."

"Got you too, have they?" I said jokingly with a drunken chuckle. I felt as though I was still in the convivial atmosphere of the pub. I didn't realise that he was the Public Examiner. There I was looking positively pissed, smiling into the face of my advocate! He looked at me with distaste and ignored my remark. I thought, 'Miserable bastard!'

On arriving in the dock in front of the judge, I looked around the court and apart from Paul and his son, the only other attendant to my demise was a journalist from the local rag. The Public Examiner (who I now realised was the man at the foot of the stairs) started to question me about my business affairs. I responded with arrogance and snide drunken remarks. Then came the point at which he hammered my weakness that his associates in my Plymouth interrogation had wheedled out of me. It was the remark he made about my mother that prompted the worst of my retorts. My poor conduct was subsequently reported in the local paper, which my family found upsetting. My contempt and arrogance towards the judge and the Public Examiner, in my drunken state, subsequently forced the judge to pronounce sine die and to send me to Exeter prison for two weeks to sober up and re-examine my attitude.

From the Torquay court, a Black Maria (commonly painted white nowadays) conveyed me to Exeter Prison. I was handcuffed to another prisoner who was unknown to me. As I arrived at the prison reception, my valuables were removed from my person and I was told to strip naked.

As I stood before the desk sergeant (naked and still pissed) he took details of my name and address and then asked, "Have you any identifying marks or scars on your body?"

"Yes," I replied. Then came a pause as he looked up from his notes and gazed at me. I assumed he must have been taking notice of all my operation scars for his notes but he was waiting for me to submit an account of them. It was like a silent stalemate. I was therefore perplexed when he said aggressively, "Well, do you think I'm psychic?"

I growled back at him, "No, I think you're blind!"

He threw his pen across the room in temper and instructed the guards, " Get him into the showers and off to his cell."

I was kitted out with my prison clothes including trousers that were four inches too big around the waist. That was the nearest they had to my size (so they claimed). I had to hold them up with one hand whilst carrying my bedding to my cell. Blanny (the prisoner I had previously been handcuffed to in the Black

Maria) shared my cell. Later I acquired a piece of string from the mailbag workshop, to serve as a belt for my baggy trousers.

Blanny was a scouse and a frequent visitor to Her Majesty's. As soon as we entered the cell, Blanny pulled a sewing needle from the cell wall that was left there by the previous occupant. He sat on a chair at a small table and industriously split each one of his safety matches long ways into two thin matches, to enable him to get two lights out of one match. He offered me a cigarette but I was beginning to sober up and it was the last thing that I wanted. I didn't smoke for four days due to my withdrawal symptoms from my booze up.

Blanny, for non-payment of a fine, was serving seven days. The fine was for not having a television licence. For short periods, Blanny was regularly incarcerated for non-payment of fines. I could never understand the trivial waste of taxpayer money. The simple answer to me would be to scrap small licences and put the tax on television equipment, or pay as you play. No licence, no crime, no fine and no jail! The same applies to road fund licences, put the money on the fuel. Using this method, the duty is paid at source and it's impossible to commit a crime. It cost more to keep a man in jail than to keep him in a five-star hotel, and jails are extremely overcrowded.

Quite large proportions of the inmates were serving similar sentences for similar offences like non-payment of child maintenance.

I thought about my time in the health farm when talking to the earl and the judge about the law for the rich and the law for the poor. Not many rich people in here, I thought. They don't have to worry about TV licences or road fund licences.

Victorian debtors' prisons were abolished but at least they were all the same category of prisoner, whereas we were rubbing shoulders with murderers.

Blanny explained the ropes to me (the rudiments of prison life) which was handy. He gave me one piece of advice which, on reflection, I should have ignored. According to Blanny, the vegetarian diet inside was the best food in the nick. I registered myself as a vegetarian, which was an irreversible choice. If you're ever inside, don't bother. I spent the next two weeks farting around. I've never eaten so many beans in all my life.

My first experience of slop-out came the next morning. The ritual was to empty your bucket of sewage into the sluice, use the toilet facility and then fill a bowl of water and return to your cell to wash. There were two toilets for about fifty men all wanting to use them first thing in the morning. The toilets had half doors fitted to them and the next guy after you invariably leant on the door moaning impatiently, "Come on, mate, hurry up." I can tell you that there's no chance of sitting on the loo reading the morning newspaper!

I didn't get a chance to use one because one of the toilets was flooded and not in use. Subsequently I was dying to go during in the day. We were locked in the cell for the rest of the day as this was the weekend and we were allocated a weekday job. Blanny suggested I ring the bell for the screw, "That's what its there for," he said. Blanny was taking the piss; I should have used the bucket provided as a toilet. There's a bell on the wall of your cell but it's for emergencies. The guard came and unbolted the solid steel door and stood there full of intimidation, menacingly thumping his truncheon into the palm of his hand. I suppose he had been informed about my arrogant nature towards the desk sergeant on my arrival and was ready for anything.

"What do you want?" he said.

"To use the toilet," I replied.

"What do you think this is, a five star hotel?" he screamed. I thought, to hell with you. I was getting a bit annoyed with this regime. I looked like a fool stood there holding my trousers up but I was not going to be treated like one.

"Do I get to go or what?" I growled.

He stood back and said, "Be quick." He followed me to the toilet and leaned on the toilet door watching me as I sat crapping on the toilet.

On the first Monday morning, I was ordered to see the governor and escorted by a warder to the governor's office. I was told to stand in a queue of prisoners outside the office. Another warder checked our names and numbers. I was looking at the floor and not paying a lot of attention to the goings on, until it was my turn to be checked.

"Name and number," said the warden to which I answered, "Shears J18 366." A period of silence elapsed causing me to look up at the warder and it was my old school friend Bert Calland.

"Christ, Bert!" I spoke out. "This is a surprise!"

I was about to shake his hand and as I reached out he yelled, "Get back in line and shut up!" You are not allowed to fraternise with the prison staff, so I did what I was told.

One of Bert's younger brothers Bob had been one of my apprentices. There were three brothers and Bert, who was the eldest, I had known at school. Bobby continued working for me for many years after he had completed his apprenticeship, during which time he got married. At the wedding, I was reunited with all his family, whom I had known in my childhood. Bert was a prison warden then at the time of the wedding and I had asked Bert if he had encountered any of our old school chums whilst working in the jail, to which he replied, "Yes, I have seen most of them." I was not surprised at this; we were the most disruptive class in the school.

Paul King later visited me in the jail and brought me three books, which were confiscated by Bert. Apparently I was not allowed gifts but later when I returned to my cell, the books were on my bunk. I read the three books whilst I was there. You have to be careful inside, knowing a screw personally can be a disadvantage. Your fellow inmates may draw conclusions from anyone fraternising with the enemy.

Blanny borrowed a half-ounce of tobacco from a tobacco baron after four days and I had a couple of cigarettes from him. The deal was arranged for Blanny to pay back three-quarters of an ounce before he left the nick. When his time came to leave, Blanny had no tobacco. I told the baron, who wanted to beat Blanny to a pulp, that I would honour the debt. I had a Rolex watch that I had been permitted to retain and decided that (as I had no money) I would barter the watch for tobacco.

How quickly the news flies around the nick! In no time at all, a fellow inmate gave me a quarter ounce of tobacco and told me he would give me two ounces the next day for the watch. He stipulated if he did not turn up the next day, the deal was off and I could keep the quarter ounce. He didn't turn up so I sold the watch to another inmate and paid the baron and thought that was that. The day after, the original inmate who had given me the quarter ounce and two other henchmen approached me in the exercise yard and they demanded the quarter ounce back. I told them to piss off and they told me not to try and draw wages in the nick.

My wages for sewing mailbags was seventy-eight pence a week and I assumed that they would be there on payday to take it from me. Whilst working in the mailbag shop the next day, the biggest scouse you ever saw came up behind me and pressed a pair of scissors under my ribs and said quietly, "Where's all the fucking hard men down here then?" He then accused me of telling one of the other prisoners that he was a grass and left. I was beginning to get the picture.

The following day a screw called at my cell to tell me I had a visitor.

"Who is it?" I asked.

"It's a solicitor," he said.

"Tell him to piss off!" I replied.

"Are you sure?" said the screw.

I thought for a moment and said, "All right, I'll see him," thinking the solicitor might have some cigarettes on him that I could scrounge. It's a good job I did see him; my arrogance was getting me into trouble.

We sat at a table and after introduction he told me that he didn't smoke. "There's nothing more I want from you!" I stated and stood up to leave the table.

"Wait a minute," he said. "If you don't calm down and change your stance, they'll throw away the key with you!" I thought about it for a moment; I was still in a temper with the way the Public Examiner had spoken about my mother. I decided that the solicitor could be right, so I sat down and listened.

He advised me that there's only one winner here and whatever I did later on when entering the courtroom for

259

sentencing, not to say anything, and to keep my mouth shut. His advice was sound.

On the morning of my departure from the prison, I was given my own clothes and possessions to travel to the court.

"Where's your Rolex watch?" asked the warden.

"Ah," I said, "I was in the toilet having a crap and as I wiped my ass, the watch strap broke and I accidentally flushed my watch down the loo."

"Come and hear this," he called out to his fellow screws and I had to repeat the whole story to their sniggers.

As I stood in the dock after my two weeks in jail, the magistrate declared, that throughout all the years he had spent on the bench, he had never before come across such a despicable man as myself. He was baiting me, hoping for an outburst, such as I had given to the Public Examiner on my first court appearance. He described all the various things that made him form his unflattering synopsis of my character. My solicitor was looking in my direction intensively. I remembered his advice and remained silent. When it was over, a collection of friends awaited me as I left the court, one of whom was Paul King.

Paul had an invitation for me to attend a staff party at the mental hospital where he had worked. I had socialised with the principal of the hospital on many occasions in the past and knew many of the hospital staff. In the car en route to the party, I found myself in the company of a titled lady who was a friend of Paul's. She told me that she did voluntary work for the Torquay police as a linguist and apparently she spoke several languages. She anxiously asked me, "What was it like in prison?" I told her that I did not enjoy the experience and although the episode was enlightening for me, as a tutorial must be, I would not recommend it to anyone else. For me, in a way, it was the therapy that fitted my situation and an ideal pause in what was, up until then, a nosedive into a wilderness of booze, uncertainty and fantasy.

The judge had given me a six-month prison sentence, which was suspended for two years. My arrogance and defiance had walked a narrow path, resulting in my humility and defeat.

CHAPTER 23

GOODBYE MUM

A few days after I had left prison, my friend John Tsigarides invited me for a few weeks' holiday as his guest in Cyprus. John was a true friend. He arranged for me to meet his bank manager, whom he had also invited, at Heathrow Airport. The manager was accompanied by his wife and daughter and found me in the bar. He addressed me as 'Your Lordship'. John had jokingly nominated me with a panjandrum, informing his family and friends that I was a titled lord. I had never met the manager before and he said he had no problem in recognising me. John must have described me to a tee.

The manager had my flight ticket and I handed it over at the departure counter. There was a long hold up and I began to wonder if there was something wrong. I thought it might be something to do with my bankruptcy.

Eventually an inspector was called over to the counter and he explained that the ticket was made out to Mrs Shears. John had purchased the ticket and being a Greek Cypriot, he hadn't noticed the error. The authorities held me there for a long time and finally agreed that I was not a woman and allowed me through to the departure lounge. My next mistake was still having my luggage with me. I should have handed it over at the luggage counter. I now had to persuade them to release me from the departure lounge to deposit my suitcase. Finally when I handed my passport over, there was something wrong with that. I had just renewed it and had forgotten to sign it.

The call came to board our aircraft and everyone started to move from the departure lounge towards the aircraft door, excluding a few other stragglers and us. This was the result of the bank manager insisting there was plenty of time but he was wrong! The airline had overbooked the flight by thirty-five seats. I was number thirty-six. I was already flying as high as a kite since being in the bar for hours. It was down to the pilot's discretion whether I was to be permitted to board.

After the pilot had inspected me and agreed that I was sober enough to board his aircraft, I was informed I would be sat in the jump seat. I thought they were joking but apparently the jump seats are situated behind the pilot's control cabin and reserved for the crew. I had a ball! I consumed four cooked meals during the flight, finished off loads of booze, and generally acquainted myself with the crew.

The co-pilot invited me into the cockpit and I chatted with the captain for a considerable time. I was a person who was happy in drink unless, like most drinkers, provoked into a change. There were three men in the cockpit and five seats.

"Why are there two spare seats?" I asked the captain. He told me it was because of technical advances in computers and navigational aids, "It won't be long before he goes through more updated equipment," he said pointing at one of his crew. I was fascinated by the pilots console and the captain pointed to the dials that were the most important to watch. I left the cockpit just before the plane had to land.

On landing at Larnica Airport in Cyprus, everyone vacated the plane except the crew and me. On reaching the exit door, the pilot stood to one side and offered me access to depart the aircraft. He was surprised when I stuffed a ten-pound note into his top pocket, as if tipping a taxi driver and said in a slurred but posh voice, "Thanks for the trip, old boy!"

He commented with a smile, "I hope I see you on the return trip."

Just when I finally thought that I had made it onto the island, machinegun-toting guards intercepted me in the reception lounge and told me that I could not enter Cyprus. I only had one hundred pounds in sterling, and should have had Cypriot currency. I also had no indication as to where I was staying.

Fortunately I saw John's head bobbing along in the crowd outside the lounge and pointed frantically to him. The guards then released me to John and I was whisked off to a hotel in a Mercedes car. I rang my mother to tell her of my experience. I was able to ring her each day.

The next day we had a different car and we stopped at a garage for petrol on our way to the beach. The garage attendant was looking under the car bonnet to check our oil and water when he noticed we had a siren under the bonnet. John had relatives in the Cyprus police and had borrowed one of their cars. This was great fun. In the heavy Cyprus traffic we simply used the siren to pass all the traffic jams.

John introduced me to a relative in Cyprus named Gibros, who was much older than me. He was a tubby man with a moustache and always smiling. I was introduced to him at a private drinking club, which is like an English Labour or Conservative Social Club. It had a nice atmosphere, with the locals sat at tables playing dominoes and baccarat. I was left with Gibros in the club one afternoon whilst John attended to his own business and found it strange that even though no one at the club spoke English but me, Gibros and I got on like a house on fire.

He introduced me to the local brandy, which was very cheap and had a distinctive taste that I grew to like. Although we could not speak a word of our language together, Gibros and I were like two long lost brothers and regularly met up for drinking sessions.

John had arranged one of his many family reunions at a hotel and Gibros and I sat down next to each other at a long banquet table. These were always great eating and drinking marathons and I was in my element. I loved to watch the band especially the balalaika and the bass player. I thought how if I had travelled the world instead of going into the sanatorium, I might have played in one of these bands.

I loved the Greek dancing and always took part in the dancing at every opportunity. Gibros too loved to dance and despite his age, he could dance well. We started to dance on the dance floor with everyone else. The higher I jumped in the air the higher Gibros jumped. We ended up as the only two on the dance floor and everyone was encircled around us clapping at our exploits. It was the best night that I had on the island.

The following week John arranged another get together at the same hotel and I took my place at the table. I was looking for my old mate Gibros but he wasn't there.

I asked John, "Where's Gibros?"

"He's barred," said John.

"What for?" I asked.

"Dancing," said John and continued, "He embarrassed the family by getting over exuberant."

"But I was dancing too," I said.

"Yes but they think you're a lord and they know Gibros is not." I never saw my friend Gibros after that but I always ask after him when I see John. He tells me that he's the same old Gibros.

Arrangements had been made for me to stay in a luxury hotel, and after settling in my daily routine on weekdays was to visit a small taverna, situated on a crossroad controlled by traffic lights. I sat outside the taverna, sipping beer and observing the hustle and bustle, as cars got up to all manners of tricks to try and beat the red lights. They even mounted the pavement to go around the back of the lights rather than stop; it was hilarious at times.

During a visit to a small place in the Trudos Mountains next to a British radar station, I purchased lots of hazelnuts that were in season. Putting two in the palm of my hand and squeezing them together to crack them made my hands sore. The local children came to my aid by cracking them with their teeth. My teeth were too soft for this and the children had beautiful white teeth. I encouraged them to form a queue and paid them a shilling for each handful they handed to me until I had eaten my fill.

The day of my departure fell on a Sunday, and I had arranged to meet a driver at the taverna to transport me to the airport. On reaching the taverna, I sat at my usual table and noticed ants at my feet; the proprietor noticed my concern and rushed to spray the offenders with insecticide. I ordered my beer, which he supplied with an array of table refreshments. It was very hot on the day and the proprietor produced a water hose to hose down the pavement, cooling the air temperature around me.

After a short time, I noticed there were no other customers there and remarked to the owner, "You're very quiet today," to which he replied, "Yes sir, we are closed." He had really thought I was a lord!

When I arrived home, John Tsigarides invited me to attend a public school open day where his son Phillious was a pupil. I accepted the invitation; I had no experience of such places and was eager to breach this bastion of knowledge that I had felt excluded from in my childhood.

Most of the day was spent meeting his son's friends and their parents and teachers. I even met John Kay the retired builders' merchant. His son also was attending the school.

The most interesting part of the day and a new experience for me was watching a play performed by the pupils. Apart from the nativity play in junior school, I had never witnessed a live acting performance in my life, not even a pantomime.

The play 'The Lord Of The Flies' was enjoyed immensely. I later reflected on its content and put the label 'indoctrination' on my thoughts. For the first time, I saw the foundation of society. It was exactly what I was meant to see, without law and order there would be anarchy. What law? Whose order?

I was also briefed on the headmaster's speech to the parents who were considering enrolling their children into the school; he spoke of their children being the future leaders of industry. How different this was to the education I had received as a child. I had been a successful businessman who had competed with these super-trained adversaries, no wonder it had been such a hard battle. No wonder that the bank manager had looked upon me as something smelly that he had just stepped in. How easy my life could have been, if I had fallen among the mirthful, instead of in the mire.

I had spent my life finding great pleasure in giving but found it hard to accept gifts from people who wanted to help. It was a fault in me to refuse others the pleasure of giving, a pleasure of which I had relished. It was something I had yet to learn.

Staying with Paul King gave me the time needed to get back on my feet. After seventeen years of business, I earned a living doing odd jobs, like gardening, roofing, labouring, all manner of things, including plumbing.

In a way, it was like a holiday, not having to worry about anyone or anything other than my own survival. My mother was safe and happy in her warden-controlled flat. If I earned enough money to have time off, I took all the time available. I must say, I had not known such freedom ever before, even though I had in the past lived like a millionaire at times. After I received my sentence in the court, my probation officer advised me to sign on the dole, with which I complied.

At the age of thirty-nine years, this was my first experience of this and I must concede; it was degrading. Around me in the dole queue were many that I recognised as good tradesmen. They felt nothing but shame at being unemployed. They were there through no fault of their own. A change was taking place in the global world of business corporations and technology, reducing the need for their skills. A more economical workforce could be found in the ill-conceivedly named Third World. The peoples of the United Kingdom now bowed to a new faceless Emperor who had learned from the British Empire that (whosoever owns all the carrots will eventually control all the Donkeys!)

The whole Social Security system was hostile to our own workforce. I found it to be a system set up to help working people during times of work shortages, but that the number of unemployed overwhelmed the system. This was a global slump. Instead of being sympathetic towards the plight of their workforce, the authorities with the face of government ministers began looking for scapegoats and castigated everyone as a potential work dodger.

It was not long before I signed off the dole and picked up small jobs of one sort or another. The face of change had stamped out long-term employment, which in a way suited me as a single man. I still needed leisure intervals and found it between jobs.

From time to time, I embarked on more ambitious jobs that lasted as long as six months. I always seemed to end up in an argument on these jobs, or a punch-up and my storming off the job, to my financial loss. I hadn't a clue as to why this was happening until I met an Irish business colleague of old. We were celebrating St Patrick's Day in a local pub and he listened intently as I told him about my altercations on these jobs.

"Bob, you're not the boss anymore," he said, as though it was so obvious but that was it! I was set in my ways! In some instances, it made me unemployable. My Irish colleague summed up my future by saying, "Bob, you're a happy man, take each day as it comes and just amble along." I thought it was good advice and crowned my thoughts. Be content with my day and leave ambition to my slumber.

In a way, I had turned full circle. My only ambition when completing my apprenticeship had been to go abroad and drift from place to place and job to job, or go to London and play the guitar. My rock and roll days were over, but I was free to go and do as I pleased. On the whole I was as happy as the day is long.

Paul King's son Ian often drove Paul and me around on our frequent drinking excursions. Ian was eighteen years old and prone to the odd scrape or bump whilst driving but he was very adept at repairing the Mark 10 Jag. Paul had a second Mark 10 Jaguar in his back yard that he kept for spares.

Staying with Paul and his wife Greta was a happy time for me. Greta and I often went out together for the evening. Paul said that he and Greta often lay in bed and listened to me coming home late at night from a spree. He said I sounded like W C Fields as I climbed the stairs to my bedroom; I always paused for a chuckle halfway.

I stayed in Paul's home for some time until eventually he sold the house.

Paul said to me, "I'm selling the house, Bob. I'm getting a small flat with two bedrooms. You had better start to look for new accommodation."

"Yes, OK," I said, not taking a blind bit of notice. If he told me once he told me a dozen times that he was leaving. Even when I walked past the house agent's for sale sign in the garden, I didn't take any notice. This went on until one day I came home from work and met the furniture removers moving Paul out. Paul always jokingly remarks when we're in company, "I only sold the house to get rid of you!" (At least I think he's joking!)

My friend John Tsigarides owned a large old house that had previously been a nightclub. He purchased the property after the nightclub was gutted by fire. The property had been standing idle for some time, whilst he contemplated what to do with it.

In the grounds of the property stood an abandoned caravan. It was still connected to the main water and electricity supplies. He had commandeered a refurbished room in the main building as his temporary office, which included toilet facilities, accessible from the grounds of the estate (in other words, the toilet door opened into the garden).

John had offered me the use of this caravan plus toilet facility rent free, for as long as it was available, should I ever need it. After leaving Paul's home so abruptly I took up his offer and moved in. This was ideal for my lifestyle.

I was not receiving Social Security money at the time; I was just getting by one day at a time. I managed to salvage some smoke-stained drinking glasses that had come from the nightclub bar and other bits and pieces of damaged goods. I cleaned them up and sold them in pubs. The most unusual item I salvaged was a large box, two feet square in size, containing two hundred small boxes of Tampax sanitary wear. They were undamaged vending machine stock. I must admit that it was not the most congenial item for me to tout around the pubs. I carried the whole box around with me until they were sold. They sold like hot cakes; it seemed they made rather good pipe cleaners for the pipe smokers.

As far as spending money was concerned, I couldn't change. I still spent every penny as fast as it was earned and enjoyed being that way.

My gallbladder was playing up, and after lying in my caravan for four days drinking nothing but water without any food I found the pain too hard to bear. I struggled to a neighbour and asked them to ring my doctor who sent me to hospital for ten days. This was my third trip to hospital but they still would not operate to remove it. When I was released, I called on my mother and told her that I had been working in London.

I was invited to stay in my friend Tommy Diamond's newly-acquired pub in Plymouth for the weekend. Tommy had taken over the chairmanship of the boxing club that was my old position. I gave my mother fifty pounds to keep for me until my return on the Monday morning. I knew I'd be skint by then if I had taken all the money with me. On my return to her flat, the warden told me that my mother had been rushed to Torbay hospital suffering from a haemorrhage.

Apparently she had a ring inserted in her in Paignton hospital as a treatment for her prolapsed womb. Our old family doctor (her friend) that she had re-registered with since returning to Torquay from Paignton had failed to read her updated medical circumstances, and was not aware of the ring implant. The ring had remained there for two years and was supposed to be replaced several times over that period of time. Subsequently the ring had festered and this had contributed to my mother's condition.

My mother was terminally ill with cancer of the womb and I naturally visited her at every opportunity. On one occasion, I had arranged with the ward Sister for me to visit before the normal visiting hours because I knew she was going through a difficult period of radiation treatment. The morphine was confusing her mind. As I sat by her side, she uttered a few words of defamation towards me that had stemmed from my brothers and sister.

Even on her deathbed my family acted out the ridicule of my being. I pleaded with my mother not to forsake me at this hour. I could not involve myself at this time in petty innuendoes. She confided something to me that I shall never forget; something that made me feel my life was worthwhile. She swore that in her life, I was the best thing that ever drew breath from her body. I took strength from her words.

As I was leaving the ward my sister Jean, who I hadn't noticed, wrenched at my shoulder spinning me around. I was quite shocked at her aggression. She said, "You can't go in there yet." She was accompanied by her husband Tony who was a nice fellow but very different in nature from me. He studied ballet and classical music and his sense of humour took some understanding. I had to force myself to laugh at his jokes. I'm afraid he caught the full brunt of my retort. I told my sister she was not my choice of sister and the days of her ridicule would soon be of no consequence to me. I turned on Tony and regrettably called him a ballet dancing classical clot! (Or near enough those words.) I then vacated the building.

On another visit, my mother wanted me to physically engage in a battle with the doctors, who she blamed for her discomfort; it was hard to comfort her in the circumstances. I could only assure her of their sincerity in their treatment.

Even after my family's attack, my mother coerced me to agree to look after the family and keep them together after her death. I agreed to this unfair request only to appease her but I had no intention of keeping my oath. I felt that this was my life and no person, even my mother, had the right to expect to burden the living after death. As a matter of self-respect, I shall treat my family with respect but their ways are their own.

My mother was moved from the hospital into a private nursing home. A nurse in the home was a friend of mine and kept me informed about the state of my mother's illness. The nurse's brother called at my caravan and told me that my mother was nearing the end. I sat with my mother until late that night talking to her in her sleep. She battled on for three more days and eventually died at night alone not long after I had left. She was eighty years old. I lay down in my caravan for four days without food and cried my eyes out. Without a doubt, she was the only person in whom I have ever confided, or to whom I could ever confess. The very fact that she had fought so hard to stay alive made me think that she could not have taken tablets when she had her illness in the flat at Paignton. This eased my mind.

I sat at the back of the church apart from my family at the funeral, accompanied by two of my old business colleagues who were known to my mother. After the funeral I shook the hands of my relatives and walked to a waiting car. As I opened the car door my sister Jean came over and asked me if I would call at her house for a family get-together. I thanked her for her offer and told her that I had already made other arrangements with my friends.

I was penniless now and my brothers and sister still had their assets and jobs, this was an opportunity for me to live a private life of my own, free from unwanted criticism. I am always polite and precise to my brothers and sister but I have noticed their lack of concern for my well-being. I told my closest friend Dennis Johns after my mother's funeral, that my brothers and sister would never darken my door again unless my fortune changed, or if a member of the family dies.

As for my remembrance for my parents, I decided that I would visit the reservoir at Henock on Dartmoor every year, their favourite spot, to pay my respects to them.

CHAPTER 24

THE SAMARITAN

With no cooking facilities in the caravan I often ate out. My old pal Tommy Diamond had returned to Torquay from his Plymouth pub and set up business in the Rendezvous restaurant. Tom was always moving from one pub to another or one restaurant to another. The Rendezvous became a regular haunt for me. One evening, I was a little unsteady on my feet after a long drinking session. I had just paid for my meal and was about to leave Tom's place.

The receipts for the meals he kept on a spike on a flat-top dresser. The spike was a six-inch curved bodkin (or darning needle) that was sticking out of a small piece of plywood.

I stumbled against the dresser leaning backward over it and the needle with all the receipts stuck in my back. It could have killed me. I was too inebriated to notice this, and was walking towards the door with them sticking out of my back.

Tom's wife Linda, who worked as a waitress, tried to pull it out but every time she called to me, I turned around and she couldn't reach around my bulky body. She thought this was hilarious and all the people in the restaurant were pointing at me and laughing.

I waved back at the customers thinking they must know me. The more I waved, the more they laughed. I thought it was a really great atmosphere. Linda eventually grabbed the needle as I was walking through the door and I knew nothing of it until she told me the next time we met.

After a long day socialising with friends, I called at Tom's place for a meal but he had closed early. A small fish and chip shop with dining facilities had just opened under new management not far from Tom's. Tom had told me that the new owner was a very religious man, a devout Christian. I was starving. Why not try it out, I thought and eagerly approached the counter to take my place in the queue. I ordered a traditional plate of fish, chips and mushy peas, to be consumed at the dining table. (There was ample room in the cafeteria section of the shop.)

To my surprise, the proprietor of the shop refused to accommodate my order on the grounds that in his opinion I was too drunk to eat in his shop. I was by no means drunk; I felt he was prejudiced. I surmised it was he who had the drink problem, not I! I had never had this problem when eating at Tom's place, or anywhere else for that matter.

He had probably caught a whiff of alcohol on my breath and that was enough for him to form his biased judgement. I was in control of my faculties, so I politely thanked him for his amateur though sincere assessment of my intoxication and vacated the shop.

Whilst leaving the shop, vexed at my prejudicial encounter, I happened upon an old gentleman of past acquaintance by the name of Walter. I had always acknowledged Walter with a courteous reception and asked after his well-being. I had known Walter for many years and he was well known as a local character. Walter was past retirement age but sold the local evening paper on a pitch near the harbour. He was harmless but always wore outrageous clothes that ranged from a grass skirt, to a cowboy outfit and he spoke an unintelligible gobbledegook.

It was rumoured that Walter had once been a high-ranking officer in the British Army and had suffered at some stage from a traumatic experience, leaving him with a debilitating mental illness, a form of shellshock.

On this occasion, he was adorned with a weird contraption on his head. It featured two long wire springs that looked like tentacles. They protruded from his forehead and culminated with two different coloured balls, bouncing around on the springs. He wore shorts and sandals, even though it was mid-winter. His spindly legs and knobbly knees reminded me of Mahatma Gandhi.

I thought that Walter was far more erudite than the fanatic in the fish shop! Some of these religious people think that everyone in the world should conform to their standards. It's a good job that they don't own all the eating houses, or I would starve to death!

"Are you hungry, Walter?" I asked to which he mumbled an incoherent gibberish, which I ignored. He then nodded his head causing his balls to undulate. I took this for an affirmative, "Come with me, Walter," I said whilst leading him into the shop, "I don't see why both of us should starve." Walter followed me with his balls bouncing, into the fish shop.

I again approached the counter, this time with a majestic gait, and inquired of the proprietor in my best authoritative vocabulary, "Would you serve this man?" indicating toward my colourful friend.

The proprietor replied, "Yes."

"Then please serve him with your finest," I requested.

I paid for Walter's meal and joined him at the table, whereupon I sat feeling ravenous and watched him whilst he gorged. Not one chip did I remove for myself from Walter's plate. The nearest I came to a meal that night was the salvo of spud and spit that purchased a hold on various parts of my face as Walter uttered more gibberish. His balls began to make sense of his oral bumble, signalling approval of his repast. Can you imagine my feelings at this time? I was extremely famished, but I bore the pangs of hunger. I was just making a point to the unenlightened proprietor of the shop of my ability to maintain myself in an order of sobriety.

There is a moral to this story and I think it has something to do with the story in the Bible about the Good Samaritan? If I was the Good Samaritan and Walter was the Philistine, who was the religious leader in the shop?

In winter, it was very cold in the caravan at night and it rocked about in storms. The caravan lay under a bank topped with large Dutch elm trees. They were all dead from Dutch elm disease and the branches clattered against one another in the wind. I wrapped myself up in a blanket and listened to a very small radio. It was only then that I learned of the explorer Earnest Shackleton and his epic exploration in the Antarctic. I thought of Henry in the sanatorium cursing me on his deathbed and wondered if he really was with Shackleton on that epic journey.

An old friend offered me the comfort of a warm room in his home on my second Christmas in the caravan (the weather was atrocious) and I gladly accepted his offer. When I returned to my caravan after Christmas, one of the large Dutch elm trees had blown over in the stormy weather and crushed the caravan. It was so badly squashed, it looked like a sardine tin. The tree blew over in the middle of the night and I would most probably have been severely injured, or even killed if I had been asleep inside. I was lucky to be alive but had to look for new accommodation.

As luck would have it, a young man approached me that day at the bar in the Old London Inn where I was contemplating where to sleep. I didn't have enough money for a deposit on a flat after the long Christmas break so I considered I might be sleeping rough.

"You know my father," said the young man, interrupting my thoughts.

"Who's your dad?" I inquired. He told me and asked me if I would mind if he spoke to me for a while. It seemed he was suicidal over problems with his girlfriend, and he requested that I might stay with him in his flat for a while. He implied that he was going to kill himself that day.

Well, I'm not saying that I'm a Good Samaritan, but this sounded like a roof over my head if I managed to keep him alive. I think I worked hard for those lodgings having listened to him going on about his girlfriend all night. I stayed there for a while free of charge until I was able to find work and pay him back. We agreed to share the flat until I was able to find a suitable flat of my own.

He was still driving me nuts about this girl all the time. Even when they got back together he was still boring me to death. He started coming back to the flat late at night drunk whereas I was not drinking at all because I was broke.

He threatened me when he was drunk and told me he was not scared of me. I could not understand what made him so aggressive towards me, as I had been listening to all his problems. Knowing my nature, I knew a confrontation was looming.

He did other things to upset me like peeing on the toilet seat. I ask you? Couldn't he lift the seat when having a pee? Just to show respect! Imagine sitting on that seat after he had done that?

I noticed he cleaned his face in the morning with a face flannel. This is something we never did in my family. We always washed our face with our hands. I used to clean the piss off the toilet seat with his face flannel and get a kick when I saw him washing his face with it.

The flat was locked when I came home from work one day. There was only one key and he had it. He was inside the flat humping his girlfriend, and I sat outside for an hour waiting for them to finish. I had told him the time I was coming home and was getting irritable because he had finished copulating and was sat in the room talking. I was starving and decided to slip the Yale lock with a piece of plastic.

When I entered the room he took an aggressive stance towards me and the moment had come for me to straighten out his false sense of bravado. I never saw him again after that day. I must have frightened him. I felt a little sorry for him, after all it was his flat, but then I did stop him from topping himself. Even a Good Samaritan can get pissed off.

CHAPTER 25

TOP OF THE HILL

Things got better work wise and I settled down in a permanent flat in Torquay. Just a few years after settling, I answered a knock on my door and my eldest brother Ron had come to inform me of my sister Jean's death and her funeral arrangements. She had died of cancer aged forty-seven. I had no idea that any of my family knew of my address. Apparently my sister had entered the hospital for one night so that she might have some tests the following day. During the night her lungs filled with fluid and she died. It was quite a shock for the family. I went to her funeral and again, as I had done at my mother's funeral, I sat at the back of the church on my own.

"It's a sad day," I said to her husband as I shook his hand when leaving the church.

He was sobbing and said, "Thank you." I then shook my brother's hands and their wives hands and made the same comment to each of them and then left.

After the funeral I met my childhood friend Benji in the local pub in Hele Village where I was born. Often I had met Benji over the years in one pub or another. He was always dressed in his working clothes and generally covered in mud. I still had a photograph of Benji as a teenager and told him I would bring it with me to the pub the next day. It was taken outside my childhood friend John's house when we were fifteen years old. It showed John and me playing our guitars with Benji in the middle, singing. (John split with his wife Liz and remarried; he now lives in Spain. His brother Allen, our bass guitarist, split with his wife and Fego the drummer never married and lives like me, from day to day. So out of the four members of The Strangers band, not one had a lasting relationship.)

I took the photograph along to the pub the next evening and gave it to Benji. His face lit up. "That's me!" he said and off he went around the packed pub, singing a rendition of 'Muleskinner Blues' and showing the photograph to everyone.

He eventually got back to me and said, "Have you seen my photograph?" I laughed and told him I had not seen it for years.

In my past as a successful businessman, if I happened upon Benji in a pub, he had a harmless habit of accepting an offer of a drink from me and then demanding a cigar. I would respond favourably to his demand. I always carried a quantity of fine cigars and this was his way of showing everyone in the bar that he could demand whatever he wanted from me because I was his friend.

The last time I met Benji was two weeks after my sister's funeral. I followed the routine formula with the pint and cigar; I had been earning good money at the time. We stood chatting for a while and Benji told me he had been conned out of his wages that day, so I gave him twenty pounds and offered to take him out for the evening, to which he accepted. During the evening, I asked Benji what he had thought of his life in general, to which he replied, "I have had the most wonderful life a person could ask for, if I lived it all over again, I would not change a thing." I must admit, I was a little surprised by his answer. For one who had so little to be so contented, took me aback.

When the evening drew to an end, I gave Benji the price of a taxi fare, to be sure of his safe journey home. I later heard he pocketed the money and walked. I suppose he was in need of the money more than the taxi ride, even though he still had the twenty pounds in his pocket that I had given him at the start of the evening. Two weeks later, Benji was killed outright, walking home from a pub; he had staggered into the path of an oncoming car.

Benji was forty-seven years old (two years older than I was) and I attended his funeral. I saw Benji's mother and father at the funeral. They looked very old and frail to me. I had not seen Benji's father since he gave me a hiding for breaking Benji's arm when we were kids. To my surprise, after all the funerals I had previously attended this had by far the largest following of mourners, and to date I have never seen it surpassed locally. It seemed that everyone had loved this harmless man of good and kind nature. I was reminded of the biblical saying 'the meek shall inherit the Earth'. Oh Benji, if that be so, I would gladly serve in your Kingdom.

The trouble with my gallbladder flared up again and something had to be done. For six weeks I had stayed in my flat, in pain and vomiting. I was living on watermelons that were brought in by my mates. My best mate Dennis Johns put a stop to it when he saw me vomiting green pus from my stomach and called my doctor. I was rushed to Torbay hospital and a tube was put up my nose and into my stomach to stop me from vomiting. The doctor told me that it was very serious and if they were forced to operate on me right away, my chances of survival were less than evens.

Fortunately the infection began to clear up and after ten days I was asked if I felt fit enough to leave. I had lost three stone in weight and had not eaten anything since entering the hospital. My only sustenance for two months had been the watermelons that I had eaten at home. In hospital I was having nothing by mouth and had survived on a saline drip. There was a shortage of beds in the hospital and the doctor was prepared to let me go if I agreed. I asked the doctor if I could have at least one solid meal and one more night to see if I could hold down a solid meal. Fortunately they agreed. I was very weak and on leaving I was instructed to lose more weight, and told that an operation would be arranged as soon as possible to remove my gallbladder. This time they had to operate and I was not looking forward to the event after the fiasco of my lung operation at Hawkmoor.

When at home I was almost too weak to do my own shopping and decided to go off the diet and eat lean steak to build up my strength. When my operation became due I was even heavier than I had been before the illness but felt fit. I was told that I would be in the hospital for ten days after the op and then have ten days in a convalescent home.

Unlike the surgeon at Hawkmoor, on the day of the op, this surgeon spoke to me before and after the operation and explained everything to me. Five days after the op I was in my local, drinking, with a ten-inch scar on my tummy and returned to work ten days later, the same day as my stitches were removed. The operation was no problem at all and the relief from gallstone problems since then has been heaven.

Fourteen years after the death of my sister Jean, her son Paul came in search of his uncle. Having heard stories about me, he was curious to see this strange relative. My friends had told me that someone was on my trail and the message I was receiving indicated that three men were looking for me all over town.

With the company I kept at times the message could have implied danger, but I suspected these were not a professional threat (more like three ghouls searching for the carcass of a dead character) and my assumption was proved to be correct.

My nephew eventually caught up with me and on his first sight of me he stated, "You're smaller than I thought!" (Paul had grown up into a big chap.) He was twenty-seven years old and this was the first time that I had set eyes on him since his mother's funeral. He made a strange claim. "All the family are afraid of you, but you don't look much to me!" ('Charming,' I thought.)

"Have I ever harmed a member of our family?" I enquired.

"No," he replied.

"Then what is the nature of their fear?" I asked.

He hesitated, looking rather sheepish and said, "I really don't know." Rightly or wrongly, I assumed that the nature of their fear lay within their own conscience.

Paul informed me that he was an accountant and was quite wealthy, implying that he was an astute businessman. I later discovered his wealth was founded on the estate of his deceased parents. My sister Jean had always bragged about how much insurance money her husband would get when she died and they were both heavily insured. The strange thing about meeting my nephew after all those years was the fact that his father Tony had recently suddenly died of a heart attack. Now my nephew and niece had inherited the money along with the house. Tony's parents had also died and left a house and money to them.

At the time we met, I was dressed in my working clothes (I had just completed a small central heating contract). He remarked, "I don't want to see you dressed like this, I want to see you dressed in your smart suits and driving a smart car. Why don't you work for me and live in one of my properties?"

I cautiously replied, "I appreciate your concern over my well-being but having lapsed from socialising with you for so many years, I would prefer to enhance our acquaintance before contemplating an acceptance of your kind offer." (I was on my guard.)

I had no intention of accepting a gift from anyone, including my family, without first consolidating a mutual respect. I therefore arranged to meet with him on a few occasions, to asses his integrity and, whilst enjoying his company, I decided to decline his offer.

Paul has since moved to London to live and I have had no further contact with him. I believe the mystery of his mad uncle is now expounded and I am no longer of interest to him. I somehow feel relaxed knowing the threat of utopia on the family scale, has been liberated.

I feel I have witnessed it all before in my own youth. He invited me into his home one day and much of his furniture I recognised as my old belongings. When I sold my home during my bankruptcy, his mother Jean looked after my furniture until my mother settled in her warden-controlled flat. My mother then took what she needed and I gave Jean the rest. On my mother's death, Jean came to me and asked me if I could provide anything towards my mother's funeral

I had inherited all my mother's worldly goods, which consisted of the antique furniture and items of value she held in store. This more than covered the funeral arrangements and I gave everything to my sister. I harbour no wish to partake of fare nor sit at a table set by the dead.

Something I saw in my nephew's home reminded me of an occasion in the past, when I had been pondering over the nature of a Christmas gift for my parents.

Everything they had wanted I always purchased as the need presented itself, and it seemed to me that they had everything. The item I noticed was a silver-plated salver. In the late 1960s I had purchased it, along with six silver-plated goblets, for the princely sum of fifty pounds.

It was an antique and the plating was in relatively good condition. It was not the antique coup of the century but it was meant to compliment a bottle of champagne, which in itself was the actual gift. My parents had often heard me mention the fact that I was drinking champagne, something that they had never sampled, so I felt it would be something different, and a thoughtful gift.

My parents took one sip of the champagne and showed their distaste for it, I had to drink the champagne. The silver salver and goblets however, was much to their tastes.

The salver that my parents had given pride of place on our mantelpiece over our lounge fireplace was now being used as a plant potholder in the hallway of my nephew's home! The silver plate had all but disappeared from its surface, owing to the rough surface of the earthenware plant pots, scouring its metal lustre.

Since my nephew moved to London, he rented out that home, after throwing out all the things that he had regarded as rubbish. I can't blame him for that. I would have done the same at his age after inheriting a considerable fortune but on that day I saw so much memorabilia.

Memorabilia like my long-playing records signed by my friend Semprini in the health farm, photographs of me in my stage costume from the rock and roll days. There was even a photograph of Jack Barnet and me when we were two childhood mates (he's become a millionaire, by the way, through his mining activities, Jack's relatives keep me informed about him). Everything went out on the refuse tip. It seems sad, but I remember in my own way. I have nothing but memories. I need no proof of my life, I have witnessed it and if anyone disputes my memory, it's of no consequence, the matter is not worth an argument.

I was recognised as an ex-member of The Vampires rock band recently by a Torquay United football fan. We met in a pub near the football grounds and he told me that the band was playing that night in Torquay. They were appearing in a local hotel at a private wedding reception. I gate-crashed the reception to say hello.

There are only two of the original members, Adrian Hall (Gunga) and Johnny Carnell the bass player still playing. They have been playing now for over forty years. Adrian's son now plays the drums. It was great to see them, I stood at the side of the stage unannounced and Johnny Carnell spotted me first. I laughed when John nudged Adrian the lead guitarist saying, "Look, it's Bob!" They both stopped playing momentarily, leaving an awful gap in the music, just to wave acknowledgement.

We reminisced during the interval and John remarked amongst other things, "The same old crap, E, A and B7!" meaning the same old songs. I stayed on until the end of the evening to talk some more and I gave them a hand in loading their equipment onto the van. It was very late at night and it reminded me of the journeys I had faced in my youth, that they still had to endure.

I could never interest myself in that lifestyle again, it made me shudder to think of it. I was facing a short walk home to a warm bed some minutes away, whereas they had hours of travel ahead of them. I arranged to call on them at some time in the future but later thought better of it; those days are gone!

Sometimes when I see famous rock bands getting awards for fifty years of their contribution to entertainment, I think of Gunga and Johnny Carnell. They have been playing for nearly that long but no awards for them. They were helpful to my first band all those years ago and how many others I wonder. When I first sat in Gunga's flat in Teignmouth fascinated by the equipment in the room. John Low, his brother and I had acoustic guitars with electric pickups that we fixed to the guitars to convert them to electric. Gunga's band had purpose-built electric guitars. I think they deserve a medal for all they have done for young musicians.

I often see Fego our drummer in Newton Abbot where he lives. He no longer plays the drums and looks like a blast from the past. My friends call him the Indian as he has long straight black hair halfway down his back and wears coloured beads around his neck.

I still visit the reservoir in Henock on the edge of Dartmoor to pay my respects to my parents once every year. I always try to visit when the rhododendrons are in bloom. My mother and I would sit in the car and chat about my father; she always brought a flask of ice cream and a flask of tea, and liked to play an Andy Williams tape. It has been a struggle for me to get there some years but I have always managed and it has been a pleasure.

I still live in the same flat in Torquay; I've been here for twenty years and no longer work. I've heard it said that a major surgical operation takes ten years off of your life, and so at over sixty I must be quite old. My problematic lungs are creating breathing difficulties and I have adopted writing as my hobby. I thought that writing a book about my life would be easy but I have had a lot to learn. I intend to keep on writing in the future as a hobby in my old age.

Many people have accompanied me to the reservoir over the years. On one occasion Ruby Murray, the famous singer, accompanied me. My mother would have loved that.

On a recent visit to the reservoir, I was sat at the edge of the water, when a crowd of country walkers strolled by. We acknowledged each other and I asked them if they had walked far, "From Bovey Tracy," they replied, "We came by way of a steep path leading from Hawkmoor Park to here." I suddenly realised that they had walked up Sputum Hill! After forty years I came to realise that my pilgrimage to the reservoir was also a pilgrimage to the lake at the summit of Sputum Hill. It seems my journey of remembrance for my parents could also have been for my past friends. It reminded me of my second birthday on Christmas Day 1963, the day my recovery began, forty years ago. It reminded me of all my friends who had died at Hawkmoor; they are always by my side. I remember their words about taking opportunities if I survived, opportunities they felt they had missed. I suppose that my visit to prison was not what they had in mind but on the whole it was a life filled with moments for which I am grateful. If I were asked the question of what would I do if I had my life over again, I would say the same as my friend Benji, and I wouldn't change a thing.

How strange it is to have chosen this spot as a memorial to my parents when my old friends in Hawkmoor also touched their lives. I remember the old saying at Hawkmoor, that if you make it to the summit of Sputum Hill you live. It seems that my friends were right, as I did finally make it to the top of Sputum Hill.

POSTSCRIPT

On Wednesday 5th January 2005 I rang my old guitarist Adrian Hall (Gunga). I wanted from him, if he had one, a photo of me when I was in the band. His daughter answered the phone and told me that he was seriously ill in Torbay hospital. She gave me the number of Johnny Carnell, our bass player, and I rang him. We arranged to visit Adrian at the hospital on the following Saturday, and John brought along a photograph of The Vampires band for me to use in this book.

As we three chatted in the hospital, Adrian's son entered the room and informed us that Fego our drummer had just been rushed into the hospital and that he was critically ill. We were not permitted to see him for at least two days.

By this strange coincidence, this was the first time in over forty years that we had all been under the same roof at the same time

I was able to visit Fego (Jeff Perkins) on the following Thursday and he seemed to be all right. We all vowed to keep in touch in the future. Sadly I heard from John two days later that Fego had died the day after my visit. I attended Jeff's funeral together with Lionel Digby, our old manager. I learned for the first time at the funeral that Jeff had a wife and two children. It seems that after fifty years the Vampires have finally disbanded.

* * *